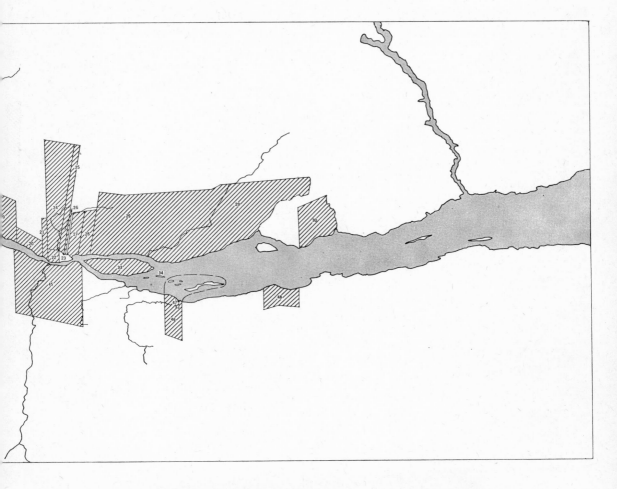

24	St-Gabriel	33	Ile d'Orléans	40	Bécancour
25	St-Ignace	34	Ile aux Ruaux	41	Dutort
26	Lespinay	35	La Prairie de la Magdeleine	42	Cournoyer
27	Notre Dame des Anges	36	Longueuil	43	Gentilly
28	Beauport	37	La Citière	44	Ste-Croix
29	Beaupré	38	Rivière de St-François des Prés	45	Lauzon
30	Malbaie	39	Godefroy	46	Rivière du Sud
31	Ile St-Paul			47	Morin
32	Ile Ste-Thérèse			48	St-Roch des Aulnaies

SEIGNEURIES IN CANADA IN 1663,
at the beginning of royal government.

The Seigneurial System in Early Canada

�֍ Richard Colebrook Harris

The Seigneurial System in Early Canada

A Geographical Study

1968

THE UNIVERSITY OF WISCONSIN PRESS
Madison, Milwaukee, and London

LES PRESSES DE L'UNIVERSITÉ LAVAL
Québec

Published by
The University of Wisconsin Press
Box 1379, Madison, Wisconsin 53701
The University of Wisconsin Press, Ltd.
27–29 Whitfield Street, London, W.1

Published in Canada by
Les Presses de l'Université Laval
Box 2477, Québec, P.Q.

Second printing, 1968

Printed in the United States of America
Standard Book Number 299–03980–3
Library of Congress Catalog Card Number 66–11799

Preface

SINCE the turn of the century when Francis Parkman wrote his picturesque history of the seigneurial system in Canada there have been a number of books, articles, and theses on the subject as well as frequent allusions to it in most of the literature on Canada during the French regime. A feudal system along the St. Lawrence has been a curiosity, and superimposed on the North American tendency to idealize life on the land, and on French Canadian veneration of the preconquest period as well, the curiosity has always had a strong romantic appeal. Moreover, the seigneurial system has been assumed to be a principal facet of the distinctive French effort in North America. Scholars and novelists have written about the seigneurial regime, a folklore has grown up around it, and a popular impression of it has become part of a Canadian mythology.

No new documents have come to light which, in themselves, warrant a re-examination of Canadian feudalism. A departing French colonial administration left behind most of the records pertaining to the civil administration of the colony, and these documents—acts of concession of land, deeds of sale, statements of vassalage, and the like—have been preserved in archives in Quebec and Montreal. The official correspondence was returned to France, but has been copied in longhand, and is available in the National Archives of Canada. This formidable mass of documentation, which is described in the bibliographic essay at the end of this book, includes nothing that has not been available to students in Canada for decades, some of it in published form.

v

However, the geographer cannot consider the seigneurial system a closed subject, nor even one that has been well opened. Most of the New World modifications of an imported legal framework have been worked out so that anyone curious about the complicated laws of *retrait* as they applied in Canada, the legal obligations of a *censitaire* towards his seigneur, or the royal *édits* aimed at forcing the seigneur to develop his seigneurie, can generally find this information scattered through the secondary literature. If, on the other hand, he wants to know why some seigneuries were hundreds of square miles in extent and others but half a dozen, whether or not the seigneurs lived on their concessions, what role they played in settling their seigneuries, or what revenue they could expect with fifteen or fifty settlers, he will find little. Should he enquire whether the size of *rotures* increased or decreased, whether the habitant held land in several seigneuries, whether settlement patterns reflected the seigneurial framework, or how the inheritance systems affected the control of land, he will find even less. And most of the scanty literature on these questions is misleading or incorrect.

Evidence about the land itself, as opposed to that in the statute books, may have been neglected because such evidence was thought to shed little light on the seigneurial system, or because it was thought to be wanting. William Bennett Munro published Catalogne's description of Canadian seigneuries in his *Documents Relating to the Seigniorial Tenure* with the explanation that it contains information about the land which "cannot be obtained from any other trustworthy source." What has been wanting, however, is not the documentary evidence, but a curiosity about the land and the patterns thereon. If the point of departure is a legal system, the patterns which it helped to create on the land are of peripheral concern; but for the geographer who, in broadest terms, has been trained to describe and interpret the variable character of the surface of this world of ours, these patterns are at the focus of his interest. There is a generic difference between the study of a legal system and the study of the patterns on the land produced in part by a legal system. Different questions need to be asked, different data collected, and many old problems rethought in a different framework.

A geographical analysis of the seigneurial system can be divided into two levels, one concerned with *seigneurs* and *seigneuries,* the other with *censitaires* and *rotures.* While both levels were integral parts of the same system—the censitaire live on a roture which the seigneur had conceded within his seigneurie—the legal positions of seigneurs and censitaires were distinct, and each group faced different problems in the development of its land. It is convenient, therefore, to look first at seigneuries and seigneurs. Against this background the organization of rotures within seigneuries and the activities of the censitaires can be examined; and, finally, an assessment of the seigneurie as a unit on the land can be made. This outline, preceded by a short description of the valley of the St. Lawrence, is adopted in the following pages.

In some chapters it has been necessary to discuss subjects which might seem more properly the concern of historians, economists, or sociologists. Crucial, for example, to an understanding of the seigneurial geography of Canada is some knowledge of seigneurial revenue. When such necessary data have not been supplied by the research of students in other disciplines I have filled them in as best I could.

A number of maps and graphs accompany this study, and it is worth reminding the reader that information presented visually is often the same kind of generalization or judgment as a paragraph of verbal argument. While there are as many statistical data on the French régime in Canada as on any colony in North America at the same time, there are frequent gaps and inaccuracies, and use of the data is constantly frustrating. Mapping from nonstatistical sources leads to even less well established cartographic hypotheses. It is possible, for example, to draw a map of seigneuries in Canada in 1663 from information in the title deeds. Although such a map is by no means accurate it is probably more nearly so than anyone in the colony could have produced three centuries ago, and is an essential first step in a reconstruction of the changing seigneurial geography. As with figures, maps can easily be designed to give a biased interpretation or may give this impression unintentionally. No maps or graphs have been included if their general impression seemed likely to be deceptive. Those that are used have been prepared with care, but their value is often chiefly impressionistic, and it can be misleading to read detailed, specific information from them.

Unless they are defined at the onset some of the terms used in this study may prove confusing; the use of "Canada" in the title is a case in point. All French possessions in continental North America were usually included under the general rubric "New France," that is, the crescent from the mouth of the Mississippi to Cape Breton. Occasionally officials in France referred to New France when they obviously meant the colony along the St. Lawrence, but those in the colony distinguished at least between Acadia, Louisiana, and Canada. The center of the last was the St. Lawrence colony, which extended from a few miles beyond the Ile de Montréal in the southwest to approximately a hundred miles below Quebec in the northeast, and in which almost all the people then considered to be Canadians lived.

More troublesome are "seigneur," "habitant," and "censitaire," and consequently "seigneurie," "habitation," and "roture." Technically a seigneur was anyone entitled to an oath of fealty for land held from him. The king was a seigneur because all land in Canada was held ultimately from him; the Companies of New France and the West Indies were seigneurs because they received *foi et hommage* (the oath of fealty) for the subgrants which they, in turn, held from the king. If the holders of the Companies' concessions could subgrant, they were seigneurs as well, and when one of these seigneurs granted an *arrière-fief,* or subseigneurie, within his concession, the holder of an arrière-fief was a seigneur. Thus Canada was part of a seigneurie, and there were several hundred seigneuries within it, the smallest of these being arrière-fiefs of a square arpent or less. In this study "seigneur" usually refers to one of the group who held land directly from one of the companies or, after the proprietary periods, directly from the king; and "seigneurie" refers to the land so held. Unless otherwise indicated "seigneur" and "seigneurie" are not intended to include the king, the companies, the holders of small arrière-fiefs, or their concessions.

In France "censitaire" referred to anyone who could not subgrant his land, for which, as a mark of this type of holding, he paid a *cens,* and because most censitaires were farmers of low income the word was broadly synonymous with peasant. Settlers in Canada were sensitive to this pejorative appellation, and the word "habitant" appeared in the colony's earliest years. As it was first used, an habitant was a permanent resident of Canada, later anyone who paid a cens, or who operated a small farm. For the purpose of this study the term has no utility if it can be applied to anyone in the colony, and because I shall use it to denote a small farmer it can be misleading if used to mean anyone and everyone who paid a cens. Most of the richest men in the colony, the senior royal officials, or important churchmen held land for which they paid a cens, and such men are not commonly thought of as habitants. I find "censitaire" a useful word and use it to mean anyone who paid a cens for a concession which he could not subgrant. I do not intend to suggest any economic or social status, but to indicate a type of ownership. Some censitaires were also seigneurs. If a seigneur fits into this category he is also an habitant, but neither seigneurs nor censitaires were necessarily habitants. An "habitation," therefore, was an habitant's house; a "roture," a concession of land to a censitaire.

Another troublesome word is "domain" which has three distinct meanings. The "royal domain" was all the land which had not been subgranted belonging to the king, in other words, Crown land; the "seigneurial domain," all land which had not been subgranted belonging to the seigneur; and "the domain," the section of a seigneurie set aside by the seigneur for his personal use.

Several attempts have been made to give a value in contemporary funds to the livre, but none is very satisfactory because the relative value of goods and services has changed so radically. One recent estimate fixed the livre at $1.00, in Canadian funds of 1958, at which rate an uncleared roture of fifty arpents of potentially good farm land on the edge of settlement might be bought for as little as $18.75; a large hand-saw of good quality, imported from France, was worth just about as much; and the ordinary laborer earned the money for either in less than ten days. Today, while ten days of unskilled labor would barely yield a down payment for the fifty arpents, they would buy fifteen or twenty hand-saws. Rather than to attempt a conversion it is more useful to think of some standard values in the colony. Although prices fluctuated widely, a laborer earned on the average two livres a day, a skilled laborer up to five, royal officials of secondary rank from 300 to 3,000 livres a year, and the governor 12,000. A capon was worth about a livre, a goose a shade more, a sheep ten to twenty livres, which was little less than the value of an average pig, a cow forty to fifty livres, an ox a hundred or so, and an ordinary horse slightly more. Wheat averaged approximately two and one-half livres for a little more than a bushel. Uncleared land was almost worthless, so that a roture of average size sold for fifteen to thirty livres, and a seigneurie of twenty-five square miles or more for well under a thousand. The value increased very rapidly when the land was cleared; the same roture with twenty cleared arpents, a one-room cabin, and a barn usually brought between one and two thousand livres and, with more clearing and buildings, could be worth five or six. All of these prices rose whenever card money was in circulation, and some depended on the harvest. These are rough averages which give some indication of what a livre could buy. The livre was divided into twenty sols, the sol into twelve deniers; and these units, as well as the livre, are frequently referred to in the following pages.

The arpent, the linear measure most commonly used in this study, was 192 feet. Eighty-four arpents usually comprised a league which was, therefore, approximately three miles. Also used from time to time is the *toise,* a unit 6.4 feet in length. A square arpent was roughly five-sixths of an acre; a square toise was forty square feet. Grain was calculated in *minots* or two *demi-minots* each of which was 1169.5 cubic inches. A *minot,* then, was 1.05 bushels.

Translation posed a number of problems in this work. Nouns like *censitaire* and *roture,* as well as phrases like *foi et hommage* or *aveu et dénombrement,* which have no simple, precise English equivalent are used throughout. A glossary of such terms will be found at the end of the book. On the other hand, a number of words like *paroisse* and *domaine* are easily translated, and the translation has been used. Other nouns of French origin—for example, *seigneur, habitant, arpent,* and *livre*—appear in the French form in most dictionaries. To avoid a cluttered look on the printed page I have used italics as sparingly as seemed consistent with clarity. The French in footnotes and quotations has not been modernized; where translated in the text, the translations are my own.

I have not consistently chosen either the French or the English spellings of place names, feeling that it would appear unnatural in an English text to write of the Fleuve Saint-Laurent, but that in most other cases the French spellings are preferable in a book dealing with the French regime. The spellings I have adopted are those which appear in the *Atlas of Canada* (Ottawa: Department of Mines and Technical Surveys, 1957).

This study would not have been possible without the assistance of many people. The staffs at the National Archives of Canada, at the Archives de la Province de Québec, and at the Archives du Séminaire de Québec were always friendly and helpful. Professor Jean Hamelin of Laval University gave encouragement when it was sorely needed, and offered much invaluable criticism of the manuscript, as did Professors Marcel Trudel and Fernand Ouellet. John and Ruth Arnold donated their summer cottage in the Gatineau as a retreat for writing, and this essay took form there under the watchful eyes of a pair of squirrels. Miss Susan Hook undertook the thankless task of checking the footnotes. However, my principal debt is owed to Professor Andrew H. Clark of the University of Wisconsin, who awakened my interest in this type of research and guided it throughout, and to the Social Science Research Council whose fellowship made a year in Ottawa and Quebec possible. As usual the responsibility for this study is my own.

R. C. H.

University of Toronto
July 1965

Contents

List of Tables and Figures

The Seigneurial System in Early Canada

1 : The Problem of the Seigneurial System

AT the beginning of the seventeenth century the seigneurial system, that is to say French feudalism, was old and effete. Seigneurs, who in the twelfth and thirteenth centuries had supplied their censitaires with needed services in return for certain payments, in the seventeenth century often lived in the glitter of an opulent court on the revenue of a burgeoning number of exactions which had long ceased to represent a *quid pro quo* for services rendered. The legal framework of an earlier feudalism remained in the *coutumes*, or codifications of French customary law, but as military power centralized in royal hands and the close functional bond between the seigneur and his vassals dissolved, that framework became a buttress of privilege and wealth.

The axiom at the heart of French feudalism, "no land without a seigneur," was assumed from the beginning to be the basis of any system of land distribution in New France. When, at the close of the sixteenth century, the Marquis de la Roche obtained the king's blessing and letters patent for his elaborate project of trade and settlement in the New World, the king stipulated that land was to be granted to meritorious individuals "en fiefs, seigneuries, châtellenies, comtés, vicomtés, baronnies et autre dignités relevant de Nous." [1] In 1623 the Duc de Montmorency, viceroy of New France, granted Louis Hébert a small fief at the edge of the fortified camp which was then Quebec. [2] And when, in 1627, the Company of New France (the Company of One Hundred Associates) was granted most of eastern North America "en toute propriété, justice, et seigneurie" and obliged to subenfeudate,[3] French feudalism, in theory at least, had been transplanted in New France. If there were Frenchmen who doubted the applicability of this French institution in a new environment, no record of their apprehension remains.

Probably there were few doubts, for at the official level New France was never more than an extension of France. The impulses which created and directed New France through a century and a half—the commercial drive of a bourgeoisie in Paris and the Channel towns, the Catholic zeal which, in the aftermath of the religious wars, was French as well, and a monarch's desire to extend the glory of his name and country—were rooted in France. The colonists themselves had been recruited by French trading companies or by the Crown. Only some five hundred came on their own, a few of them to escape creditors, others because they had been deluded into believing that fortunes were to be made, or simply because the spirit of adventure ran strong in them. No one came as part of a group which objected to specific conditions in France. Such groups were excluded from a colony which was the creation of the ruling class for solid, Catholic Frenchmen, and which was as minutely supervised by the home government as any colony in the New World.

The Frenchmen who crossed the North Atlantic to Canada found themselves on the edge of an immense wilderness inhabited by a scattering of Stone Age people. The potentialities and the demands of this new land were unknown. Initially no one knew what wealth in furs, timber, and minerals the land contained; or what reception the Indians would give to European intruders into their domain. No one could be sure how French crops would do in a different climate, or even whether men could be induced to till the land as long as the fur trade beckoned. When agricultural settlement began, no one knew how much land a censitaire had to clear before he could produce an agricultural surplus, or a seigneur had to control before he could hope to profit from his seigneurie. Least of all, if anyone had thought about it, was it possible to be certain whether a feudal system which had been shaped in France where land was scarce and the economy predominantly agricultural could be made to function in a rough, new environment which had attracted French interest primarily because of its furs.

Almost everyone who has written about the introduction of the seigneurial system to Canada has pointed out that the vestigial feudalism of seventeenth century France was transformed along the lower St.

Lawrence. Some laws were altered, but the background of the decisive changes has been seen in a Canadian way of life which was significantly different from the French. In France there was an economic gulf between seigneurs and censitaires. In Canada many seigneurs were no better off than their censitaires, and nowhere were there those extremes of wealth which characterized an effete feudalism in its waning years. In France the seigneurial system was woven into a rigid class hierarchy. There was little economic basis for class in Canada, and although some seigneurs were addressed as *sieur* and almost all were entitled to certain privileges, the Old World distinctions were blunted when seigneur and censitaires worked side by side on the land. A submissive French peasantry was replaced in Canada by independent, self-reliant habitants who, with an intendant's support, would not accept many of the more burdensome charges of seventeenth-century French feudalism. These points have been made many times, and there is no reason to dispute any of them.

The transformation of the seigneurial system in Canada has been interpreted in several ways. William Bennett Munro, and both Benjamin Sulte and Edmé Rameau before him, have suggested that Canadian seigneurialism was a return to "pristine feudalism shorn of the excrescences which in France barnacled its later days."[4] The seigneur is described as a judge of petty disputes, a provider of indispensable services, and a leader, along with the curé, of a community which he had created. The seigneur depended on the revenue from his censitaires; they on the services, protection, and leadership which he provided. Later scholars, pointing out that a seigneur's power was closely circumscribed in Canada by royal edicts and watchful royal officials, and that the king's intendants regularly by-passed the seigneur to deal directly with his censitaires, regard the seigneurial regime as a system of colonization which gave Canada a social and economic structure which was only slightly reminiscent of medieval feudalism.[5] Léon Gérin has departed even more radically from the earlier interpretation to suggest that most Canadian seigneurs were French gentlemen who were totally unequipped to deal with the problems of agricultural development in a new land. They turned instead to the fur trade or to the civil service and added to a bureaucracy which was already top-heavy.[6]

Each of these interpretations envisages in the seigneurial system what Canon Lionel Groulx describes as "une des lignes de force du Canada d'autrefois."[7] Munro, Sulte, Rameau, and most other writers at the end of the last century and the beginning of this, thought of the seigneurial manor as "the recognized social center of every neighborhood."[8] The seigneurie was the basic unit of social and economic organization, and the close bond between seigneur and censitaires was indispensable in a difficult new land. Most later writers have emphasized the censitaires' independent temperament and the control of the seigneurs by royal officials, but have agreed nonetheless with Gérard Filteau that "l'habitant ne peut s'empêcher de respecter cet homme [his seigneur]."[9] Guy Frégault considers that the system supplied "une grande partie du peu de bien qui s'est fait en ce pays"[10] because as he, Trudel, Groulx, and others agree, it provided a social and economic framework in which the development of a new colony could proceed. Canon Groulx does suggest that in the eighteenth century parish and curé began to supplant seigneurie and seigneur as the cornerstone of social organization.[11] Even Léon Gérin, whose outright condemnation of the Canadian seigneurs is unique in the literature, implies that because the seigneurs were indifferent to the responsibilities of settling and developing their seigneuries, the colony was seriously weakened. The seigneurial system is seen as the center around which Canada developed, and it is Gérin's contention that the center was defective.

The assumption that the seigneurial system was *une ligne de force* in early Canada, widely accepted as it is, leads directly to several apparent contradictions. Accompanying general agreement that the system provided a framework for colonization, is the admission that few seigneurs brought settlers to Canada, and that the colony's chronic failure was its inability to attract immigrants. The picture of independent and often unmanageable habitants which was frequently painted by royal officials during the French regime and by some writers since, ill fits that of an influential seigneurial system, for seigneurialism, however modified in Canada, was at heart a system of social and economic organization and control. Why the habitants depended on their seigneurs, who were seldom more prosperous and frequently less experienced in a Canadian environment than themselves, is certainly not clear, especially if it is remembered that many of these same habitants were *coureurs de bois* and as capable as any white men of fending for themselves in the North American wilderness. Nor is the attitude of the habitants fifteen years after the conquest, when in spite of the remonstrances of seigneurs and clergy the majority remained neutral or sided with the American invaders, in accord with the traditional picture of kindly seigneurs and dependent habitants. If, as Mason Wade suggests, the habitants were reacting against the reimposition of seigneurial control,[12] and if the traditional picture of the seigneurial system is correct, then one can only say that a short and misleading exposure to some of the ideas of American republicanism and democracy was enough to raise serious doubts in the mind of a fickle population about the way of life which it had long enjoyed. None of this rings true.

It is a basic assumption of this study that if the seigneurial system were *une ligne de force* in early Canada, if much or even a small fraction of the social and economic life of the colony developed within a seigneurial framework, then the patterns of social and economic activity which appeared on the land would reflect the connection. Whereas earlier studies of the seigneurial system have looked to the statute books and to the official correspondence for evidence, the geographical analysis which follows has looked to the land, a fundamentally different point of view which has forced different questions to be asked, neglected documents to be opened, and others which have been much perused to be examined in a different light. Data have been collected which previously had been neglected, and an attempt has been made to demonstrate that this geographical evidence about the land in the broadest sense—about the size, shape, and distribution of seigneuries and rotures, the influence of an inheritance system on the amount of land controlled by individual seigneurs, the distribution of population, the character of the habitants' farms, the spatial arrangement of their settlements, and so on—is indispensable to the clear understanding of the seigneurial system as it developed in Canada.

The evidence presented in this study leads to the conclusion that the seigneurial system left an altogether insignificant impression on the geography of early Canada. Settlement expanded along the St. Lawrence and patterns of social and economic activity developed there in ways that rarely reflected a seigneurial framework. The seigneuries were indefinite units on the land; in the early years their boundaries were usually known only vaguely, and later when boundaries had been surveyed, they served little more than to separate censitaires who paid the annual dues to one seigneur from those who paid them to another. Some of the legal superstructure which accompanied the seigneurial system to Canada, as for example the laws of inheritance, was of great importance in shaping the geography of the colony, but these legal details could apply to many social and economic systems. The seigneurial system itself was largely irrelevant to the geography of early Canada, and it is reasonable to conclude that it was equally irrelevant to the way of life which emerged there. The evidence which leads to this conclusion, and the reasons for the rapid collapse of the seigneurial system in Canada during the French regime are discussed in the following chapters.

2 : The St. Lawrence Valley

THE trickle of settlers that crossed the Atlantic from France to the New World was deflected around a buffer of Dutch and English claims along the eastern seaboard of what is now the United States to a few islands in the West Indies, to the lower Mississippi, and, in the north, to a fringe of land around the southern margin of the Canadian Shield. As drawn by French cartographers, France's possessions in North America formed a crescent extending from New Orleans on the Mississippi delta to Louisbourg on Cape Breton Island. Others claimed some of this land, and with a handful of forts in several million square miles France never really occupied it. Unlike the cartographic dream, New France consisted of several pockets of isolated settlement, one on the tidal marshes around the Bay of Fundy, another along the lower Mississippi, a third along the St. Lawrence, eventually a few villages in the Illinois country, and a scattering of forts between. After 1608 when Samuel de Champlain moved his base of operations from Port Royal on the Bay of Fundy to Quebec, the St. Lawrence pocket, or Canada as the French began to call it, was the principal French settlement in North America. It was to the St. Lawrence that most Frenchmen came, and it was with the problem and potentialities of the St. Lawrence environment that they had to contend.

Although French explorers, traders, and missionaires quickly pushed by canoe and portage trail up the St. Lawrence and its tributaries to the Great Lakes and beyond to the rivers draining into Hudson Bay and the Gulf of Mexico, agricultural settlement along the lower St. Lawrence was

9

narrowly constricted. There the Canadian Shield presses in upon the river from the north. Relief in this section of the Shield rim is in the order of one to two thousand feet, and most of its surface has a slope of more than 10 per cent. As elsewhere in the Shield, there are innumerable swamps and lakes, and bedrock often juts through the heavily podzolized soils which have developed on a mantle of glacial drift. Here and there delta kames or strips of postglacial alluvium form pockets with soils suitable for cultivation, but even today agriculture often ends where the Shield begins. During the French regime the lure of beaver pelts or of heathen souls to win pulled men into the Shield; agricultural settlement stopped wherever it reached the margins.

The Shield and the St. Lawrence intersect twenty-five miles below Quebec, and at the point of intersection hills rise sharply from the river for a thousand feet or more. To the east the wall of hills is broken in several places; and the valleys, inundated by the postglacial Champlain Sea, are covered with sedimentary deposits on which fertile soils have formed.[1] Such a valley at Baie Saint-Paul opposite Ile aux Coudres was settled before 1700, but most of the north shore was cut off to settlement twenty-five miles below Quebec. From there the river swings away from the Shield to a maximum distance, midway between Quebec and Montreal, of more than twenty miles.

South of the river is the northeastward extension of the Appalachian Roughlands. The relief in these hills and mountains is not unlike that of the southern fringes of the Shield, and the effects of glaciation are almost as marked. A mantle of glacial drift covers the underlying sedimentary rocks, but soils developed on this ground moraine are generally more fertile and more easily cultivated than those in the Shield. Before the end of the eighteenth century parts of the Appalachians began to be cleared and settled, but during the French regime, when better land along the St. Lawrence was available, the northwestern boundary of these rough highlands was a barrier to settlement. At Montreal this boundary is forty miles away, at Lake Saint-Pierre at least thirty, and only well below Quebec does it approach the river to pinch out the lowland strip altogether.

Settlement west of the Ile de Montréal was restricted by Canadian governors and intendants who would not grant seigneuries along either the upper St. Lawrence or the Ottawa River, two of the principal routes of the fur trade. Farms along either route would have been exposed to

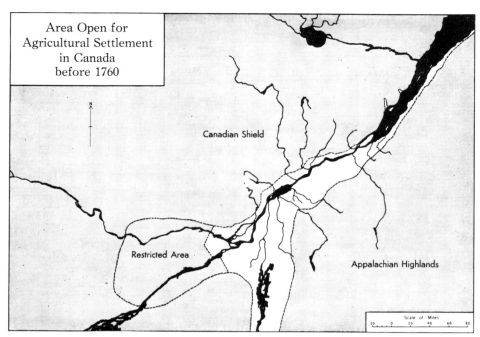

Fig. 2–1.—Area available for agricultural settlement (white area) along the St. Lawrence River and its tributaries, before 1760.

Indian attack and, even more serious in official eyes, would have exacerbated the baffling problem of policing the trade. Of course, habitants used these routes both legally and illegally with almost equal impunity, but did not establish farms along them when agricultural land was available closer to the markets along the lower St. Lawrence, and when an isolated and illegal farm to the west would have been taken by officials as tangible proof of participation in the fur trade. Thus while the St. Lawrence waterway drew on an enormous hinterland, agricultural settlement—and, for all practical purposes, the seigneurial system—expanded within the narrow limits shown in Figure 2–1; that is, within the area bounded by the Shield, the Appalachian Roughlands, and the western limit of seigneurial concessions.

The core of this new land was the river itself, the second largest in North America (by volume) and, like the Mississippi, an avenue to the heart of the continent. From Montreal to Quebec the river is seldom less than half a mile wide, and below Quebec the width expands to many miles as the river opens slowly into the Gulf of St. Lawrence. The largest ships from France anchored in the shadow of the rock at Quebec, and although currents and winds made navigation more difficult upstream, small sailing vessels could get as far as Montreal. In the early years most habitants used canoes to take vegetables to the town market or to visit their neighbors, and in winter they also travelled on the river by snowshoe or sleigh. Seigneuries were conceded along the river in long narrow trapezoids so that as many seigneurs as possible would benefit from river frontage. Partly for the same reason rotures were similarly elongated, and at any time before the conquest at least nine out of ten Canadians lived within a mile of the river. The St. Lawrence was an omnipresent element of Canadian life.

The land rises gently from the St. Lawrence towards the Shield or the Appalachians. The underlying sediments are folded and faulted, but repeated glacial scouring, morainic debris, and the succeeding deposition in the postglacial Champlain Sea have left a plain through which a few relic igneous masses protrude as the Monteregian Hills. Mount Royal in Montreal is the best known, and five others extend in a line to the east towards the Appalachians. In general the St. Lawrence lowland from Lake Saint-Pierre to Montreal and well up the Richelieu is remarkably level; even the river banks are only a few feet high. East of Lake Saint-Pierre the underlying strata dip towards Montreal; and the river, flowing in the opposite direction, has cut through them, its banks becoming steeper and higher until they approach three hundred feet at Quebec. Often there are narrow flats below these cliffs, and during the French regime lines of farmhouses appeared either on the flats or along the rims of the cliffs. Where the Shield or the Appalachians press close to the river, there is often a succession of terraces or a slope which is so steep that erosion was a problem on the long strip farms which were conceded at right angles to the river. However, within the limits shown on Figure 2–1, the roughness of the land surface rarely presented serious barriers to agricultural settlement.

The most important of the many tributaries of the St. Lawrence which cross the lowland are shown in Figure 2–2. These rivers and streams generally have low banks, but even though bridges were quickly built across some and by the 1740's ferries operated on others, they impeded land travel along the St. Lawrence axis. With approximately forty inches of rain a year everywhere in the colony the tributaries were not needed

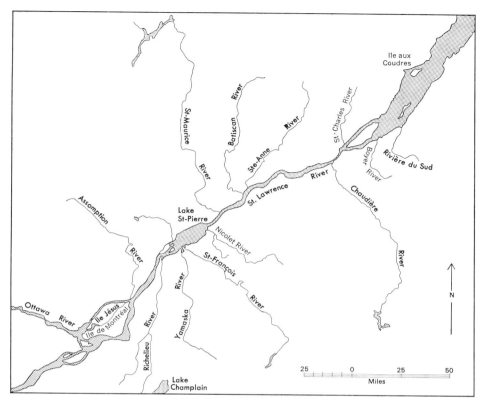

*Fig. 2–2.—*Principal waterways in Canada.

for irrigation, but many provided power for saw- or gristmills, water for stock, and water for household use. When a tributary was navigable and access to it from the land was easier than to the St. Lawrence, settlement often followed its course, and seigneuries were conceded along the most important tributaries as they were along the St. Lawrence.

While there are very few lakes on the St. Lawrence plain, swamps and bogs and large areas of inadequately drained land are common. Consolidated dunes along the river are likely to have swamps behind, and wherever the slope of the plain is slight there are drainage problems. Peter Kalm, the Swedish naturalist who visited Canada near the end of the French regime, remarked that he saw no ditches anywhere although they were often needed.[2] Drainage ditches were used in Canada but not nearly frequently enough, and water on the land often must have held up spring planting and thus shortened the effective growing season. Wherever poor drainage and poor soils combine, as in a broad belt several miles south of the river, which extends roughly from Lake Saint-Pierre to Quebec and beyond, the land was not farmed and in most cases has remained uncultivated to the present.

The St. Lawrence plain was covered by a dense forest. Broadleaf deciduous species predominated near Montreal, but the coniferous representation increased steadily towards the northeastern end of the colony.[3] The association west of Lake Saint-Pierre comprised a wide variety of species—sugar maple, beech, yellow birch, white elm, red maple, basswood, white ash, red, white, and burr oaks, and large-toothed aspen. In the river valleys there were some butternut, cottonwood, and slippery elm, and in the poorly drained areas tamarack (larch), eastern white cedar, black spruce, and black ash. Below Lake Saint-Pierre, where summers were slightly cooler and winters longer, species from the boreal forest of the Shield had invaded the lowland. Sugar maple, red oak, white ash, butternut, yellow birch, and white elm were still common, but so were tamarack, balsam fir, spruce, and white birch. Here and there were stands of white pine. The Crown set aside the oaks in these forests for shipbuilding, some merchants attempted to export white pine masts, and others built sawmills to cut planks and beams for construction in the colony and, occasionally, for export. Great quantities of wood were burned in "the prodigious Fires" the Canadians made to keep out the winter's cold, and many habitants supplemented their incomes by supplying cordwood to the towns.

Although wood was indispensable the forest stood in the way of agriculture. As was often the case in North America, trees were girdled and burned and the stumps usually left in the ground until they rotted, but even by this method clearing was inordinately slow. In the early years a few seigneurs hired men to clear land or paid their tenants a bonus for each arpent cleared, but such costly methods were soon discontinued, and the habitant with a new concession had a forest between himself and a farm. Uncleared land in most parts of the colony was almost worthless.

When Champlain camped on the Ile de Montréal in 1611 he found sixty arpents of meadow in what must have been originally an Indian clearing,[4] but except for the natural meadows along the river bank, there were few other holes in the forest cover. Tides affect the river level as far up as Trois-Rivières, and some of the low flats below the river banks were fresh-water tidal marshes. Above Trois-Rivières the difference between seasonal high and low water levels was sufficient where banks were low to inhibit tree growth and produce strips of grassland which were dry for part of the year. As the Canadians did not bother with dikes these strips were seldom cultivated. They were moderately good pasture, provided some winter hay of indifferent quality, and were regularly set aside for such purposes.

Frenchmen settling in Canada found themselves in a continental climate with winters colder and summers as warm as or warmer than those they had known. Air masses that move eastward over the St. Lawrence valley come from the land, and when the same air masses reach western Europe they have been moderated by an ocean. Largely for this reason the January mean temperature in Quebec and Montreal (10° F.) is almost thirty degrees lower than in coastal Brittany, and twenty-five degrees lower than in Paris. The July mean in Montreal is several degrees higher than anywhere in western France. Almost every visitor to Canada remarked on these extremes, particularly on the winter temperatures which, they pointed out, froze the holes which fishermen cut in the river ice to a depth of six inches overnight in a land at the latitude of Nantes. The river is frozen from mid-December to the end of March, and from the beginning of December until April snow accumulates to a depth of four or five feet. This winter isolated Canada from the outside world, although within the colony the frozen river remained a transportation route, and it may actually have been faster to travel upriver on snowshoes or in a sleigh in winter than by boat during the rest of the year. But when winter settled down around the colony most of its activity slowed, and from time to time the intendants complained of "La longeur [*sic*] de l'hyver pendant tout lequel le peuple ne fait rien, que se chaufer." [5]

Summers along the lower St. Lawrence and in western France are less different. Showers are more abrupt and intense in the continental climate of eastern North America, but total summer precipitation along the lower St. Lawrence and in western France is roughly equivalent. The frost-free period of approximately one hundred and fifty days at Montreal, one hundred and thirty at Quebec, and barely a hundred below Baie Saint-Paul, is shorter in each case than that in western France; but mean July temperatures at Montreal (70° F.) and Quebec (68° F.) are both above the Paris mean for the month, and the July mean at Baie Saint-Paul

(64° F.) is only slightly below. While almost every habitant near Montreal grew a few melons, summers were usually too cold elsewhere in the colony.[6] Corn became marginal near Quebec, and wheat which matured near Montreal was often frost damaged in other areas. Well below Quebec pasture tended to replace grains. French pear, peach, and walnut trees did not survive anywhere in Canada,[7] but the Canadian climate exacted few other casualties in the transfer of plants from western France.

Soils along the lower St. Lawrence are rarely of exceptionally good quality.[8] Most are slightly acid, deficient in some nutrients, heavy in texture, and poorly drained. The best soils are on the Montreal plain, but there were few areas even there that would not have been improved during the French regime by better drainage. Clay and silt loams cover more than two-thirds of the Montreal plain. Although these clay loams have a heavy texture and tend to dry out, their humus content is high and they can be very fertile. The silt loams are heavy soils on the south shore but their texture is ideal on Ile Jésus and the Ile de Montréal, and these are probably the best soils along the lower St. Lawrence. There are only limited areas of less fertile sandy loams near Montreal and some pockets of gley soils which have never been cultivated.

Soils similar to those on the Montreal plain extend east to the valleys of the Richelieu and Yamaska and beyond, in an ever narrowing ribbon along the south shore, to Rivière du Loup a hundred miles below Quebec. Sandy loams are more common in this strip, acidity more marked, and drainage more of a problem than on the Montreal plain. However, these soils along the river are substantially better than those extending behind in a broad belt to the Appalachians. In this belt drainage is extremely poor and the glacial drift a mixture of sand and gravel on which a shallow, acidic soil has formed. Most of the land is still uncultivated, and the characteristic vegetation along the south shore a few miles from the river is spruce bog with a few stands of jack pine in particularly sandy areas. It was equally unattractive during the French regime, and settlement expanded away from the St. Lawrence only in river valleys like the Nicolet and Chaudière where good soils had formed on recent alluvial deposits.

On the north shore near Quebec and on the Ile d'Orléans sand and silt loams mixed with gravel predominate. Slopes are steeper and drainage is seldom a problem, but soils are deficient in many nutrients and are much less fertile than are those near Montreal. The belt of easily worked land along the north shore above Quebec is often less than a mile wide and composed of sandy soils in which many crops do not thrive. It widens north of Lake Saint-Pierre in an area of clay and silt loams, and extends up the Assomption, Berthier, and Sainte-Anne rivers in pockets that include some of the best land in the colony. However, little enough of the land between the river and the Shield is good farmland.

All in all, the soil resources of early Canada were scanty. There were bands of potential farmland along either shore of the St. Lawrence and up some of the tributaries, and a triangle of fertile land from the Ile de Montréal to Lake Saint-Pierre and south towards Lake Champlain, but the best land was to the west in what is now Ontario, and was then the territory of the fur trade. Agricultural practices were rudimentary: land was rarely fertilized and crop rotations were inadequate or nonexistent; and although officials claimed that the best soils could be cultivated continuously for twenty years without obvious deterioration,[9] the fertility of even these soils declined in time. Reports of soil exhaustion began in the 1660's and continued fairly steadily thereafter. New farmland was always available in Canada during the French regime (although not always near the towns) because the population was small. After the conquest, as the population continued to rise and the outlet to the west, which would have been opened sooner or later by the French, was closed by English settlement, rural overpopulation became serious. The problems created by a large rural population on a small amount of good land have plagued Quebec to the present.

The riparian St. Lawrence colony had three principal outlets: one by way of the St. Lawrence or the Ottawa to the Great Lakes and beyond, another by the Richelieu–Lake Champlain route to the Hudson River and New York, and the third through the Gulf of St. Lawrence to the North Atlantic. The St. Lawrence route to the heart of a continent was the easiest along the eastern seaboard; and, partly for this reason, French-speaking explorers and traders had pushed across half a continent before many Englishmen had taken their first timid steps on the western flank of the Appalachians. Thousands of Canadians, some on authorized but most on illegal trading expeditions, left the lower St. Lawrence for the upper Ottawa and the Great Lakes beyond. A man could vanish into this wilderness of water and forest, and there was next to nothing French officials could do to stop him or to apprehend him when he returned. The land connection with New York was also easy, and although association with the heretical English and their cheaper trade goods was condemned and serious penalties (hanging in at least one case) awaited the lawbreaker who was caught, the connection was always maintained. Canada was part of a North American matrix of trading connections and contending national aspirations. Its inhabitants dealt with Indians and Englishmen and these contacts were instrumental in shaping the distinctive character of early Canada.

The other outlet led by way of the Gulf to the North Atlantic and thence to France, the French possessions in the West Indies, and even to the English colonies along the Atlantic seaboard. Quebec was no farther from La Rochelle than Boston was from London, but it was almost twice as far by water from the West Indies, and was closed to sailing vessels for a third of the year. For these reasons alone Canadian merchants were enormously handicapped in comparison with the ubiquitous Bostonians operating out of a more central, year-round port. A rigid French mercantilism, which could be relatively easily enforced in Canada because most exports and imports by sea had to pass through a single port, compounded their difficulties. The St. Lawrence opened the heart of a continent to the Canadians, but a colony along its shores was a poor base from which to maintain sea connections with the lands of the Atlantic rim.

Officials in Canada quickly recognized this. In 1663 Governor Avaugour suggested establishing a French fort on the Hudson River.[10] Three years later Jean Talon, the king's first intendant in Canada, urged Louis XIV to negotiate with the Dutch for the acquisition of New Holland (he did not know that the Dutch colony had come under English aegis), a move which, he argued, would give Canada two ports and undisputed control of the fur trade.[11] When this suggestion was turned down Talon recommended a road to the Bay of Fundy.[12] In 1689 the Chevalier de Callières, governor of Montreal, proposed that a Canadian contingent by land and French forces by sea attack New York,[13] and the king was intrigued enough by this foolhardy scheme to allocate two ships for the siege.[14] The attack never materialized, but it was mooted for more than a decade with one of the arguments in its favor being that Canada would be provided with a year-round port closer to the French possessions in the West Indies. However, such a port was a pipe dream, and Canada remained poorly situated with respect to the Atlantic world until the conquest.

Although there were frequent protestations to the contrary, Canada had been established primarily for the fur trade for which it was an admirable base. No other site could have been as advantageous except possibly one in Hudson Bay, and because of the difficulty of entry to the Bay and the distribution of beaver before the southern fringes of the Shield were depleted, probably even Hudson Bay did not have as much to offer. So easy was the St. Lawrence route that almost any inhabitant of Canada could, if he wished, become a fur trader with a minimum of effort. On the other hand, as a base for agricultural settlement the lower St. Lawrence was wanting in two respects: there was very little good land, and the outlet to the markets was difficult. Furs, a high-value, low-bulk export, could be shipped easily to France, but Canadian agricultural products, essentially the same as the French, could not have competed in French markets at French prices after a trans-Atlantic haul, even if they had been admitted freely. Most of the small market was in the West Indies, in respect to which Canada was extremely poorly situated. If the French companies which were given charters to trade in and colonize North America had made agricultural settlement their primary objective, they would probably have established a colony to the south as close to Jamestown as possible, and the French or English destiny of most of North America would have been decided very much earlier. But the companies were formed for the fur trade, for which the St. Lawrence was the obvious base, and the side effects of their venture in the New World had to fit in as best they could. When the relative importance of the fur trade declined, as it had by the end of the seventeenth century, the broad lines of European penetration in North America had been set and France could not expand to the south into land which by then was claimed and occupied by others.

3 : Land Division among Seigneurs

PROBABLY few of the Europeans who came to North America in the seventeenth century thought of the move as a creative venture. There were forests to clear, houses and roads to build, and fields to plow, but immigrants envisaged in European terms the settlements which would grow out of these labors. However, a new environment forced creativity upon its settlers, and the building process inevitably modified many European institutions and ideas, and particularly, because land was the outstanding new resource, European policies of land distribution and settlement. Out of this rethinking came impractical utopian experiments, quite workable approaches to land granting and colonization such as the New England proprietary township, and, eventually, the American Land Ordinances of the 1780's and their subsequent modifications. In many cases a sharp break was made with European traditions, but in French Canada, which retained a feudal system of land tenure until the mid-nineteenth century when it had outlived its French parent by more than sixty years, the persistence of French land policy would appear to be much more remarkable than its change.

However, because there was no equivalent in France of the great river, the endless forest, the Indian raids, or the lure of the fur trade, there were no French precedents for many of the decisions about land policy, or there were precedents which fitted poorly. Furthermore, there were many French systems of landholding, loosely united, within the jurisdiction of the coutumes, around certain common assumptions about the nature of property. The introduction of the Coutume de Paris about 1640 [1] as the Canadian civil code did not fix the nature of Canadian landholding, for a coutume was no more than a set of laws applicable to many landholding types. The Canadian system was to be seigneurial; that is, all land was to have a seigneur to whom a statement of vassalage (*foi et hommage*) and, perhaps, specific payments were due. But if the banks of the St. Lawrence had been divided into a handful of baronies, each baron the king's vassal and free to subenfeudate at will; or if the king's officials had granted plots of a few square arpents in return for a statement of *foi et hommage* and a nominal *cens* * which they received in the king's name, the system would have been nonetheless seigneurial. Neither extreme was excluded by the coutume nor was without precedent in France. Thus, although Canada acquired the legal structure of French land tenure, there quickly began an intermittent process of experimentation and adaptation as French forms were introduced and modified and as Canadian innovations appeared. In spite of these modifications the legal system remained predominantly French, although by the end of the French regime it was encrusted with intendants' ordinances and royal edicts which applied only in Canada. Patterns on the land changed more rapidly, and at the heart of these changes were the effects of decisions about the size and shape of the Canadian seigneurie.

In the spring of 1627 Cardinal Richelieu granted the Company of New France all those lands bounded by the Arctic Circle, Florida, Lake Superior, and the sea. This vast territory was held directly from the king and was charged with only the usual statement of *foi et hommage* and a golden crown upon the accession of each new monarch. In return for the grant and the exclusive trading privileges that accompanied it, the Company was to bring two to three hundred men to New France in 1628 and four thousand more during the next fifteen years. In establishing these immigrants or anyone else who requested land in the colony the associates were free to

improve and arrange the said lands as they will deem it to be necessary, and distribute them to those who will live in the said land and to others in such quantity and by the means that they will judge proper; give and attribute to

---

* A token payment to a seigneur which was levied only on the final concessions of land in the feudal ladder. These *en censive* concessions, or rotures, could not be subgranted, and the censitaire usually worked the land.

them such titles and honors, rights, powers, and options that they will judge to be good, needed, or necessary according to the qualities, conditions, and merits of the people, and generally with such charges, reserves, and conditions that they will deem to be needed. And nevertheless in case of the creation of duchies, marquisates, counties, and baronies letters of confirmation from His Majesty will be required.[2]

The Company was expected to subgrant through most of the feudal range, although not without royal consent at the higher levels. The size, shape, and title of the grants, and the choice of the grantees were left to the Company's discretion.

The capital and enthusiasm that created the Company of New France were not attracted by the modest and distant returns which could be expected from the concession of land. The associates envisaged spectacular profits in the fur trade, and against this happy prospect the task of building an agricultural community along the St. Lawrence was an unwelcome chore. Yet hanging over the Company was the knowledge that its predecessors in the fur trade, Guillaume de Caën and his associates, had lost their charter for establishing no more than forty or fifty Frenchmen in Canada,[3] and that theirs might be the same fate. Although the Company brought out a few settlers (never in sufficient numbers to approach its charter obligations), it was more interested to find some formula by which its responsibility would devolve on others. The most obvious was to subenfeudate with the hope that the new seigneurs created by the Company would bring the settlers on whom the king insisted. To this end the Company's first seigneurial concession, which it granted in 1634 to Robert Giffard, stipulated that the men whom Giffard or his successors sent to New France would be credited to the Company's account, thereby diminishing the number of settlers which it was required to recruit.[4] Over the next thirty years the Company granted some seventy seigneuries, most of them with this clause in the title deed, in a half-hearted attempt to spur others on to an activity which it found so onerous. From time to time the Company brought out settlers and usually gave them rotures,[5] but it relied mainly on the seigneurs it had created to fulfill the obligation to colonize, and would give a substantial concession to anyone who showed any interest in doing so.

The front endpaper of this book shows the seigneuries granted during the proprietary period, other than those within the villages of Quebec and Trois-Rivières or around the Gaspé shore.[6] Seigneuries were clustered in a group around Quebec where most of the settlers in the colony lived, and secondary concentrations appeared near Montreal and Trois-Rivières. The smallest seigneuries were only a few square arpents in the towns (too small to appear on the map); the largest, hundreds of square miles. Most, but not all, were trapezoidal with their long axes at right angles to the river. Some seigneuries overlapped. The dimensions specified in the title deeds of Saint-Ignace, Saint-Gabriel, and Sillery, three seigneuries just west of Quebec, did not fit the available land. Morin, a small seigneurie thirty miles downstream, was granted within an earlier concession, while a similar distance upstream from Quebec Portneuf overlapped an earlier concession to Henry Pinguet, so that different seigneurs apparently paid *foi et hommage* for the same land.[7] Several seigneurs were left to choose the sites of their concessions. In 1640 François de Chavigny was granted half a league along the river by three leagues in depth somewhere between Quebec and Trois-Rivières.[8] Most seigneuries were neither inhabited nor surveyed and no one had a very clear idea of the land that had been conceded. One element of order was introduced in the 1630's when a *rhumb de vent*, a survey line roughly perpendicular to the river, was fixed as the axis of most seigneurial concessions,[9] a decision which is reflected in field patterns along the St. Lawrence to the present day.

These concessions are not as puzzling as they seem if it is remembered that the Company had no precedent for, and little interest in, the concessions it was making. In 1640 no one could be very precise about the amount of land that a seigneur might be expected to clear, or about the minimum size of a potentially profitable seigneurie. (See Chaps. 5 and 6 for discussions of seigneurial revenue and the problems of attracting settlers to individual seigneuries. It is apparent that seigneuries in Canada had to be many square miles in extent before their seigneurs could hope to make a profit, but of course no one could have known this during the proprietary period.) Certainly the Company was not very interested in finding out. However the Company did have some criteria for its seigneurial concessions, and if the title deeds are read in conjunction with the map of grants during the proprietary period, then the outlines—such as they were—of its land policy are fairly clear.

Initially, the Company had no plan for the shape of Canadian seigneuries. Of its earliest concessions, Beauport was a league along the river and a league and one-half deep; La Citière, an enormous triangle;

Lauzon, a square; and Beaupré, an approximate rectangle, its long axis parallel to the river. Because the river was the route to the interior and to France, as well as the avenue of intracolonial transportation in winter and in summer, all seigneuries were on the river, and no one would have wanted one away from it. Apparently it was not until 1637 that the Company realized that river frontage might become valuable and should be conceded with restraint. In this year appeared the first of the long, thin trapezoids: Sainte-Croix and Grondines, each one league wide and ten deep; Linctôt, three-quarters of a league by three leagues; and Dautré, half a league by two leagues. From time to time thereafter there were concessions of other basic shapes. Cap des Rosiers was an arc ten leagues wide around the Gaspé shore; and, in the heart of the colony, De Maure was greater in length along the river than it was in depth. However the trapezoid suited the colony. It gave most seigneurs access to the river, and its boundaries were easily fixed. Posts at either corner along the river were a fairly accurate indication of a man's property,[10] and to be absolutely certain a seigneur had only to hire a surveyor to extend two lines along a standardized *rhumb de vent*. The backline could be left for years. No system could have been easier or, provided the original title deed was clear, more foolproof. As it was seigneurs were fairly frequently in the courts, but probably would have been there steadily if a less straightforward system had been introduced. So the trapezoid remained the standard shape for the seigneurial grant, a ratio of width to length of one to two, three, or four replacing the extreme ratios of some of the early concessions.

As the map of seigneuries in 1663 shows, there was no uniformity in the size of the Company's concessions. Associates, influential friends, and the Jesuits were granted the largest seigneuries ever distributed in Canada. La Citière contained at least a thousand square miles, and its seigneurs granted concessions that differed from the Company's only in the person to whom the grantee paid *foi et hommage*. Beaupré, Lauzon, Ile de Montréal, Batiscan, Cap de la Madeleine, and Cap des Rosiers were well over a hundred square miles each. On the other hand, Dautré was no more than seven, and Pointe du Lac and Morin even less. Although the Company tended to give these smaller concessions to less important individuals, proprietors of the largest seigneuries also controlled some of the smallest. Not one of the largest seigneuries, to be sure, was the property of an inconsequential seigneur. Obviously the Company had not reached any conclusion about the appropriate size for a Canadian seigneurie; as a general rule, the more important the individual the larger the grant he could expect, but there was probably almost the same degree of correlation with the ability to argue a good case. In a different class were twelve seigneuries granted in the village of Quebec and nine at Trois-Rivières. These were intended as sites for churches and hospitals or as residences for persons of some distinction, and usually contained only an arpent or two.

Most of the Company's concessions were made between Montreal and Quebec. Concessions above Montreal were avoided partly because the Iroquois would have made life in them even more precarious than it already was in a colony where habitants were ordered to take a gun as well as a pick to their fields,[11] but primarily because such concessions would have invited competition in the fur trade. While most of the Company's grants expressly excluded the seigneurs from the trade, the first of a great many ordinances condemning unauthorized coureurs de bois, appeared during the proprietary period,[12] and from the Company's point of view it made no sense to exacerbate a situation already getting out of control by conceding along the fur routes. Below Quebec the agricultural potential declined as the shore became more rocky and summers cooler and shorter so that when seigneuries were granted below Ile aux Coudres they tended to be developed as fishing stations or lumber camps. The heart of the colony during the proprietary years was the Quebec-Montreal axis, and the reasons for a concentration of Company grants in this two hundred mile strip did not change significantly during the rest of the French regime.

The Company's charter was revoked early in 1663. In 1627 the fort at Quebec had been a fur trading post, and thirty-five years later Canada was little more. Near Quebec some land had been cleared and planted, but with just over two thousand Frenchmen in the entire colony most seigneuries were entirely undeveloped. The attempt to add the responsibility for settlement to the fur trading monopoly had not worked; nor, considering the inherently conflicting nature of the two purposes, could it really have been expected to work. Throughout the French regime there was a tension between the fur trade and agriculture as the former drew habitants into the woods in the unauthorized expeditions which were the bane of all attempts to regulate the trade. Had the two occupations been more nearly complementary, the organizational and logistical problems of an uncertain trading venture spread over a large segment of a new continent would have been sufficiently absorbing. The understandable failure of the Company of New France to promote settlement did not deter the king from reconceding New France in 1664 to the Company of the West Indies with powers, in theory, as extensive as those of its predecessor. But after 1663 it was young Louis XIV, his advisors, and his appointees who directed the settlement of the colony. Royal officials in France sent copious memoranda to their counterparts in Canada, and for several years the king allocated funds for regular contingents of settlers.

The king was concerned not only with the indifference of the Company of New France to settlement, but also with what he considered to be serious flaws in its land policy. One of the principal reasons why Canada was not developed, he concluded, was that its settlers held more land than they could possibly clear, and in March 1663 he ordered all land grants in Canada which were not cleared within six months to be returned to the royal domain.[13] In May the king sent a special commissioner primarily to investigate land policy,[14] and in his instructions to Talon two years later reiterated his convictions that "one of the things which presents the greatest obstacle to the settlement of Canada has been that the habitants . . . have taken very large areas of land for their concessions which they have never been able to cultivate because of their overly large extent, and being thus separated find themselves exposed to Iroquois ambushes."[15]

Over the next several years most letters from France touched on this point. Concessions were too large, they could not be cleared, and they resulted in isolated farmsteads which were impossible to defend. At first these objections were directed less at the Company's seigneurial concessions than at the rotures within them, although the scope of royal criticism widened as more explicit information reached France.

In 1667 Talon pointed out in his annual report that "the large, free concessions which have until now been made in Canada result in demands for such large tracts of land that I shall soon be short of it for those families which you will send hereafter if I fulfill everyone's wishes. M. de Saurel [Sorel] shows signs of being dissatisfied that I have not conceded him a holding of more than fifty thousand arpents of land."[16] This and other observations of a similar nature led the king and his advisors to the decision in June, 1672, to reduce the size of Canadian seigneuries. The king ordered Talon to compile an inventory of all seigneuries granted more than ten years before and to withdraw half of the undeveloped land in each.[17] As soon as he received this royal edict, Talon issued an ordinance requiring all those holding more than four hundred arpents to inform him of the amount of cleared land and of the numbers of settlers and livestock in their seigneuries.[18] However, while Talon reconceded several smaller seigneuries which had existed only on paper during the proprietary period, and which had probably been forgotten by the time Talon arrived in the colony, he never withdrew fractions of unsettled seigneuries as the king had ordered.*

The decision to reduce the size of seigneuries was reflected, however, in Talon's own concessions. Figure 3–1 shows his grants in 1672, and as most of these grants were made in the last days before he sailed for France, they were his final judgment about the size of seigneurial concessions in Canada. By earlier standards they were all small. Malbaie, the largest, was an earlier grant which had been reconceded, while Chambly, which was almost as large, occupied a strategic position around a fort on the Richelieu and owed its size to the special importance which Talon attached to it. The extremes of the Company's concessions were gone; Talon did not concede plots in the towns, while fifteen of his seigneuries filled a fraction of the area which had been the seigneurie of La Citière.[19] Most of his concessions were one or two leagues along the river and two or three in depth, but the smallest were little more than a square mile, or roughly six to eight times the size of an average roture.

However, one hundred and fifty to three hundred rotures grouped in four to eight small villages could have been conceded within most of Talon's seigneuries. When fully settled such a seigneurie would have provided a yearly revenue from the censitaires alone of approximately 2,500 to 5,000 livres—enough to have enabled the seigneur to live more comfortably than most of his censitaires, but not so large that he would necessarily have been a person of influence anywhere in the colony. (See Chap. 5 for a detailed analysis of seigneurial revenue.) Although Talon may have been thinking along these lines it is entirely possible that he divided the available river frontage by the number of prospective seigneurs, to arrive at some rough standard for the river dimension of the

* Talon left Canada shortly after he issued this ordinance, and there was not another intendant in the colony until 1676. Perhaps the royal edict would have been followed up if Talon had remained, but as it was no action was ever taken.

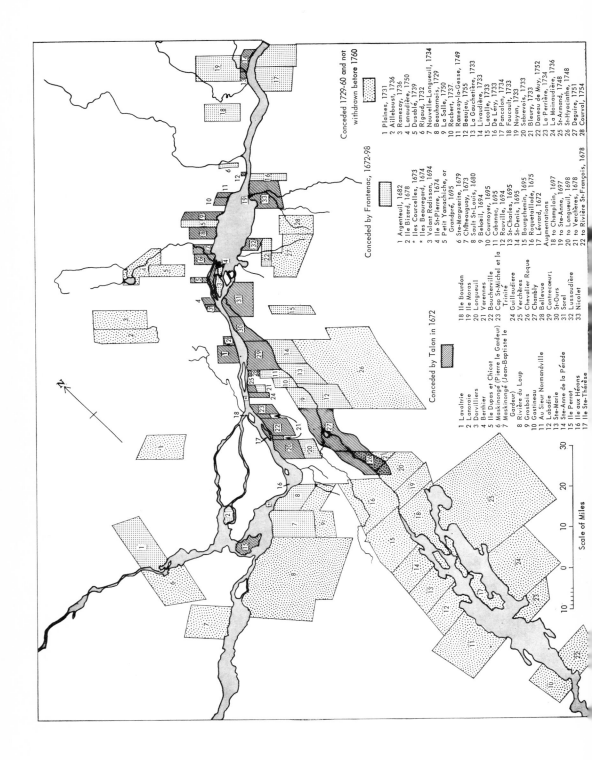

Conceded 1729-60 and not withdrawn before 1760

1 Plaines, 1731
2 Ailleboust, 1736
3 Ramezay, 1736
4 Lanaudière, 1750
5 Dusablé, 1739
6 Rigaud, 1732
7 Nouvelle-Longueuil, 1734
8 Beauharnois, 1729
9 La Salle, 1750
10 Rocbert, 1737.
11 Ramezay-la-Gesse, 1749
12 Beaujeu, 1755
13 La Gauchetière, 1733
14 Livaudière, 1733
15 Lacolle, 1733
16 De Léry, 1733
17 Pancalon, 1734
18 Foucault, 1733
19 Noyan, 1733
20 Sabrevois, 1733
21 Bleury, 1733
22 Daneau de Muy, 1752
23 La Perrière, 1734
24 La Moinaudière, 1736
25 St-Armand, 1748
26 St-Hyacinthe, 1748
27 Deguire, 1751
28 Courval, 1754

Conceded by Frontenac, 1672-98

1 Argenteuil, 1682
2 Ile Bizard, 1678
* Iles Courcelles, 1673
* Iles Beauregard, 1674
3 Volant Radisson, 1694
4 Ile St-Pierre, 1674
5 Petit Yamachiche, or Grandpré, 1695
6 Ste-Marguerite, 1679
7 Châteauguay, 1673
8 Sault St-Louis, 1680
9 Beloeil, 1694
10 Cournoyer, 1695
11 Cabanac, 1695
12 Rouville, 1694
13 St-Charles, 1695
14 St-Denis, 1695
15 Bourgchemin, 1695
16 Roquetaillade, 1675
17 Lévrard, 1672
Augmentations
18 to Champlain, 1697
19 to Ste-Anne, 1697
20 to Longueuil, 1698
21 to Verchères, 1678
22 to Rivière St-François, 1678

Conceded by Talon in 1672

1 Lavaltrie
2 Lanoraie
3 Dorvilliers
4 Berthier
5 Ile Dupas et Chicot
6 Maskinongé (Pierre le Gardeur)
7 Maskinongé (Jean-Baptiste le Gardeur)
8 Rivière du Loup
9 Grosbois
10 Gastineau
11 Au Sieur Normandville
12 Labadie
13 Ste-Marie
14 Ste-Anne de la Pérade
15 Ile Perrot
16 Ile aux Hérons
17 Ile Ste-Thérèse
18 Ile Bourdon
19 Ile Moras
20 Longueuil
21 Varennes
22 Boucherville
23 Cap St-Michel et la Trinité
24 Guillaudière
25 Verchères
26 Chevalier Roque
27 Chambly
28 Bellevue
29 Contrecoeur
30 St-Ours
31 Sorel
32 Lussaudière
33 Nicolet

Scale of Miles

30   20   10   0   10

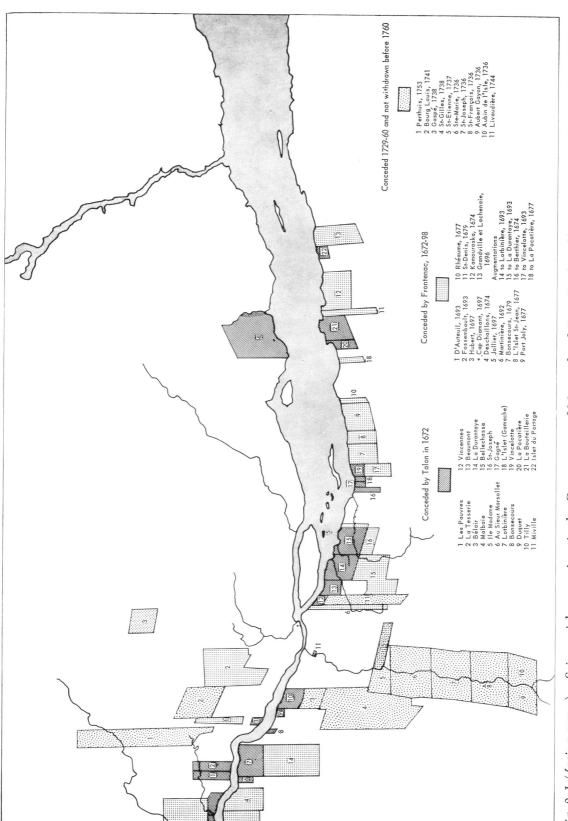

Fig. 3-1 (facing pages).—Seigneurial concessions in the Governments of Montreal and Trois-Rivières (*facing page*) and Quebec from 1672 to 1760. Prepared by the University of Wisconsin Cartographic Laboratory.

seigneuries which he conceded. Without the range of wealth and social position among the grantees that had characterized the earlier period, such a system was possible. Certainly, Talon was convinced that seigneuries of a hundred or more square miles were unsatisfactory. Experience had shown him that they could not be developed, and such concessions to individuals who, if they could develop their seigneuries entirely, must wield great influence in the colony were out of keeping with the centralizing approach to colonial development of which Talon was a representative. Whatever the other considerations, Talon's concessions in 1672 reflected the king's decision to keep the colony's control firmly in his own hands, and they insured that no large landowners would acquire title to most of the agricultural land in the colony.

The largest cluster of Talon's concessions was along the south shore between Montreal and Trois-Rivières, where, after La Citière had reverted to the royal domain, most of the unconceded river frontage between Montreal and Quebec was located. From Trois-Rivières to a point fifty miles below Quebec gaps left by the Company were filled in so that when Talon left the colony in 1672 only a few patches along either bank of the St. Lawrence for two hundred miles had not been granted. Chambly and Chevalier Roque, Talon's only two concessions away from the St. Lawrence, reflected his concern to bar the Iroquois and the English from the Richelieu gateway to Canada, as perhaps did Sorel, Saint-Ours, and Contrecœur, although these three would probably have been conceded regardless of Talon's decision about the strategic significance of the Richelieu. For the most part Talon conceded where land along the river was available, and more land was open on the south shore towards the Montreal end of the axis. With few exceptions his concessions were contiguous either with his own or with earlier grants.

In spite of Talon's smaller concessions the authorities in France were still convinced that many of the seigneuries in the colony were too large and, throughout the 1670's, emphasized this point in their dispatches as if it were the crux of the colony's ills. The royal ordinance of June 4, 1672, which ordered officials to reunite uncleared seigneurial land to the royal domain, was reissued in 1675 and reinforced with a clause stipulating that new concessions not cleared within four years would be withdrawn as well.[20] The next year Governor Frontenac and Duchesneau, the intendant who arrived in the colony in that year, were instructed to extend this period to six years, but when Duchesneau gave the seigneurs who had held concessions in Canada for some time one year to clear their seigneuries he was roundly rebuked by Colbert, who stated that such leniency "not only does not conform with, but changes entirely the provisions of the said decree [June 4, 1672, and the reissue] for the nonfulfilment of which you must explain yourself."[21] As Duchesneau had strayed from his instructions only in the matter of the year of grace, Colbert's caustic response is some measure of the importance he attached to the reduction of the size of Canadian seigneuries. In 1679 another royal edict pointed out that potential seigneurs would not be attracted to Canada because almost all the cultivable land had been conceded, and ordered that a quarter of the undeveloped land in all seigneuries in 1679 and a twentieth of the remainder every year thereafter was to be reunited to the royal domain.[22]

The curious feature of these royal edicts is that neither Duchesneau nor later intendants paid any attention to them. While several of Talon's small concessions were reunited to the royal domain when their seigneurs returned to France,[23] the large seigneuries which had survived from proprietary days remained unaltered. If an undeveloped portion of a seigneurie was ever withdrawn no record of the transfer remains even though as late as 1700 not more than 4 or 5 per cent of all the seigneurial land granted in Canada had been cleared (my own estimate, if anything a little high). Far from reducing the size of seigneuries the governors and intendants were increasing it as seigneurs asked for, and usually received, augmentations to their original concessions. At first the augmentations were small offshore islands which had not been specified in the original concession and were too small to be conceded separately, but before long, tracts as large as or larger than the original seigneuries were being added behind the older riparian grants. After 1672 augmentations were almost as common as new concessions and were regularly sent to France to be ratified by the king. These augmentations were not being added to seigneuries dating from the proprietary period; rather, Talon's small seigneuries were being enlarged.

The paradox of a king who insisted on the one hand that seigneuries in Canada were too large and on the other ratified almost all the augmentations sent to him is not easily explained. Some of his ministers in Canada were not above greasing a friendly palm, and most were likely to be sympathetic to a seigneur's lamentations about the difficulties of developing his land, but as augmentations were not valid until ratified in France they could have been stopped at any time. However, the king's remedy for flagging settlement was not very helpful, and his ministers in Canada, recognizing this, probably were able to mollify their superiors. With only 6,000 settlers in Canada in 1672 it was impossible to clear all the conceded land; and, with the distractions of the fur trade, land was probably being cleared as rapidly as could be expected. Furthermore, from 1689 until almost the end of the century, while the colony was fighting for its life against the Iroquois, clearing new land was out of the question when many established farms could not be cultivated. If there had been a press of immigrants from France, if unused land in an established seigneurie could have been given at once to a new seigneur who could have settled it, the situation would have been entirely different. As it was, the king's proposals for the withdrawal of land could not have accelerated the pace of settlement and, by discouraging seigneurs even more, might have retarded it.[24] Undeveloped seigneuries were a symptom of the colony's basic failure, its inability, for one reason or another, to attract settlers.

Rather than returning land to the royal domain, governors and intendants regularly backed seigneurs' requests for augmentations with glowing and often inaccurate reports of the applicants' devotion to the development of their seigneuries. If a proposed concession to the Sieur de Longueuil appeared a little large, His Majesty was asked to consider that Longueuil had been put to some "dépenses extraordinaires" to clear all of his seigneurie and to establish his nine children in several fine buildings, that he planned several villages in the near future, and that he had served the king well in the recent Indian wars.[25] Replying to the minister's usual admonitions to reduce the size of seigneuries, Frontenac and the Intendant Champigny pointed out in their last dispatch in 1694 that the original concession needed to be "d'une étendue assez grande" if eventually it was to have enough settlers to make up a seigneurie,[26] and were more specific in subsequent dispatches:

> We have . . . taken the liberty, Monseigneur, to inform you that when we give concessions which appear to be too large we ordinarily do so only because of the small amount of land suitable for cultivation which is found there, most being filled with rocks which make the greatest part uncultivated and useless. It often happens that it would be equivalent to not giving any land at all if we gave other than those concessions which seem to be more than they should be. It is done to give them [the seigneurs] the means to develop their seigneuries in these spots and to establish habitants on them.[27]

We have received confirmation of the concessions which you accorded last year, about which His Majesty recommends that we apply ourselves more to reduce those which seem to be too extensive than to increase and extend them into distant parts. On this subject we take the liberty of pointing out that although vast holdings had formerly been given here, we notice that as soon as they are divided among several children, each one of them finds himself too restricted in his particular holding.[28]

The minister would reply to such statements that it had long been His Majesty's policy to reduce the size of seigneuries, but the minister rarely turned down the requests.

Although these observations about bad land and the inheritance system were excuses for by-passing the royal edicts, they were good excuses. A seigneurie in Canada, like a township along the Ohio, included bad land with the good, so that although a seigneur usually selected the general location of his seigneurie, he could not adjust its boundaries to exclude poor land. In the larger concessions a considerable percentage of unworkable land did not matter a great deal, but if half or two-thirds of the land in one of Talon's average seigneuries was swamp or sand there was hardly enough cultivable land left to support a seigneur on the revenue from his censitaires. In 1688 the seigneur of Rimousky complained that more than a league of the two he held along the river was nothing but ."Rochers escarpes," [29] and the seigneur of Ile Verte argued similarly a year later.[30] Both requested augmentations. These two seigneuries were along the south shore well below Quebec, where the edge of the Appalachian Roughlands approaches the river, but seigneuries anywhere in the colony were likely to include as much unproductive as productive land. Even more important in reducing the operational size of a seigneurie were the inheritance laws, which will be discussed in some detail in Chapter 4. It will suffice here to describe a hypothetical division among eight children of a seigneurie of one by two leagues: the eldest son would inherit half a league of frontage, and each of his brothers and sisters an eighth of the other half, that is, strips approximately three hundred and fifty yards wide and five miles deep. One of these small units could not support a seigneur unless he treated it as a roture and became a farmer himself. Considerations such as these explain why governors and intendants began conceding larger seigneuries and adding to some of those conceded by Talon in the face of opposing royal pressure.

Figure 3–1 shows most of the seigneuries and augmentations granted by Frontenac or by Frontenac and an intendant. The offshore islands which had not been specified in the original titles were added to a number of seigneuries, and augmentations on the mainland, some of which were larger than the original seigneuries, were added to many others. Frontenac regranted a few seigneuries because the original titles were lost, and made approximately thirty new concessions. Most of these were almost as large as Talon's largest concessions, and none was smaller than a square league. Except for a few overlooked slivers of land, all the river front from Montreal to well below Quebec was conceded by 1700, and some new seigneuries were granted behind old concessions along the river. In 1694 and 1695 Frontenac filled in the unconceded land along the Richelieu between Chambly and Saint-Ours in what was probably another attempt to reinforce this defensive artery. He had been instructed to make contiguous seigneurial grants and generally he did. But Frontenac was not above facilitating his many illicit fur-trading schemes by occasional seigneurial grants. Fort Frontenac (on Lake Ontario at Kingston), which he conceded to La Salle, cannot be entirely explained by considerations of defense or settlement, or by his claim that the fort reduced the flow of furs to New England.[31] Argenteuil also was well away from earlier concessions and squarely on the Ottawa fur route. Frontenac had given the Sieur d'Argenteuil permission for several trips to the interior, at least one of which had been extremely profitable,[32] and this seigneurie was undoubtedly intended to be a base for Argenteuil's operations in the fur trade.

Louis XIV and his advisors in France never entirely abandoned their conviction that seigneuries in Canada were too large. As late as 1709 Jacques and Antoine-Denis Raudot, the father and son who shared the intendancy from 1705 to 1711, assured the French minister who had been enquiring about the matter that they would concede smaller seigneuries than had been the custom in the past, although they doubted that anything could be done about existing seigneuries because each had passed into many hands.[33] A different approach had been suggested fifteen years before by Frontenac and Champigny who had told the minister that no new seigneuries should be granted until the land which had already been conceded was developed.[34] Gideon de Catalogne's seigneurie-by-seigneurie description of the colony in 1711 [35] probably directed the ministers to the same conclusion, and preoccupation with the number of Canadian seigneuries became to the ministers in the eighteenth century what preoccupation with size had been to their predecessors in the seventeenth. The new orientation was defined first in the Royal Edicts from Marly in 1711 which ordered, among other things, not that fractions of seigneuries be withdrawn as in the past but that all seigneuries which were still without a domain and some settlers a year after the edict was published should be returned to the royal domain.[36] Supplementing this edict was the king's warning three years later that he was "absolument résolu" to grant no new concessions.[37] He agreed to a concession to the Sulpicians in 1717 and another, twelve years later, to Governor Beauharnois, but all other requests were turned down.[38] Seigneurial grants were not made regularly again until 1732.

This diagnosis of seigneurial ills was somewhat more realistic than its predecessor. There had been well over a hundred concessions during the forty years after Talon's departure, and altogether more than two hundred and fifty seigneuries had been conceded by 1715. Some of these had disappeared as others were conceded over them or had been returned to the royal domain, and a few were plots in the towns. Nevertheless, at least one hundred and eighty seigneuries were open for rural settlement in 1715 in a colony of barely twenty thousand people. Five thousand people lived in the towns and seven thousand more on a dozen important seigneuries; if the remaining eight thousand were evenly divided there were only seven or eight families for each seigneurie. In this situation it made some sense not to add more seigneuries to the many which were already undeveloped, and if the intendant had revoked some of these concessions it was possible that development could have been speeded on the remainder.

In any case the governors and intendants in Canada were as loath to withdraw seigneuries as they had been to act on the edicts of 1672, 1675, and 1679. What ministers in France considered indispensable for the establishment and growth of the colony [39] was much less pressing to their counterparts in Canada who would point out in reply that most seigneurs were doing what they could to develop their seigneuries, that almost all seigneuries were settled (an observation which was only true if a few farms in a corner constituted a settled seigneurie), and that the unsettled seigneuries were generally unfit for agriculture.[40] From the Canadian point of view the crux of the argument was the same as before. As the Intendant Bégon told the Minister, he had not withdrawn undeveloped seigneuries because with no one else asking for them the withdrawn land would not be settled, and he argued that it would be much more useful to help the seigneur to establish his seigneurie than to threaten to take it away. Although ministers in France knew enough about Canada by this time not to expect that a seigneur would develop all of his seigneurie, they did insist that the seigneur had to make some effort to develop his land,[41] and under this steady pressure, officials in Canada were eventually forced to take some action. In 1737 they returned one unsettled seigneurie to the royal domain and four years later returned sixteen others which were spread out along the Richelieu and Lake Champlain.[42] That this was a major stimulus to seigneurial development, as Munro and Frégault suggest,[43] is not very likely. Several of the withdrawn seigneuries were reconceded to their original seigneurs a few years later; and, in the face of the difficulty and expense involved in settling a seigneurie, the withdrawal of a few empty seigneuries, not one of which was worth half as much as an ordinary habitant's farm, was not of great consequence. (The discussion of seigneurs as land speculators, in Chap. 4, sheds further light on this question.)

After 1730 the hold-the-line policy on seigneurial grants was relaxed in the face of an increasing number of requests for new seigneuries. The ministers in France had decided that it was not in the colony's interest to exclude an energetic new seigneur, but they were still concerned about the number of seigneuries, and their later concessions were neither as frequent nor as automatic as those granted before 1714. Nevertheless, some fifty concessions were made during the last thirty years of the French regime, and most of these are shown in Figure 3–1.

These later seigneuries were large by Talon's or even by Frontenac's standards. The smallest was twenty square miles, the standard grant was two by three leagues or approximately forty square miles, and the largest contained as much land as did any but two or three seigneuries from the proprietary period. The trend away from the small seigneurie which had begun shortly after Talon's departure was very definite after 1730, and because there was a century of Canadian experience behind these last seigneurial grants of the French regime, their size is of considerable significance. By 1730 there was ample evidence that most of Talon's concessions had been too small. With a trickle of immigration to the colony from France seigneuries were bound to fill slowly, and if new settlers were divided among many small seigneuries no one seigneur could expect to have more than a handful of settlers during his lifetime. The most energetic seigneur could not attract all the flow because few potential censitaires would take land away from the river as long as there was unconceded river frontage in an adjacent seigneurie. If there were a number of new seigneuries the river front of all of them had to be filled before there was a move into the interior, and this, coupled with a scarcity of settlers, meant that the settlement of any seigneurie was slow. The number of settlers in each seigneurie and, consequently, the seigneurial revenue, increased if there were fewer grants in the same area. Moreover these larger seigneuries might be divided among a seigneur's progeny into units which were potentially profitable. When Beauharnois and Hocquart explained to the minister in 1736 that they had granted four leagues along Lake Champlain instead of the usual two because the seigneur had fourteen children,[44] they knew that only a small fraction of this seigneurie of over one hundred square miles had any chance of being settled for decades. They hoped that a slightly larger seigneurie would result in more settlers and more revenue for the seigneur, and were thinking ahead to the division of the seigneurie among a numerous progeny. The size of seigneuries had increased with good reason, even though no one expected that most of each new concession would be anything but forest for as long as anyone could foresee.

The distribution of these later seigneuries is more easily accounted for. With no unconceded river frontage between Quebec and Montreal, the only new concessions along the St. Lawrence were at the two extremities of the colony. Several concessions were granted above Montreal although, for the same reasons as before, officials were not anxious to expand far in that direction, and at least one prospective seigneur who requested land above Montreal was granted it instead along Lake Champlain.[45] There were a few seigneuries behind earlier grants along the river, their odd shapes determined by the backs onto which they were grafted, but most new concessions were along two tributaries of the St. Lawrence: the Richelieu–Lake Champlain system and the Chaudière. With westward expansion along the St. Lawrence axis restricted, these were obvious areas for new settlement. There were also sound strategic reasons for settling the Richelieu, which was the easiest avenue to and from the English colonies, and the Intendant Hocquart, like Talon and Frontenac before him, would have felt easier with a bastion of French settlement along it. However, as long as agricultural land was available along the St. Lawrence, few habitants would settle away from the colony's principal axis, and the group of seigneuries along the upper Richelieu and around Lake Champlain was withdrawn in 1741. Most were regranted a few years later, but as the English menace increased, the likelihood that settlers could be tempted into this area declined and none of these seigneuries was settled at the conquest. The few seigneuries along the Chaudière fared better, and in 1760 there were several dozen families there.

At the end of the French regime there were almost two hundred and fifty seigneuries in Canada, excluding the small grants within Quebec and Trois-Rivières. Concessions extended in an uninterrupted line along the south shore of the St. Lawrence for more than three hundred miles, and for almost as far along the north shore. There were only a few sections of unconceded land within twelve miles of the river between Montreal and Quebec, and in the last years seigneuries lined the upper Richelieu and the Chaudière. The back endpaper of this book, which shows seigneuries in 1760, is a patchwork suggestive of a more chaotic approach to seigneurial concessions than had been the case. Different sizes and shapes had been tried at different times, and if a century and a half of experimentation had not resulted in a standard seigneurial grant, some possibilities had been eliminated. Large seigneuries which would have permitted a few seigneurs to control all of Canada were not attractive to a king whose influence could only have been weakened thereby, and the proprietary years had shown that there was nothing in Canada to induce the holders of such grants to develop them. On the other hand, because Canadian seigneuries were settled slowly, because the censitaires paid little for their rotures, and because seigneurial control usually fragmented after the original seigneur's death, a seigneurie smaller than thirty or forty square miles was seldom profitable, and consequently the small seigneurial grant was abandoned in the later years. The trapezoid, the characteristic shape of a Canadian seigneurie, had been introduced in the 1630's, and because it suited a river-front colony it remained throughout the French regime. Departures from this basic shape were common only when all the river front was conceded. It was understood from the first that bad land would be conceded with the good, and by 1672 there was agreement that seigneurial grants should be contiguous. Although this latter rule was not always followed there were two solid lines of seigneuries by 1760. Seigneuries were arranged in a simple, geometric pattern not ill-adapted to life in a riparian colony. Certainly the pattern would have been more simple if there had been a greater degree of standardization, but no one in 1630 had any idea what the standard should be, and almost a century of experimentation was required before a general consensus emerged which seemed to fit the special conditions of a new land.

Most of the conceded land within these seigneuries was held by censitaires who paid certain annual dues to the seigneur for the rotures which he had conceded, but there were also subseigneuries, or *arrière-fiefs,* which were conceded by and held from the seigneur of the larger seigneurie. The arrière-fief was itself a seigneurie; its seigneur granted rotures and received the revenue from them. There were half a dozen or more arrière-fiefs in many large seigneuries, and they were not rare in seigneuries of twenty or thirty square miles. Perhaps two hundred arrière-fiefs were granted during the French regime, and although the area they occupied was only a small fraction of the total conceded land, they were a significant type of seigneurial grant.

Arrière-fiefs were of two types: a few were concessions of several square miles and were expected to be developed as a seigneurie; most were no larger than an average roture and were intended to become farms. The former type had been conceded during the proprietary period by some of the most important seigneurs. The seigneur of La Citière granted La Prairie de la Magdeleine to the Jesuits in 1647, and the same seigneur made four more substantial seigneurial grants—Longueuil, Saint-François des Prés, Ile Sainte-Thérèse, Ile Saint-Paul—before his enormous seigneurie disappeared shortly after 1667 (see front end-paper). While these seigneuries were eventually held directly from the Crown, originally they were all arrière-fiefs. By the mid-1660's the Ile d'Orléans was divided into eight arrière-fiefs, some of them large enough to contain more than a hundred rotures. Throughout the French regime these were held from the seigneur of the Ile d'Orléans, and from the censitaires' point of view the island was eight distinct seigneuries. The second type of arrière-fief was much more common. Of seven arrière-fiefs granted in Beaupré in the 1650's and 1660's none was more than two or three arpents along the river; of fourteen on the Ile de Montréal, the largest was just over four hundred square arpents; while in 1693 the seigneur of Boucherville conceded an arrière-fief that was one arpent square.[46] Arrière-fiefs of this sort were given to children, friends, religious orders, creditors, or to anyone to whom the seigneur wanted to give a little land free from the annual dues which were levied on rotures. All arrière-fiefs reduced the effective size of seigneuries and the potential revenue of the seigneur, although they were much less important in these respects than the system of seigneurial inheritance which is discussed in the next chapter.

4 : The Seigneurs' Control of the Land

T HE Canadian seigneur has been pictured by some as the benef-
icent guardian of his flock, and by others as a member of an
insouciant privileged class.[1] His admirers write of the seigneur as
a leader who settled his censitaires' small disputes and calmed their
anxieties, and who was the fulcrum of a community which he had created
and watched over with loving care; his deprecators write of him as a
parasite who lived off royal appointments and *gratifications* * and illegal
dealings in the fur trade, while totally neglecting the welfare of his
censitaires. Probably there were both types, for Canadian seigneurs were
drawn from most social and economic strata in the colony, and had taken
seigneuries for a variety of reasons. Governors, religious orders, merchants in Paris as well as in Canada, military men, doctors, parish priests,
and habitants—all were seigneurs. Further complicating the problem of
understanding the seigneurial class in early Canada has been the scarcity
of documentary evidence. Many documents have been preserved which
deal with the financial and legal relationship between the religious orders
and their censitaires, but there are at most two or three statements of *foi
et hommage,* a title deed, an act or two of sale or exchange, and an *aveu
et dénombrement* for each of the lay seigneuries.† These documents,

* Seigneurs often applied to the king for small cash presents which, for one reason or
another, they thought they had earned, and the king frequently looked favorably on these
petitions and accorded the requested *gratifications.*

† The *aveu et dénombrement* was a list of the landholdings within a seigneurie, including the buildings, cleared land, and livestock on them, and the dues with which the landholdings were charged. This list was required of the seigneur after any change in seigneurial control, or on the special request of the intendant.

some of which are more revealing than has been supposed, are the basis of this and the next two chapters, in which an attempt is made to assess more accurately the seigneur's influence, as a central figure in the land system, on the use of land in the colony.

CHURCH SEIGNEURS

More than half of some thirty seigneuries held by religious orders at the end of the French regime had been conceded to them by the Company of New France in the years before 1663. One of the Company's charter obligations was to spread the knowledge of God in the New World; it counted priests and devout laymen among its associates, and it controlled the colony at a time when the Jesuit *Relations* and their accounts of the suffering and the glory of serving God in Huronia were exciting French imaginations. Concessions to the Church satisfied pious souls, they were at least as likely to be settled as other seigneuries, and they cost the Company nothing. In all, the Company made almost twenty concessions to the Church, many of them plots of a few square arpents in Quebec and Trois-Rivières, but others, like Batiscan and Cap de la Madeleine, among the largest grants in Canada.

With the advent of royal government, concessions to the religious orders almost stopped. The young Louis XIV, anxious to assert his own authority in the colony and convinced that Church holdings were already too extensive, instructed his ministers to ensure that royal authority in Canada was not impinged upon by the Church. In those few instances when the king proposed to grant land to a religious order, one of his officials in Canada usually reminded him that the Church's holdings were already large and suggested that His Majesty's interests would be better served if the land were given to a different seigneur or kept in the royal domain.[2] Usually the king and his ministers in France agreed, and in 1743 Louis XV tightened royal policy still further in this regard in an ordinance which stated that additional concessions to the Church "can only be regarded as contrary to the common good" because "they take a considerable part of the wealth and land of our colonies out of circulation."[3] Henceforth there were to be neither new concessions to any of the Orders nor any sales or gifts of land and buildings to them without His Majesty's express permission.

Although the Crown had granted only five new concessions to the Church in the eighty years between the establishment of royal government and this ordinance, the amount of land controlled by the Church had more than doubled. Bishop Laval bought up Beaupré and the Ile d'Orléans in the 1650's and 1660's, exchanged the Ile d'Orléans for Ile Jésus, and in 1680 gave Beaupré and Ile Jésus to the Séminaire de Québec in what was the largest of many donations of land to religious institutions. Occasionally the Orders bought seigneuries. The Jesuits, for example, acquired Bélair by a number of purchases after 1710, and the Ursulines of Trois-Rivières bought Rivière du Loup in 1723. On the other hand the Jesuits who controlled Ile Jésus during the early years of the colony gave the seigneurie to a Paris merchant in recognition of his services to the Company,[4] and the sisters of the Hôtel-Dieu in Quebec sold their seigneurie of Grondines. However, the Orders acquired in one way or another more land than they disposed of, so that in spite of royal reticence about new grants Church holdings steadily increased. These accretions were almost stopped by the royal ordinance of 1743.

The rural seigneuries held by the Church at the end of the French regime are shown on the map of seigneuries in Canada in 1760 (back endpaper). Not on the map are the arrière-fiefs and rotures which the Church had acquired in lay seigneuries. The Orders themselves gave occasional arrière-fiefs to laymen, but because they acquired in this way more land than they granted, the map shows somewhat less land than they actually held. All in all the Church controlled a little more than a quarter of the conceded land, and because much of it was located close to a town, approximately a third of the population of the colony lived on this land. The north shore within a fifteen mile radius of Quebec and both shores within a similar distance of Montreal were the most valuable and densely settled land in the colony, and almost all of it belonged to the Church. The Jesuits, the Séminaire de Québec, and the Sulpicians were easily the most important seigneurs in Canada, and the Church as a whole controlled enough land to make the king's apprehension on the point understandable. Yet as the Church provided education and care for the sick and indigent as well as religious guidance, it is an open and, from the point of view of this study, not very important question whether or not it controlled a disproportionate share of the land.

Most of the Orders appointed a priest to manage each of their seigneuries. These directors knew the censitaires, listed unpaid dues, and kept a close check on the value of a man's property when his dues were in arrears (see Chap. 5). The censitaire knew what dues he had to pay and that he had to pay them. If he abandoned his roture the director would quickly apply to the intendant for permission to reunite it to the seigneurial domain so that it could be reconceded at the first new request (see Chap. 7). As was the case in most church seigneuries in France, the censitaire's relationship with his seigneur was clearly defined, and the director saw to it that the relationship was maintained. Occasionally lay seigneurs were as meticulous, but because their seigneuries were divided when they died control of lay seigneuries was never as even or as thorough in the long run.

LAY SEIGNEURS

Because almost everyone in the colony could acquire a seigneurie, the amorphous group of lay seigneurs is extremely difficult to characterize. In theory the habitants were excluded from seigneurial grants, and when one of them requested a concession officials were apt to react like Governor Beauharnois and the Intendant Hocquart, who forwarded such a request to the minister with the terse comment that "il ne convient point qu'un simple habitant possède des fiefs." [5] In fact, however, prosperous habitants occasionally acquired seigneuries by outbidding competitors when a seigneurie was offered for sale,[6] and thus were represented among the seigneurs. From this level the seigneurs ranged upward in wealth and social position to the leading merchants in the colony, the most senior government officials, and wealthy men in France. As long as he was Catholic and French and a bare notch above the ordinary habitant level, anyone interested in acquiring a seigneurie and able to convince the governor and intendant that he intended to develop it could usually expect a favorable response to a request for land. In 1731 Hocquart and Beauharnois wrote a strong letter supporting a widow's application for a small pension and a seigneurie even though the poor woman was in such financial straits that she had barely survived the winter.[7] Such a seigneur was in no position to put very much effort into developing a seigneurie. In the Company period, grants to indigent seigneurs were less common because the Company, with its large concessions and small experience in a New World environment, certainly envisaged the Canadian seigneur as an individual of considerable importance. With the later insistence on smaller concessions and the discovery that seigneuries often involved their seigneurs in more expense than revenue, the conception of the seigneur as a man of consequence beyond the limits of his concession disappeared. Although some of the most influential men in the colony were seigneurs, no one was ever important only because he owned a seigneurie, and as royal officials came to expect less of the seigneurs it became less necessary to restrict concessions to people in certain financial and social strata. Hence the great variety of Canadian seigneurs.

It might be expected that military men, merchants, royal officials, and habitants would develop their seigneuries differently, and that the division of lay seigneurs into occupational groups would be a fruitful point of departure for the study of the seigneurs' influence on the land. There are enough data so that many seigneurs can be roughly classified by occupation,[8] but such divisions are deceptive. As seigneuries changed hands the occupations of their seigneurs changed as well; no lay seigneurs in Canada were engaged generation after generation in one occupation for which successive fathers passed on the family skill and capital. To the contrary, a single seigneur was likely to be involved in several activities, so that to label the officer who was trading furs, or the holder of a government sinecure who shipped grain to the West Indies and had an interest in the fur trade as one type or another, is to create a stereotype that rarely existed. In the ways of making a living, life in Canada was extremely fluid, and without data for precise empirical classifications it is probably only misleading to sort seigneurs into distinct occupational groups.

Seigneurs Who Controlled less than a Seigneurie

A division more closely approximating reality can be made between seigneurs who, as inheritors of a fraction of the family estate, controlled less than one seigneurie and those who held one or more. With the exceptions of Beaupré and the Ile d'Orléans, which were conceded to a company of eight men, and the concessions to the Church, seigneuries in Canada were granted to individuals. However, the seigneur could sell, exchange, or donate part of his seigneurie, and his property was divided among his progeny at his death. Consequently the two hundred and fifty rural seigneuries in Canada in 1760 had several times as many seigneurs. This fragmentation of seigneurial control took many forms, but inevitably a seigneurie belonging to several individuals who divided the obligations and the profits was managed differently from one controlled by a single seigneur. The reasons for these divisions and the forms that they took need to be thoroughly understood.

Although in a few cases the fragmentation of seigneurial control was the result of transactions during the seigneur's lifetime, it usually began at his death. The system of inheritance followed in most of the French coutumes and introduced into Canada without legal modification in the relevant articles of the Coutume de Paris was a modified form of primogeniture, a compromise between the assumption that an individual had a "natural right" to land and the desire to preserve the integrity of the family estate.[9] By the provisions of the coutume the eldest son inherited the seigneurial manor, its courtyard, and half of the rest of the seigneurie; the other half was divided among the other children. If there was no manor on the estate, the eldest son could claim an additional square arpent of land, while a manor without surrounding land went entirely to the eldest son. If there were only two children the eldest son received the manor, the courtyard, and two-thirds of the rest of the estate; if all the children were girls, manor and land were divided equally. If a seigneur's death preceded his wife's, the estate was divided between the widow and the children although the widow's half was held in usufruct and passed to the children at her death. These rights were rigorously protected and were lost only if an individual accepted something in their stead (e.g., a donation which was larger than the inheritance), renounced his claim, or entered the Church. A seigneur could sell his seigneurie, but his wife and children could reimburse the purchaser and take over the seigneurie themselves (the *retrait lignager*).[10] A more important check on sales was the *légitime* (an individual's right to half his original inheritance), and any transaction could be invalidated for interfering with it.[11] This was a thoroughly protective system which by giving the eldest son the manor and half the land preserved the estate as a unit, if a truncated one, and by giving his brothers and sisters equal portions of the remainder satisfied their right, as offspring of a seigneur, to own land.

Although these provisions of the Coutume de Paris were applied without legal modification in Canada, they did not have quite the same effect in a new environment. When the eldest son inherited the manor and half the land in a seigneurie at the outskirts of Paris, he inherited substantially more than half the value of the seigneurie. The manor had been the family home for generations, and had a much greater value in relation to the rest of the seigneurie than its simple Canadian counterpart. Until towards the end of the French regime most Canadian manors were built of roughly squared logs (a construction known as *pièce sur pièce*) and could be put up by two or three workmen in less than a season, and stone manors which became common in the eighteenth century were not often more than forty feet long and a story high. Even though labor was expensive and land was cheap these manors were not the substantial part of an inheritance that they were in France. Because there was no manor on many Canadian seigneuries many an eldest son acquired another square arpent of land, an addition which could be quite important in a small seigneurie near Paris but which meant nothing along the St. Lawrence. For these reasons, the eldest son's inheritance tended to be substantially less important in Canada than it was in France. It is probable also that Canadian seigneuries were being divided among more inheritors. Eighteen or twenty children were relatively common in Canada, and an average family included five or six.

The extent to which seigneurial control was divided in Canada is difficult to overestimate. Intendants and the Sovereign Council judged hundreds of disputes which turned one way or another around problems created by divided seigneuries. As often as not statements of *foi et hommage* were made by one seigneur acting in the name of several or, when a seigneurie was minutely divided, by a notary hired for the purpose. When the notary Dulauret rendered *foi et hommage* and presented an *aveu et dénombrement* for the seigneurie of Cap Saint-Michel he represented François Messier, the principal seigneur (the seigneur who controlled the largest percentage of the seigneurie, usually the eldest son), and twenty-four others who had some interest in the seigneurie.[12] Occasionally the ownership of a seigneurie became so complicated that a special investigation was required to unravel the tangle. A *mémoire instructif* was prepared for the arbiters investigating a property dispute on Ile Bizard, to sort out the seigneurs of the island after three eldest sons had died in quick succession leaving so many inheritors that, even with this *mémoire*, it is clear neither who the several dozen seigneurs were, nor what fraction of the seigneurie each of them controlled.[13] A simpler division is described in the preamble to a *papier terrier* * for the seigneurie of Varennes:

In proceeding with the drawing up of the said *papier terrier*, there has come before us in our hotel René Gaultier, squire, Sieur de Varennes, Lieutenant of the troops of a division of the marine in this country, eldest son and inheritor

---

* A *papier terrier* was a list of documents pertaining to the ownership of a seigneurie, arrière-fief, or roture. It made mention of the original deed of concession, and all subsequent transactions relating to the ownership of the land at the time when the *papier terrier* was prepared.

of the deceased René Gaultier, squire, Sieur de Varennes, Governor of Trois-Rivières, and in this capacity proprietor of half of the half of the fief commonly called Varennes situated on the south shore of the St. Lawrence joining to the northeast the fief of Saint-Michel belonging to the Sieur de Saint-Michel and to the southwest the twenty-six arpents explained below, comprising a half of a third of the fief of Boucherville and another third in the sixth of the other half of the said fief, given to him by his sister, one of the Ursulines of this city [Montreal]; the said Sieur who has come before us acting also for dame Marie Boucher, his mother, widow of the said deceased Sieur de Varennes, proprietor of half of the said fief of Varennes because of the *communauté des biens* which existed between her and the said deceased Sieur de Varennes and, because of the gift which she received from the deceased Pierre Boucher, squire, Sieur de Grosbois, her father, at the time of her marriage with the deceased Sieur de Varennes, of a third of the old seigneurie of Boucherville, also situated along the south shore of the St. Lawrence, consisting in part of twenty-six arpents adjacent to the said fief of Varennes and extending to the southwest to the fief of Demuy, and in twenty-six other arpents of frontage and the same depth commonly known as Tremblay . . . ; acting also for Mre. Jean Baptiste Gaultier, Sieur de Varennes, archdeacon of the diocese of Quebec . . . ; Pierre Gaultier, squire, Sieur de La Vérendrye, thirty-six years old and ensign of the troops of the company; Madeleine Gaultier, forty-eight years old and widow of the Sieur Petit de Levillier, Captain in the said detachment of the marine; Marguerite Gaultier, forty-four years old and widow of the Sieur de Puisgibault, Lieutenant in the said detachment; Marie Renée Gaultier, forty years old, widow of the Sieur de Lagesmeraye, Captain of a company in the said detachment, and at present spouse of the Sieur Lilvin; each one an inheritor of a sixth in the other half of the said half of the said fief of Varennes; the said Sieurs Jean Baptiste and Pierre Gaultier each inheritors of a third of the said sixth given to them by their said sister who, with the others mentioned, vows and declares to hold from His Majesty the said fief, and portions of the said fief explained above.[14]

This bewildering legal statement, which is illustrated cartographically in Figure 4–1, describes a straightforward inheritance. On the death of René Gaultier, governor of Trois-Rivières and seigneur of Varennes, half of his seigneurie passed to his widow because of the *communauté des biens*, a contract which husband and wife had entered into when they married.[15] By the terms of this contract all fixed property (*immeubles*) acquired by husband or wife other than through direct inheritance or gift in the line of succession, belonged commonly to both, and half of it reverted to the widow when her husband died. The third of the seigneurie of Boucherville which Marie Boucher had acquired from her father was not in the communauté because it was a gift in the direct line

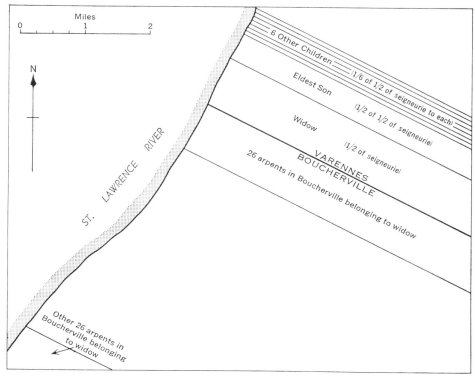

Fig. 4–1.—Division of the seigneuries of Varennes and Boucherville after the death of René Gaultier.

of succession. The other half of the communauté passed to the children of Marie Boucher and René Gaultier. René Gaultier (junior), the eldest son, acquired half of this half and each of his six brothers and sisters a sixth of the remaining half of the half which was not the widow's. Because one of the six had entered a religious order, she could not hold her inheritance,[16] and had divided it among her three brothers. The widow, Marie Boucher, would hold her half of Varennes and a third of Boucherville until her death, at which time they would be divided among her children in the usual ratios. If she remarried, the children of both marriages would have claims on the land and the inheritance would become more complex. The widow could sell the land to a third party or she could give it to her offspring. Five years after the first division she did the latter. The widow owed some 4,000 livres and gave her land to her children on condition that they retire the debt. She retained the revenue from the land, a small house, and a garden plot until her death.[17] By this arrangement, land which otherwise would have been sold was kept in the family. However, 4,000 livres was a substantial debt, and the eldest son would have had to pay half if he had insisted on his right to half the land. The widow's portion was divided, therefore, into equal parts so that the eldest son eventually acquired much less than half of the original seigneurie (in this case a quarter plus a fourteenth). Although there were great variations in detail, almost all lay seigneuries in the colony were divided at one time or another roughly along these lines.

Not only the land but also the seigneur's *banal*, or communal, mill rights and occasionally his Church privileges were affected by this fragmentation of seigneurial control. The Sieur de Livaudière acquired the *banal* mill on the seigneurie of Beaumont after seven separate purchases.[18] The coseigneurs of Rivière des Vases agreed to share mill costs and profits,[19] and the principal seigneur of Lauzon refused to build a mill unless either he were given all the revenue from it, or those who owned fractions of the mill defrayed their share of the cost.[20] The principal seigneur of Vincelotte discovered that the coseigneurs who owned the land on which the Church had been built had "thrown his pew out of the church" and barred him from its door until he contributed to the Church's upkeep.[21] In this case the intendant upheld the principal seigneur's rights and his coseigneurs had to replace the pew, but the incident is indicative of the pervasive influence of a system of inheritance which divided seigneurial control among many seigneurs.

Once divided, control of a seigneurie tended to work back into the hands of one individual. When his brothers and sisters all agreed to sell, the eldest son was able to buy the seigneurie at a type of public auction. He, or someone acting for him, would read a statement in front of the parish church after mass on three successive Sundays which announced that the seigneurie of which he owned half was to be sold. Prospective buyers were invited to make offers. A prospective buyer himself, he would usually make the first bid. Jean Baptiste Le Moyne, who acquired all the seigneurie of Cap de la Trinité in 1702 by this method, opened bidding at 1,200 livres, and after several interested parties had made ten other bids he finally acquired the seigneurie for 3,250 livres.[22] As he already owned half of it, the cost to him was 1,625 livres, or just over 270 livres to each of his six brothers and sisters for a sixth part in half a seigneurie. The auction guaranteed a fair price for the six who were selling and was the most rapid means by which the eldest son could acquire all the seigneurie. He ran some risk of being outbid, but since he was able to deduct half the cost, he was in a strong competitive position. In other cases the guardian of several young inheritors could sell their inheritance if the sale appeared to be in their interest. After the death of the seigneur of Chambly his widow called a meeting of relations and friends of the family at which it was decided that the children would benefit most if their inheritance were sold and the money put towards their education.[23] Such a sale had to be ratified by the intendant, but when it was the seigneurs were reduced to two, the widow and whoever bought the children's half of the seigneurie.

Often one of the seigneurs drove independent bargains with each of his coseigneurs and after several years or decades regained control of the entire seigneurie. One seigneur bought out the others to regain control of the seigneurie of Deschambault between 1716 and 1719,[24] another acquired Carufel after six purchases between 1741 and 1758,[25] while the Jesuits acquired Bélair in nine transactions spread over thirty-three years.[26] Occasionally a seigneur would exchange the "sixth of a half" he held in one seigneurie (perhaps his wife's inheritance) for land in another, and some of these trades, as well as fairly frequent gifts of portions of seigneuries, tended to concentrate seigneurial control. On the other hand, it could happen that reunification was not complete, and occasionally not even begun, by the time the eldest son died twenty, thirty, or forty years after he had inherited half the seigneurie. In this case his half, two-thirds, or whatever it had become was subdivided, one half going to the eldest son and the other half to the rest of the progeny. The process of reunification would begin again on less land, and for this reason there was a tendency for seigneurial control to become slowly more fragmented with successive generations.

Occasionally the division of seigneurial control led to the creation of two or more small, independent seigneuries. In 1676 the Sieurs Jacques Le Moyne and Michel Messier held the seigneurie of Cap de la Trinité conjointly. Deciding that they would rather divide the seigneurie in two, Le Moyne and Messier visited a Montreal notary who drew up documents which defined seigneurial boundaries and gave each seigneur the right to "jouyr et disposer" of his seigneurie as he saw fit,[27] and the two seigneuries (one still called Cap de la Trinité, the other Saint-Michel) became entirely independent. However, such divisions were uncommon.

Although Le Moyne and Messier might have improved their social status, they had almost certainly increased their expenses without changing either their actual or their potential revenue. Two gristmills were now required where previously one sufficed, and if officials had often over-looked a missing mill in 1676 when this division was made, they were more insistent on this point a few years later.[28] Any coseigneur who created an independent seigneurie out of his inheritance faced either a decrease in an already slim revenue when his censitaires took their grain elsewhere, or the outlay for a mill; and a mill on a small seigneurie was seldom profitable. (See the discussion of the *banalités,* in Chap. 5.) When one seigneurie was divided into two independent seigneuries one of the new seigneurs was likely to complain before long to the intendant that the new units were of too little value to constitute separate seigneuries, and to request their reunification.[29]

The position of the coseigneur differed from that of the seigneur of an entire seigneurie only in that, unlike the latter, he did not have sole responsibility for the development of the seigneurie. He was not, therefore, required to *tenir ou faire tenir feu et lieu* (to live on or have someone else live on his seigneurie for him), to subgrant land, or to build a seigneurial gristmill. The king's officials might have prodded a seigneur if there was no settlement or mill on the seigneurie, but they never exerted any pressure on a coseigneur if there were a well-established domain, a number of tenants, and a communal mill on another fraction of the seigneurie. The coseigneur could live at the other end of the colony, send someone around once a year to collect the dues from those censitaires who happened to live in his inheritance, and contribute occasionally to the upkeep of the mill. If his revenue was not large, his expenses were small, and an inheritance could be profitable which, had it been an independent seigneurie with its own gristmill, would have lost money.

If there were only two or three coseigneurs, each commonly operated his portion as a separate unit except in those matters mentioned above. Such a coseigneur was the Sieur François Chorel Dorvillier, who lived on and paid *foi et hommage* for half of the seigneurie of Sainte-Anne de la Pérade.[30] For some years three seigneurs owned Ile Dupas et Chicot, a seigneurie comprising some islands and a small holding on the north shore at the head of Lake Saint-Pierre. In 1723 Jacques Brisset drew up an *aveu et dénombrement* for half of the seigneurie, and a year later

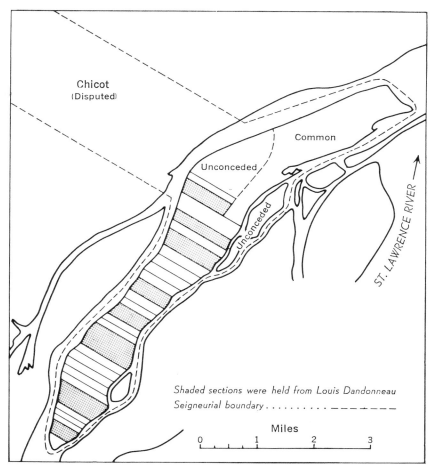

Fig. 4–2.—Division of the seigneurie of Ile Dupas et Chicot between Jacques Brisset and Louis Dandonneau, 1723.

Louis Adrien Dandonneau another for the other half.[31] Brisset operated a domain containing a small house, a barn, a cowshed, a stable, and over thirty arpents of cleared land; in his half Dandonneau reported two domains and several farm buildings on one of them. Brisset claimed that he controlled the eastern half of the property on the mainland; Dandonneau, that this land, none of which had been cleared, was not divided. Unable to agree on a permanent division of Ile Dupas the two had worked out a modus vivendi by which each received the dues from alternate strips of rotures (see Fig. 4–2). These coseigneurs lived on different domains and collected dues from different censitaires in one seigneurie. The third seigneur, who also was a Dandonneau, did not live in the seigneurie although a domain and an uncleared roture belonged to him. The roture had probably been conceded to him by his father, from whom he eventually inherited part of the seigneurie. As a censitaire he contributed to the seigneurial revenue of which, as a coseigneur, he was entitled to a sixth. His business at both levels was apparently handled by his brother.

The relationship between the Dandonneau brothers is a simple example of the way in which most divided seigneuries were controlled. When a seigneur held a substantial portion of the seigneurie, he often acted as an agent for the others. Usually he lived on the seigneurie, and paid *foi et hommage,* prepared the *aveux et dénombrements,* and collected the annual dues for each of his coseigneurs. In some of the divisions of this type the seigneurie was divided so that each coseigneur held a specific fraction and expected the revenue from it. More usually each coseigneur claimed a percentage of the total income from the seigneurie. In either case the arrangement was a convenient one for the coseigneur who did not hold enough land to warrant operating it as a separate unit, who was too young to look after his holding, or who was thinking about a trip to Michilimakinac. He could expect an income from his inheritance without any responsibility other than that of contributing occasionally to the maintenance of the communal mill.

When a seigneurie was well divided in this way, control of it tended to be lax. From the censitaires' point of view the principal seigneur was *the* seigneur, while he lived on the seigneurie without very much interference from or contact with his coseigneurs. However, unless he was willing to pay the bills he could not make general improvements to the seigneurie without consulting his coseigneurs. Should he build and pay for a mill without an agreement, each of the coseigneurs could claim a share of its revenue; and to persuade half a dozen widely scattered coseigneurs to renounce their shares in a projected mill or to contribute to its construction was a troublesome, time-consuming business. Usually the principal seigneur did not bother, and the necessary new mill or repairs to the old one were neglected until a clamor from the censitaires led to an intendant's ordinance. In this way a number of coseigneurs tended to inhibit seigneurial initiative. Even when only one of the seigneurs lived on the seigneurie, he collected his dues and perhaps those of his coseigneurs; he farmed or had someone farm the domain. There was little incentive to do more as long as seigneurial control and revenue were split several ways.

The exact number of divided seigneuries at any given time is difficult to determine. However, documents which give some indication of seigneurial control are relatively plentiful for the period from 1720 to 1740, and information about the seigneurs of most seigneuries can be obtained for some date during these years. An analysis of the documents of this period pertaining to the fifty-nine rural seigneuries spread along the north shore from Argenteuil to Malbaie gives the following results:

Lay seigneuries with one seigneur	22
Lay seigneuries with two or more seigneurs	21
Church seigneuries	12
Seigneuries lacking data, 1720–40	4

Although there are certainly errors in these figures,[32] the assumption that at any time during the last eighty years of the French regime half of the lay seigneuries in the colony were divided among two or more coseigneurs cannot be seriously incorrect.

Seigneurs Who Controlled more than One Seigneurie

A few seigneurs owned several seigneuries. The Company of New France had granted one seigneur a number of small seigneuries as freely as it made concessions of several hundred square miles. Robert Giffard, seigneur of Beauport, received four concessions from the Company.[33] Jean Bourdon, engineer, surveyor, king's attorney, jack-of-all-trades, and seigneur of Saint-Jean (a doubtful distinction as Saint-Jean was a roture of fifty square arpents on the outskirts of Quebec), was granted a small seigneurie in 1636 and another in 1637.[34] In 1639 the Company conceded the roture of Saint-Jean to Bourdon, and another small plot near Quebec a few years later. In 1652 the same Bourdon was one of a group of associates granted most of the coast of Gaspé under the name Cap des Rosiers; a year later he acquired Malbaie and Dombourg, two substantial seigneuries on the north shore; and finally, in 1665, a small arrière-fief in Lauzon. With the exception of the arrière-fief, all of these concessions had been made by the Company.[35]

The king's officials looked upon prodigality of this sort with very jaundiced eyes, and during a century of royal government no seigneur received as many grants as the Company had made to Jean Bourdon. A few, however, received two or three grants, and added to their holdings by purchasing additional land from other seigneurs.

One of these, Aubert de la Chesnaye, came to Canada as a clerk of the Company of New France and soon was engaged on his own in the fur trade, the grain trade, and the sedentary fishery, and became for a time the richest man in Canada. In 1662 La Chesnaye bought one-eighth shares in Beaupré and the Ile d'Orléans.[36] Two years later he bought another eighth of each and then sold the land to Bishop Laval. The Intendant Talon in 1672 and Governor Frontenac a year later granted him respectively Ile Percée in Gaspé and Rivière du Loup along the lower St. Lawrence for the establishment of sedentary fisheries. A few years later he bought Bourdon's old plots in Quebec. During the 1680's La Chesnaye bought three seigneuries along the lower St. Lawrence, was conceded another in Acadia and extensive fishing rights in the Gulf, and was given a seigneurie on Lake Saint-Pierre. Somehow he also acquired Ile Dupas et Chicot and a seigneurie near the Saguenay. After the turn of the century he sold Ile Dupas et Chicot and L'Assomption, and gave away the concession near the Saguenay, but he seized a small seigneurie near Trois-Rivières from a debtor, and was granted another along the lower St. Lawrence.

Although Aubert de la Chesnaye controlled more seigneuries than anyone else in Canada ever did, he died heavily in debt and his holdings were divided among creditors. On a smaller scale the same fragmentation was repeated several times as fractions of the two or three seigneuries which one man had acquired during his lifetime were distributed among inheritors and creditors on his death. Mille Iles and Sainte-Thérèse had belonged to one seigneur for several years before they were divided between inheritors in 1743.[37] In 1756 one seigneur paid *foi et hommage* for Rivière du Loup and Madawaska,[38] and some years before Pierre le Gardeur had done the same for Lachenaie and a fraction of Repentigny.[39] Seigneurs had trouble enough to acquire the exclusive control of one, much less of two or three seigneuries, and these few blocks of seigneuries controlled by single seigneurs were always broken up when they died.

SEIGNEURS AS LAND SPECULATORS

Aubert de la Chesnaye's career suggests that some Canadian seigneurs may have speculated in land, and Figures 4–3 and 4–4, which show the number of times individual seigneuries were sold, have been prepared to shed more light on this question. Although there were sales for which the records have been lost, and alienations which were not sales, the graphs make several points clear.

Either there was no rush to sell seigneuries or there were few buyers. The few sales were fairly well distributed, although there was a slight tendency for sales to be more common during the first decades after the initial concession and towards the Montreal end of the colony. After 1725 the sale of an entire seigneurie was particularly rare; only nine such sales are indicated for more than one hundred and thirty seigneuries. On the other hand, the graphs do not suggest a great rigidity in landholding; land may have been changing hands more rapidly in Canada than in France. Speculation in seigneuries was another matter, for with only two or three sales in the entire colony in any given year, the Canadian seigneur who held his land as a speculation had the patience of Job.

The Coutume de Paris placed several checks on speculative schemes. A tax which was a fifth of the sale price was levied on the sale of seigneuries, and royal agents in Canada saw to the collection of the *quints*. Any close relative who objected to a seigneur's sale of his land could take over the seigneurie by reimbursing the purchaser, according to the provisions of the *retrait lignager*. No sale could interfere with the children's *légitime*, and more than one seigneur had to return portions of a seigneurie years after he had acquired the land.[40] The inheritance tangle slowed sales even more. When the Jesuits were negotiating for their fourth purchase of a fraction of Bélair, twenty-three years after their first, they pointed out that the land was about to be divided again, and that, if they did not acquire it at once, they would spend years negotiating with another generation of inheritors.[41]

Nevertheless the checks inherent in the coutume would not have stopped the buying and selling of seigneuries if the practice had been profitable. Seigneurs were not land speculators because an unsettled seigneurie in Canada during the French regime was almost worthless. In 1712 the seigneur of Gastineau sold his seigneurie of fifteen square miles for two hundred livres, that is, for approximately three cows.[42] At the end of the French regime the seigneur of Ailleboust, a seigneurie of twenty-five square miles on which there was a house and thirty square arpents of cleared land, sold all the land and buildings for 1,800 livres.[43] Years before, the seigneur of La Chevrotière had exchanged his seigneurie of approximately ten square miles for a small farm on the Ile d'Orléans[44]

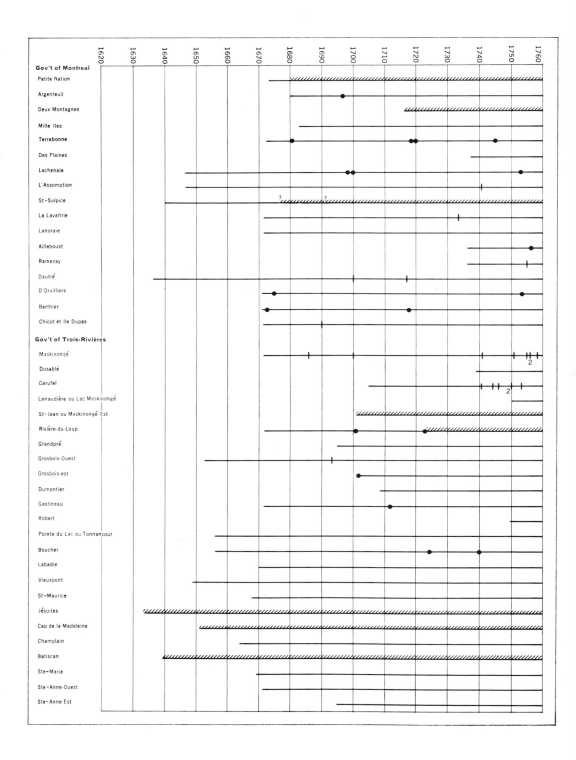

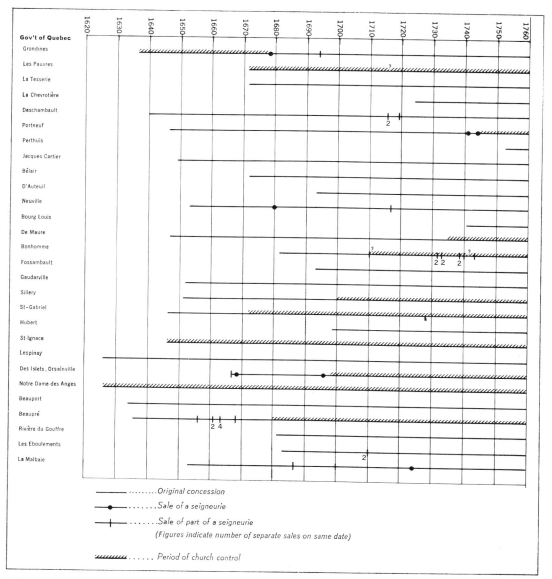

Gov't of Quebec

Grondines	
Les Pauvres	
La Tesserie	
La Chevrotière	
Deschambault	
Portneuf	
Perthuis	
Jacques Cartier	
Bélair	
D'Auteuil	
Neuville	
Bourg Louis	
De Maure	
Bonhomme	
Fossambault	
Gaudarville	
Sillery	
St-Gabriel	
Hubert	
St-Ignace	
Lespinay	
Des Islets, Orsaïnville	
Notre Dame des Anges	
Beauport	
Beaupré	
Rivière du Gouffre	
Les Eboulements	
La Malbaie	

——————— .... Original concession

●——————— .... Sale of a seigneurie

——+——— .... Sale of part of a seigneurie

(Figures indicate number of separate sales on same date)

⫻⫻⫻⫻⫻ ...... Period of church control

Fig. 4–3 (facing pages).—Sales of seigneuries along the north shore of the St. Lawrence during the French regime. Based on P. G. Roy's *Inventaire des Concessions en Fief et Seigneurie,* and on some uncatalogued documents in the Archives de la Province de Québec.

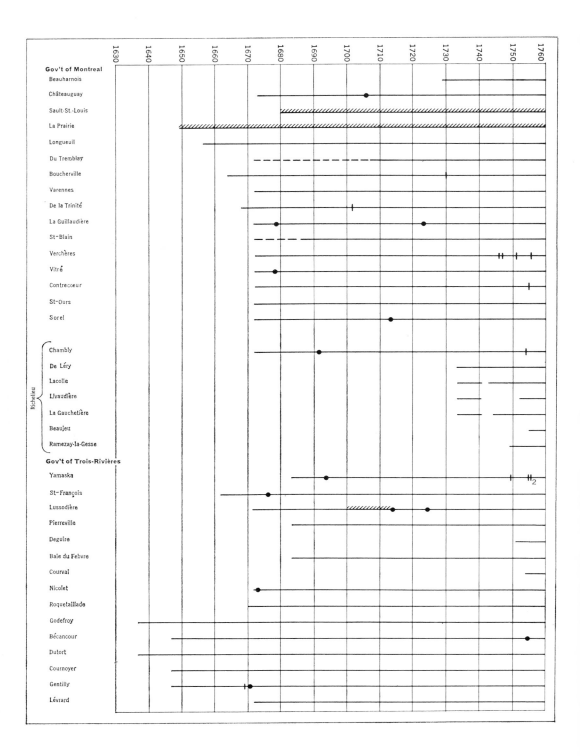

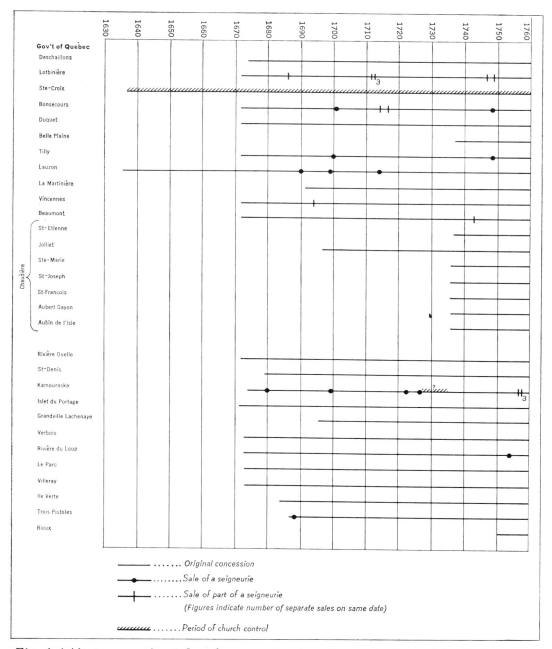

Fig. 4–4 (facing pages).—Sales of seigneuries along the south shore of the St. Lawrence during the French regime. Based on P. G. Roy's *Inventaire des Concessions en Fief et Seigneurie,* and on some uncatalogued documents in the Archives de la Province de Québec.

and, by the standards of the day, probably had the better of the bargain. Anyone who wanted to speculate in land could have bought up hundreds of square miles for next to nothing, but what he would do with the land was another question.

A seigneurie became valuable only when the domain was settled and some rotures were developed. If there were a manor house, several farm buildings, a mill, and fifty square arpents of cleared land on the domain, as well as thirty or forty settled rotures, the seigneurie was likely to be worth 8,000 to 12,000 livres.[45] However, as the domain could be rented for several hundred livres a year and as the censitaires paid several hundred more in yearly dues, it was seldom good business to sell such a seigneurie which, built up at considerable expense over many years, was beginning to repay the effort.

In summary, the religious orders, which controlled more than a quarter of the seigneurial land in Canada and which were seigneurs for almost a third of the Canadians, were the most methodical seigneurs in the colony. A director was appointed to supervise development and to collect annual dues in each seigneurie, and under the watchful eyes of this priest a censitaire's obligations towards his seigneur and vice versa were regularly met. The lay seigneurs are more difficult to characterize. Although it is misleading to divide these seigneurs into occupational groups, an important distinction can be made between those seigneurs who controlled less than a single seigneurie, and those who controlled one or more. Fragmentation of seigneurial control almost invariably followed a seigneur's death; in extreme cases one seigneurie belonged to twenty or thirty coseigneurs. This division of seigneurial control took many forms, but whenever there were several coseigneurs, seigneurial control was more diffuse and, consequently, more passive. Even the repairs to the gristmill required the consent of all the coseigneurs, and when the coseigneurs were scattered around the colony, their consent was not readily forthcoming. On the other hand, a few seigneurs acquired several seigneuries, although these blocks of seigneuries were broken up after the seigneur's death. When there was only one seigneur, a seigneurie was likely to be more carefully managed than when there were several. Apparently none of the seigneurs who acquired several seigneuries was speculating in land; with a small population in Canada there was so little pressure for land that large tracts of forest were almost worthless.

5 : The Seigneurs' Revenue from their Seigneuries

IF it can be assumed that a seigneur's interest in his concession rarely stemmed primarily from altruistic considerations, then the revenue that a seigneurie produced, or might be expected to produce, was probably what motivated him to develop his land. Thus there was a direct correlation between actual or expected revenue and the enthusiasm, energy, and capital the seigneur invested in his seigneurie. If these assumptions are correct, information about revenue is, indirectly, information about the seigneurs and their role in shaping the development of the land.

William Bennett Munro has studied the types of seigneurial revenue to which the Canadian seigneur was legally entitled, but has not assessed the seigneur's average or potential revenue from his seigneurie. Nor has Munro dealt with all the sources of revenue, or estimated the return from most of those he mentions. It is necessary, therefore, to re-examine the question of seigneurial revenue. In order to do this two sources of revenue need to be considered: that which the seigneur received from his censitaires in payment for the rotures, the common, and so on; and that from the domain, which depended primarily on the seigneur's initiative.

REVENUE FROM THE CENSITAIRES

(1) *The cens.*—All censitaires owed a cens, which was a small cash payment intended less as a source of revenue than as a mark of the last type of concession on the feudal ladder. Unlike the quit rent in the English colonies, the cens was not intended to absolve the censitaire of

other charges, but to indicate that land was held *en censive* and could not be subgranted. In the early years of the colony the cens was only a couple of deniers; * later, six deniers, or a sol for every arpent of frontage, or five or six sols for the entire concession became a fairly common cens. The cens was never fixed at one level, and it fluctuated from one title deed to another within the range of a few deniers to half a dozen sols. Towards the end of the French regime the most common rate was one sol per arpent of frontage. At least once, a cens of six deniers per square arpent, that is two and one-half livres for one hundred arpents, was charged, but as total payments for the concession were not unusual, cens and *rentes* were apparently confused in the title deed.[1] Ordinarily the cens was a token payment, no more than 5 per cent of the dues a censitaire paid for a roture.

(2) *The rente.*—Most censitaires paid a rente which was a heavier charge than the cens and intended as a major source of revenue for the seigneur. In the seventeenth century the rente was usually a money payment plus one or more capons; in the eighteenth century wheat often replaced the capons. A few rentes were paid in money and turkeys,[2] others entirely in grain and capons, and still others in furs.[3] Towards the end of the French regime the rentes were usually stipulated as straight cash payments,[4] and whenever the title deed permitted payments in cash or kind, the seigneur almost always insisted on cash if he had any hope of collecting, since the conversion rate on capons or wheat was fixed at a level which was higher than the average market price. (In periods of inflation, to be sure, seigneurs often preferred payments in kind.) Sometimes a seigneur appealed to the intendant for a judgment against censitaires who insisted on paying in kind, and if the phrase "à la choix du seigneur" was in the title deeds, the judgment the seigneur requested was always forthcoming.[5]

The rate of these rentes was never fixed in Canada although early in the eighteenth century the French minister charged with colonial affairs took the first steps in this direction. He informed the intendant that he strongly favored a uniform rente, and consulted several legal experts in France about the technicalities of the move,[6] but no legislation came of these efforts. Occasionally rates were dictated to individual seigneurs. When the Sulpicians in Montreal received the seigneurie of Deux

---

* A denier was to a livre as a penny is to an English pound. Thus 12 deniers made 1 sol, and 20 sols made 1 livre.

Montagnes in 1718 they agreed to charge twenty sols and one capon for each arpent of frontage in all of the rotures,[7] and a few years later a curious augmentation to Sainte-Marie fixed the rate of the rentes (see Chap. 6). These two regulatory attempts took place in the period of greatest official disenchantment with the Canadian seigneur. More often seigneurs were enjoined from charging more than *les cens et rentes accoutumés,* a vague phrase which, as Governor Beauharnois and the Intendant Hocquart assured the minister,[8] left the seigneur free to charge what he wanted, up to twenty sols for each twenty square arpents, plus a capon or the equivalent in wheat. This rate, they claimed, was the *pratique constante* in the colony.

The rente stipulated in the majority of the many hundreds of title deeds surviving from the French regime was close to a standard one sol per square arpent, or a somewhat lower rate of twenty sols for each arpent of frontage. In some title deeds issued in the 1640's and 1650's, thirty rather than twenty sols was often the charge for each arpent of frontage.[9] On the other hand seigneurs sometimes reduced their rates to attract settlers or to favor a friend or relative. Village plots were much more expensive; the Jesuits charged six deniers per square *toise* (forty square feet) for their concessions in the village of La Prairie de la Magdeleine, or just over twenty-three livres a square arpent.

In his 1707 report on seigneurial abuses[10] the Intendant Jacques Raudot charged that the seigneurs were manipulating the rate of the rente. Concessions, he pointed out, had been made without any regularity. Some censitaires held correct title deeds; others, vaguely worded notes; and many, no written agreement at all. Profiting by this uncertainty, the seigneurs charged exorbitant rates and even forced censitaires off the land if they refused to meet the new conditions. When seigneurs exercised their choice of payment in cash or kind and demanded cash, they fixed the value of the capons or wheat at three times the market price. Consequently there were great variations in the rentes from seigneurie to seigneurie and even within a seigneurie. It would be advisable, Raudot told the minister, for His Majesty to make a declaration fixing the rates for once and for all.[11] Almost a century and a half later the question of the rate of the *cens et rentes* became a crucial point in the debate over the abolition of seigneurial tenure. A commission made a thorough investigation of the subject and found that there had been an unofficial standard rate during the French regime, and that there was no evidence that it had been exceeded.[12] Although the commission's findings have generally been accepted, conversations with several scholars who have worked on the French regime reveal that they are by no means convinced of their validity. The evidence needs to be briefly re-examined.

There is no doubt that a censitaire who held a written title deed paid no more than it stipulated. This contract was legally binding, and it is hard to imagine any of the colony's naturally litigious inhabitants, who could appeal to generally sympathetic courts in the towns or to the intendant, paying more than was required legally. Often they tried to pay less, claiming that money had been devalued, that a capon was not worth as much as the seigneur demanded when he insisted on cash payment, or that because the contract had been given when card money was in circulation, the payment should be smaller when made in French money,[13] for censitaires were at their creative best in court. But a contract was a contract, and if it could be produced there was seldom any case. When the stipulated rates were higher than the average, the censitaire had to pay them; when lower, there was nothing a seigneur could do,[14] and a contract given in 1650 was perfectly good a hundred years later.

The highest charge stipulated in a title deed for a roture of two by thirty arpents in the two most populous Jesuit seigneuries—Notre Dame des Anges and La Prairie de la Magdeleine—was six livres; that is, one livre and one capon (valued at a livre) for twenty square arpents. This was the most common rate in Notre Dame des Anges between 1690 and 1730, and there were occasional grants at the same rate in La Prairie de la Magdeleine. More common in La Prairie de la Magdeleine was a rate of one sol per square arpent and one capon per arpent of frontage; thus the rente for a concession of two by thirty arpents involved two instead of three capons, making a total yearly rente of five livres. All the concessions in Notre Dame des Anges between 1665 and 1672 were also made at this rate. For two decades after 1673 the Jesuits attempted to attract settlers to La Prairie de la Magdeleine by reducing the rentes from one to one-half sol per square arpent, a reduction which fixed the annual rente for such a roture at three and one-half livres. After 1730 the value of a capon in Notre Dame des Anges was reduced to fifteen sols, and the total rente fell from the usual six to five and one-quarter livres. These four rates— twenty sols and a capon for twenty square arpents; twenty sols for twenty square arpents and one capon for each arpent of frontage; ten sols for twenty square arpents and one capon for each arpent of frontage; and twenty sols and a capon valued at fifteen sols for each twenty square arpents—are found in at least 95 per cent of all the preserved title deeds for rotures within the two seigneuries. Except for the two decades after 1672 in La Prairie de la Magdeleine rentes fluctuated in the limited range of from five to six livres. Rentes were not rising or falling in a perceptible trend, and probably there was no more stable price in Canada during the French regime than the rente charged for a roture in a Jesuit seigneurie. Nothing in the documents suggests that censitaires were treated differently in seigneuries belonging to other religious orders.

Rentes in lay seigneuries probably fluctuated a little more. However none of the several hundred title deeds which have been preserved for rotures in lay seigneuries list rentes higher than one livre and one capon or half a minot of wheat for twenty square arpents. The commision reported this correctly in 1843. Occasionally, to be sure, twenty-five or thirty sols were fixed as the exchange for a capon, a figure well above the usual market price, but in many seigneuries after 1730 an exchange rate of fifteen sols became standard. No exchange was fixed when half a minot of wheat was charged instead of the capon, and because the price of wheat fluctuated widely around an average of at least two and one-half livres, the seigneur could often increase his revenue. But there was no over-all tendency for rentes to be pushed up. Indeed, they may have been decreasing slightly; in the last three decades of the French regime fifteen sols for an arpent of frontage, or fifteen sols for thirty square arpents was quite commonly charged.[15]

If rentes were being manipulated, the censitaires who suffered must have been those who did not hold proper contracts. However, very few complaints of juggled rentes reached official ears, although as late as 1700 probably a third to a half of all censitaires did not have written contracts. The commission of 1843 stated that "upon the subject of the rate of concession, no difficulty appears to have existed in the colony, as a usual and accustomed rate was by universal consent acknowledged to be settled . . . ."[16] This is not quite exact, for there were occasional complaints, but in all the documents there is apparently only one reference to a dispute over rentes specified in a lost or a verbal contract, and that on an unsigned, undated scrap mixed in with the seigneurial documents in the Archives de la Province de Québec.[17] A Sieur Doyon (?), who may have held an arrière-fief in Notre Dame des Anges, bought seven and one-half arpents of frontage in the same seigneurie from Pierre Jean and resold the land to whoever was responsible for the note. As Pierre Jean did not know the charges on the roture, Doyon fixed them at a level "qu'il Luy plait" when he resold it. Somehow the new buyer found out that the original charges had been twenty-five sols per arpent of frontage and two capons (therefore originally conceded by the Jesuits around 1650) and took issue with Doyon's new rates. He had consulted several knowledgeable people who had assured him that the rentes could not be changed, and warned that "nous vivrons en paix et de bonne intelligence" only if they were maintained at the original rate.

This isolated case is most interesting for what it indicates about a censitaire's efforts to demonstrate that he did not have to pay an increased rente. He had found out what the original rente had been, and argued that the prescription laws which equated uninterrupted tenure of property for a certain period with a clear title to it did not apply to the *cens et rentes.** Thus, even if a former censitaire had been exempted from the rente, his successor argued that Doyon had no right to increase the rente when he reintroduced it. This argument broached some of the finer points of the coutume, but habitants were often capable of fairly sophisticated legal arguments. Had many seigneurs been tampering with the rentes, even rentes verbally given, the courts would have been deluged with complaints. Some rentes must have been fixed at the going rate when no one could remember what the original concession had been, or when a censitaire could not prove what they had been, but probably no seigneur ever succeeded in or, with the above exception, may ever even have tried to raise rentes above the standard level. Any censitaire knew what was usually paid; had he been overcharged he would have gone at once to the courts in Quebec, Trois-Rivières, or Montreal, or to the intendant, and the record of his appeal would be preserved.

Most of Raudot's points were accurate but somewhat misleading. Although rentes fluctuated from seigneurie to seigneurie, the differences were slight; and although seigneurs did demand cash or kind payment depending upon prices, the rente was not large in either case. Occasionally seigneurs raised rentes if the terms of the original contract were forgotten, but never beyond the prevailing level. Raudot handled dozens

---

* The censitaire who wrote this was not on absolutely sure legal ground. He would have no trouble demonstrating that the cens was nonprescriptable, but would have had more difficulty with the rentes.

of cases a month involving every sort of dispute and no one was in a better position to assess the need for more uniform seigneurial charges. His 1707 dispatch was a brief for this reform in which he made as strong a case as he could, but it does not follow that because the system was not legally standardized, seigneurs were raising rentes above the unofficial ceiling. When Beauharnois and Hocquart pointed out in 1734 that "concessions doivent être quasi-gratuites" [18] they were reiterating a tacit assumption of officials in Canada since the 1660's. This official stand along with the disputatious temperament of the habitants made it virtually impossible until the end of the French regime for a seigneur to increase the rentes and get away with it.

(3) *The corvée as a charge added to the rente.**—At the beginning of the eighteenth century, the *corvée*, or compulsory work day, began to appear in roture contracts as a charge supplementing the rente. In 1708 the seigneur of Bonsecours conceded two hundred square arpents which were charged with five sols, five capons, and five livres, an ordinary *cens et rente*, and also one day of corvée in March or two additional livres, an addition which was without precedent in the colony and without sanction in the coutume.[19] Before the re-emergence in the later Middle Ages of a money economy in France, villeins were regularly required to work two or three days a week in their lord's fields, although long before the seventeenth century this corvée had been replaced by payments in kind or cash. The few corvées in France in the seventeenth century were for public services for the parish. Although the Canadian corvées referred to in this section were only a day or two a year, they were definitely of the earlier French type, and after several seigneurs had listed them in their roture contracts, the intendant reported this violation of the coutume to the minister. The affected censitaires had reacted more quickly. By 1716, when the censitaires of La Chevrotière petitioned the intendant to abolish their corvées, there had been several complaints. The intendant, agreeing that the corvée was an illegal charge, ordered that no seigneur could insert it in any contract, but ruled that the censitaires from La Chevrotière must pay the corvées stipulated in their contracts and, insult added to injury, supply their own tools and food,[20] a

---

* This is not to be confused with the *corvées* charged for the common, which appeared much earlier. The *corvée* referred to in this paragraph was not a payment for a particular right or service, but simply an added charge, to all intents and purposes part of the rente but listed separately.

remarkable indication of the strength of a contract even when the intendant disagreed with its terms. This ordinance almost ended the corvées as supplements to the rentes, although they appeared again in 1733 in the title deeds for rotures which Governor Beauharnois granted in his new seigneurie.[21] But all in all, these corvées were rare. Although they appeared in a few seigneuries in the first two decades of the eighteenth century, they were quickly discouraged, and never constituted an important source of seigneurial revenue.

(4) *Charges for fishing rights.*—Usually seigneurs had been granted the *droit de pêche* in their seigneurial title deeds, and Vaudreuil and Beauharnois told the minister that seigneurs passed on the right to their censitaires [22] in return for a small cash payment or a fraction, usually between a tenth and a twentieth, of the catch.[23] However, as they do not appear in many title deeds it is doubtful that these charges were as common as the two ministers thought. If they were, they must have been almost impossible to collect, for the seigneur had no way of knowing if the censitaire who brought around an occasional fish or basket of eels was paying his required fraction or not, while a cash payment which had not been stipulated in the contract was even more elusive. Some disputes over fishing rights reached the courts. When several censitaires in Saint-François complained that their seigneur had no right to prevent them from fishing in the Saint-François River or along the shore of Lake Saint-Pierre, the seigneur replied that he had this right by virtue of a clause in his seigneurial title deed, an intendant's ordinance on the subject fifty years before, and the fact that the six livres a year which he charged each of his complaining censitaires for the right to fish had never been paid.[24] The intendant agreed with the seigneur, but his judgment may well have served only to turn the censitaires into more skillful poachers. In another litigation the seigneur of Portneuf complained that two of his censitaires had established an illegal eel fishery which was reducing the catch in his own traps. The two fishermen in question replied that they had never intended to farm their rocky roture. They did not have a contract which permitted them to fish, but as everyone else in the seigneurie was fishing they had not thought that a contract was necessary. The two fishermen eventually agreed to pay four barrels of eels a year to their seigneur,[25] and this charge, backed as it was by an intendant's ordinance, was undoubtedly collected. In such a case the revenue from fishing privileges may have been an important percentage of the total seigneurial revenue,

but the charges were usually difficult to collect and small enough so that few seigneurs bothered with them.

(5) *Charges for wood rights.*—Although many seigneurs reserved the right to cut a certain amount of timber within their subgrants, these wood rights were not, strictly speaking, a source of revenue coming from the censitaires. On the other hand, when in 1725 the Jesuits in Batiscan conceded a roture to Michel Baribaud for a modest *cens et rente* and, as well, a twelfth of all the planks and timbers he cut, this was a distinctive new charge.[26] Depending on Baribaud's success with his sawmill, such a charge could have been very profitable for the Jesuits. But if similar charges were stipulated in other title deeds, record of them has been lost.

(6) *Charges for a common.*—Common pastures—sometimes an island in the St. Lawrence, sometimes a strip of natural grassland along the bank, sometimes considerable tracts of forest—began to be set aside in the 1660's and 1670's, and hundreds of disputes over the right to use these commons, the number of animals that could be grazed on them, or the fences that were built around them attest to their importance for both seigneurs and censitaires.[27] By 1700 there were commons on a third to a half of all settled seigneuries, and two or more on some of the larger ones. In some cases charges for commons were specified in the title deeds, but more often the seigneur drew up a special document in which he granted a common to his censitaires in return for certain prescribed charges. The terms in these donations were quite as binding as those in the title deeds, and charges were rarely the issue in all the disputes over commons if they had been specified in one document or the other.

Charges for the common were sometimes based on the number of livestock pastured in it. Five sols per head was a fairly standard rate, although even when a cowherd was hired to tend the common these charges were difficult to collect. Censitaires were frequently accused of spiriting cattle in and out. To avoid this difficulty most seigneurs charged a flat rate for the right to use the common regardless of the number of head pastured in it.[28] This rate averaged approximately two livres per year, but there were marked variations from seigneurie to seigneurie. Five sols, and later thirty, were charged for the common in La Prairie de la Magdeleine, fifteen in Notre Dame des Anges, three livres payable in wheat or peas in Saint-Antoine, five livres in Berthier, and four days of corvée or seven livres in Boucherville. These corvées, like those added to the rentes, had no legal support in the coutume, and most of them were commuted by a cash payment of from one and one-half to two livres per day.

(7) *The banalities.*—The banalities were charges for services which the seigneur provided rather than for the use of land which he had granted. In seventeenth-century France the banalities were a much greater burden than service to the censitaires, but probably only two of the many banal charges in France came to Canada. One was a bake-oven banality, so incongruous in a land where the seigneur's oven might be miles away and the dough frozen long before it got there, that it was quickly abandoned. The other, a gristmill banality, was always insisted upon when a seigneur had a mill, and often became an important source of seigneurial revenue.

In 1667 the gristmill banality was fixed at a fourteenth of the grain ground [29] in either water or windmills.[30] As the censitaire had to take only that portion of his grain which was for his domestic consumption to the banal gristmill, it cannot be concluded that a seigneur's revenue from his mill was a fourteenth of the grain grown in his seigneurie. The censitaire could take his surplus to be ground elsewhere, or could sell it to an itinerant merchant. But if the mill turned out acceptable flour, and if the service was reasonably rapid, most censitaires probably did take their surplus to the seigneurial mill.

The seigneur was expected to build a mill, and after 1686 to build it within a year or sacrifice has banal rights.[31] The construction of this mill was his principal seigneurial expense. The largest of them, like the stone mill on Terrebonne which was one hundred and twenty feet long and forty wide, three stories high, and fitted with granaries on the top floor and four pairs of water-powered millstones below,[32] or a similar mill belonging to the Séminaire de Québec at Petit Pré in Beaupré, probably cost the seigneurs at least 10,000 livres. When the English burned part of the mill at Petit Pré in 1759, repairs alone amounted to more than 3,500 livres.[33] Most mills were less elaborate; windmills were commonly round stone towers approximately twenty feet high and twelve to fifteen in diameter, and water mills often resembled small farmhouses from the outside. Yet one of these mills must have cost the seigneurs at least 2,000 livres. Maintenance costs were also high. The Séminaire de Québec spent over 1,000 livres a year on its mill at Petit Pré, and almost as much on a smaller mill at Le Sault à la Puce.[34] With depreciation, repairs, and a miller's salary, the yearly expenses for the simplest mill must have been in the order of 500 livres a year.

Assuming an average price for wheat of approximately two and one-half livres a minot, the seigneur had to take in two hundred minots in some combination of his own and his censitaire's grain (that is, to grind 2,800 minots) to break even on his mill. When wheat prices rose, less grain was required to make it profitable because the rise in the price of wheat, while triggering a general inflation, regularly exceeded that of wages and capital goods. On the other hand, when wheat prices fell below two and one-half livres a minot, wages and the price of capital goods dropped more slowly, and more wheat had to be taken in if the mill were to break even.[35] In either case the seigneur could reduce expenses by operating the mill himself. If there were a mill in his seigneurie, he also saved the milling charges for the grain which he had grown on his domain.

A rough estimate of the profitability of a mill can be obtained by dividing a fourteenth of the grain grown on a given seigneurie by the number of mills there, although in assuming that all the grain was handled at the banal mill, a definite bias is introduced in favor of profitability. The first census which includes enough data for this simple calculation was taken in 1688. Of the forty-four gristmills then in the colony approximately half were profitable or marginally profitable (180 to 220 minots revenue); the rest were definitely unprofitable. The profitable mills were on the older, established seigneuries like Beauport and the Ile d'Orléans and the others on more recently settled seigneuries. The mill for Longueuil and Tremblay produced almost three times the revenue of that for Contrecœur and Saint-Ours although it served only a dozen more inhabitants. Longueuil and Tremblay had been settled a few years before Contrecœur and Saint-Ours, and farms were therefore producing more. The last census to give wheat yields was taken in 1739. By that year all but a handful of the one hundred and twenty mills in the colony were solidly in the black, and a few on older seigneuries produced a gross return of nearly 1,000 minots. Most of the unprofitable mills were around Lake Saint-Pierre or along the south shore well below Quebec in areas which had been settled only a few years before.

The profitability of the seigneurial gristmill was broadly determined by the number of settlers in a seigneurie and by the length of time they had been there. A dozen families settled for one year were not producing as much grain as a similar number who had been established for a decade. If two seigneuries were settled at the same time and one contained ten, the other twenty families, the latter was likely to produce more grain and, therefore, more revenue for the seigneurial gristmill. It should be possible to determine under what combination of these two factors gristmills tended to pass from the red to the black side of the seigneurial ledger.

An examination of census data for seigneuries settled less than fifteen years suggests that in such seigneuries the mill banality averaged approximately three minots per family (seigneur included), being as much as five or as little as one. At this rate a seigneur broke even on his mill during these early years if he had sixty-five families in his seigneurie, and showed a profit with seventy-five. If, as was many times more likely, he had ten families, he stood to lose four hundred livres a year on his gristmill. When a seigneurie had been settled for more than fifteen years the revenue per family from the banal mill rose to no more than four or five minots in some seigneuries and to nearly fifteen in others, depending upon a number of variables—rate of clearing, soil quality, land utilization for other crops, and so on. Eight minots per family was roughly the average. At this rate the mill was marginally profitable with twenty-five families settled in a seigneurie, and definitely so with thirty. If there were a hundred families, the seigneur cleared six hundred minots or, at two and one-half livres a minot, 1,500 livres. However, a hundred families (or any number beyond fifty) usually produced more grain than a small mill could handle, and the seigneur had either to enlarge his old mill or build another.

In general, then, the gristmill was a liability to a seigneur until there were at least twenty-five families in his seigneurie, or more than twice that many during the first years of settlement. Settlers in Canada were seldom easily come by, and only a few seigneuries ever attracted even twenty-five families within fifteen years. More often a generation or perhaps two or three passed before this number was reached, and all the while the banal gristmill lost money. On the other hand, when the seigneurie was well settled the mills were a steady source of revenue. Seigneurs often rented the mills on such seigneuries, and were generally able to charge a hundred minots or more a year for a small mill, and two to three hundred for a larger one.[36] Mill rents were much lower in seigneuries comprising less than twenty-five families, but with relatively little grain coming to the mill, the miller almost invariably had difficulty with his payments.

Throughout the seventeenth century there were complaints that seigneurs were not building or maintaining mills. A surprising number of mills were built years before they could be profitable, but most seigneurs procrastinated because of the debts they knew a mill in a sparsely settled seigneurie would incur. Complaints became less frequent in the eighteenth century as the increase in population, coupled after 1718 with a period of inflation, made gristmills profitable. Very few settled seigneuries at the end of the French regime were without a mill, and some had four or five.

(8) *The lods et ventes.*—Whenever a roture was sold out of the line of direct succession, the seigneur was entitled to a twelfth of the sale price, and this twelfth was known as the *lods et ventes*. There was no argument about the charge; as long as a sale could be proved and the seigneur bothered to collect, one-twelfth of the price was indubitably his. Censitaires could avoid or reduce the *lods et ventes* by disguising sales as exchanges or gifts (the authenticity of at least a few of the many such transactions can certainly be questioned), or by fixing the sale price in the deed of sale below what actually was charged. To protect themselves against the latter practice, Canadian seigneurs usually inserted a *retrait roturier* in their contracts. This *retrait,* which had come to Canada in the Coutume de Normandie,[37] enabled the seigneur to acquire a roture by paying the purchase price to the buyer within forty days of the sale. In 1707, Raudot complained that there was no authority in the Coutume de Paris for the *retrait roturier,*[38] and a decade later Bégon commented in the same vein,[39] but whenever the *retrait* was stipulated in a title deed it was apparently legal.[40] In the last decades of the French regime the *retrait roturier* was given precedence over the *retrait lignager,* a change which was contrary to an article in and violated the entire spirit of the Coutume de Paris. In France the *retrait lignager* was a bulwark protecting family property from an ill-considered alienation, and the fact that this right was degraded in Canada is extremely significant. It is an understandable but not often recognized fact that the family land did not mean to Canadians during the French regime what it did to Frenchmen.

That the *retrait roturier* was applied at all, much less strengthened in this way, is a clue to the importance of the *lods et ventes* as a source of seigneurial revenue. Many rotures changed hands frequently in the first years after their concession; some had four or five owners within a decade. (See the discussion of sales of rotures, in Chap. 8.) Sales were less common thereafter, but a seigneur's revenue from his *lods et ventes* probably did not decrease very much in older, established seigneuries because even if there were not so many sales, the value of a single roture was many times greater. Although there are no complete records of sales in any seigneurie over an extended period, an estimated return from the *lods et ventes* of two to three hundred livres a year for every hundred rotures cannot be too far from the mark.

(9) *Sales of rotures.*—Although seigneurs rarely sold unimproved land, cleared land had some value and a price was always charged for it over and above the usual conditions. In the proprietary years some seigneurs rented concessions and paid their tenants a bonus for each arpent they cleared in the hope that cleared land could some day be sold.[41] This practice disappeared—at least there is no record of it—after 1663, but a seigneur could always buy a cleared roture, claim one in payment for debts, or reoccupy one when it was abandoned.[42] Once cleared land was in his possession, the seigneur could sell it, and in the 1730's Beauharnois and Hocquart pointed out to the minister that seigneurs were selling entire rotures for substantial sums whenever there were small clearings on them.[43] However, if these sales had been common, court cases involving them surely would have been more plentiful, and the intendants much more insistent. It is safe to assume that sales of cleared land constituted so spasmodic and generally insignificant a source of seigneurial revenue that it is probably misleading to indicate a yearly average.

(10) *Interest.*—Seigneurs occasionally lent money to their censitaires on the security of the roture, or permitted purchase payments on rotures to be spread out over a number of years. In either case the interest rate (*rente racheptable*), which was reduced with the principal, was invariably 5 per cent per annum. Another procedure occasionally followed by a censitaire in need of money was, in effect, to sell his land to the seigneur. The seigneur acquired title to the roture, but the censitaire stayed on it as long as he paid the 5 per cent yearly interest on the sale price. The land was legally his again as soon as he had paid back the principal.[44] Lay seigneurs probably seldom had the cash for these loans, but they were a fairly common, if modest source of revenue in Church seigneuries. From the seigneur's point of view it was a safe arrangement;

either he received the land at a price substantially below the market value, or he got his money back plus interest; and in those cases where payments lapsed after some years, he received the one and part of the other. The religious orders may have averaged fifty to one hundred livres from these interest charges for each one hundred rotures.

(11) *Miscellaneous charges.*—Some seigneurs required their censitaires to plant a Maypole in front of the seigneurial manor each year, although this picturesque and apparently disliked obligation was stipulated in very few seigneuries.[45] Censitaires who were priests were sometimes required to say a number of masses for a departed seigneur. Here and there censitaires brought their seigneurs bouquets of flowers on certain dates. These payments, which have prompted many nostalgic comments, were rare.

It is possible to estimate a seigneur's total revenue from his censitaires by adding the revenue from each of the sources listed in this inventory. Table 5–1 shows estimates of total revenue for seigneuries with ten, twenty, fifty, one hundred, and five hundred families. The assumption is made throughout that individual rotures were three by thirty arpents, and that when a seigneurie was well established each family held two rotures, one of which was partially cultivated. The usual revenue from each source is given first, then the minimum and maximum possible. These latter figures are based on the minimum and maximum rates that were charged with any regularity. The common charge for the cens was a sol per arpent of frontage, the minimum a sol per roture, the maximum approximately five sols a roture. The customary rente was a livre and a capon for each arpent of frontage; the extremes, a livre per arpent of frontage at the lowest level, and a sol for each square arpent plus a capon for each twenty square arpents at the highest. Usually habitants did not pay a corvée added to the rente or a charge for fishing privileges, but when they did there were usually two days of corvées a year (at two livres a day) and fishing rights amounting to approximately four livres a year. Revenue from payments made for wood rights was so rare that it has not been included in the table. Habitants usually paid approximately two livres a year for the common, but sometimes as much as six. The banal mill revenue is calculated on the basis of an average yearly expenditure for the maintenance of the mill of five hundred livres, a minimum of four hundred, and a maximum of six hundred. It is estimated that

TABLE 5–1

Seigneurial revenue, in livres

Source of revenue	10 newly settled families	20 newly settled families	20 established families	50 families	100 families	500 families
			Probable return			
Cens	1.5	3	6	15	30	150
Rente	60	120	240	600	1,200	6,000
Corvée added to rente	. . .	. . .	. . .	. . .	. . .	. . .
Fishing rights	. . .	. . .	. . .	100	200	400
Common	20	40	40	100	200	1,000
Lods et ventes	25	50	100	250	500	2,500
Sales of rotures	. . .	. . .	. . .	. . .	100	500
Interest	. . .	. . .	. . .	. . .	100	500
Banalities						
Revenue	100	200	400	1,000	2,000	10,000
Expenditure	500	500	500	500	1,000	5,000
Net profit or loss	−400	−300	−100	500	1,000	5,000
TOTAL	−293.5	−87	286	1,565	3,330	16,050
			Minimum return			
Cens	0.5	1	2	5	10	50
Rente	30	60	120	300	600	3,000
Corvée added to rente	. . .	. . .	. . .	. . .	. . .	. . .
Fishing rights	. . .	. . .	. . .	. . .	. . .	. . .
Common	. . .	. . .	. . .	. . .	. . .	. . .
Lods et ventes	10	20	40	100	200	1,000
Sales of rotures	. . .	. . .	. . .	. . .	. . .	. . .
Interest	. . .	. . .	. . .	. . .	. . .	. . .
Banalities						
Revenue	50	100	300	625	1,250	6,250
Expenditure	600	600	600	600	1,200	6,000
Net profit or loss	−550	−500	−300	25	50	250
TOTAL	−509.5	−419	−138	430	860	4,300
			Maximum return			
Cens	2.5	5	10	25	50	250
Rente	90	180	360	900	1,800	9,000
Corvée added to Rente	40	80	160	400	800	4,000
Fishing rights	40	80	160	400	800	1,600
Common	60	120	120	300	600	3,000
Lods et ventes	50	100	200	500	1,000	5,000
Sales of rotures	20	40	80	200	400	2,000
Interest	10	20	40	100	200	1,000
Banalities						
Revenue	150	300	750	1,825	3,750	18,750
Expenditure	400	400	400	400	800	4,000
Net profit or loss	−250	−100	350	1,425	2,950	14,750
TOTAL	62.5	525	1,480	4,250	8,600	40,600

three minots (at two and one-half livres a minot) was an average payment per family for the use of the gristmill in a newly settled seigneurie. Two minots is suggested as the minimum, six the maximum. On established seigneuries eight minots was probably nearer the average, five the minimum and fifteen the maximum. Revenue from sales and from interest charges was unusual, but estimates are included in the "maximum" columns. The miscellaneous charges were negligible in even the largest seigneuries, and have not been shown on the table. As it is highly unlikely that any seigneur charged consistently at the maximum or minimum levels, these extreme totals were probably never reached. On the other hand, the probable columns give a clearer impression than any other available of the revenue a seigneur could expect from his censitaires.

It is apparent from Table 5–1 that a seigneur lost money if he had ten or twenty newly established families and a mill in his seigneurie. After some years the seigneurie would begin to show a modest profit because many of the original censitaires had applied for additional rotures, and because the twenty families were taking more grain to the banal mill. When there were fifty families, a seigneur received a net revenue from his censitaires of approximately 1,500 livres, a sum which would buy a dozen oxen, thirty cows, or a farm with twenty or thirty cleared arpents and several wooden farm buildings. With one hundred families, this revenue had more than doubled; with five hundred, the seigneur's revenue from his censitaires was over 16,000 livres a year, a sum which could hire a hundred laborers for seventy-five days, buy over three hundred cows, or pay for ten small farms at average prices. Although only one Canadian seigneurie—the Ile de Montréal, excluding the city—was in the five-hundred-family class at the end of the French regime, there were a dozen with more than a hundred. Even at the low rates charged in Canada these seigneuries could have been very profitable.

It cannot be too strongly emphasized that the seigneurs did not always collect the revenues shown in Table 5–1. Not only the marginal sources, but even the *cens et rentes* were frequently neglected, so that some censitaires made no payments whatsoever for twenty or thirty years. Sometimes censitaires refused to pay because they were unhappy with the charges. Pierre Lanouette and his seigneur in Sainte-Anne could not agree whether payments should be in cash or kind, and after thirteen years of intermittent haggling, Lanouette owed twenty-six capons, thirteen chickens, and six and one-half minots of wheat for the rente as well as one livre six sols for the cens.[46] A censitaire on the Ile d'Orléans owed twenty-one years of back dues because he thought that he should pay only three-quarters of the stipulated charges (the contract was drawn up when card money was in vogue), and that he was owed a considerable sum for work he had done for his seigneur. The *jugement définitif* in this drawn-out case ran to more than 10,000 words,[47] but whether the seigneurs ever collected the dues stipulated in this compromise is not clear. Julien Rivard Lanouette, another censitaire in Sainte-Anne, backed his refusal to pay with the claim that one of the coseigneurs had ordered him not to pay.[48] More frequently, however, dues were avoided because no one had bothered to collect them. Such was the case in De Maure, where in 1734 censitaires were ordered to show their contracts to the seigneur and to pay him twenty-nine years of uncollected dues.[49]

The breakdown of contact between seigneurs and censitaires occurred in two situations. If the seigneur of a sparsely settled seigneurie of ten, twenty, or thirty families lived in one of the towns, the dues were often not worth the trouble of collecting. Probably the seigneur had not built a mill, and if he paid any attention to his concession it was only to collect the *cens et rentes* every five or ten years. Quite possibly he knew neither his censitaires nor what dues they were supposed to pay. A similar situation could have developed when a seigneurie was well divided among a number of coseigneurs. The principal seigneur collected the dues from his fraction of the seigneurie and sometimes from the remainder, but when he did not, the coseigneur who lived miles away and controlled a small fraction of the seigneurie seldom bothered to collect the pittance which was his. In either situation the feudal axiom *nulle terre sans seigneur* had evaporated in any practical sense.

Because there was a direct correlation between the number of censitaires and the seigneur's income, the more populous a lay seigneurie became the better it was likely to be managed. Church seigneuries, on the other hand, were usually carefully tended whatever their population. Censitaires in these seigneuries were allowed to build up considerable debts—four censitaires in Notre Dame des Anges owed the Jesuits over 650 livres in 1754[50]—but the director kept a close check on these outstanding dues and as long as they were well below the value of the roture, his Order was assured of the dues or the roture sooner or later. When a censitaire owed twenty or thirty livres on an undeveloped roture, the director or, for that matter, any lay seigneur who tended his seigneurie carefully, was likely to apply to the intendant for the right to withdraw the roture because the land was not worth enough to cover the debt. Herein lay the principal difference between Church and lay seigneuries. Control was steady in the former; censitaires knew what they had to pay in dues and back debts, and that they had to pay. In lay seigneuries, especially those with fewer than forty or fifty families, control was much more spasmodic; the seigneur could be more demanding than the Church usually was, or could completely neglect his seigneurie for decades.

It is a simple matter to calculate from Table 5–1 a representative amount which the individual censitaire paid his seigneur every year. In newly settled seigneuries the total payment for a single roture was just over twenty livres; in older seigneuries where more land was cleared and hence more grain taken to the banal mill, it reached approximately thirty-three livres. Thirty-three livres would buy fifteen days of manual labor, a small cow, or between ten and fifteen minots of wheat at average prices. It was probably under 10 per cent, and may have been no more than 5 per cent of an habitant's yearly income. In return his grain was ground at the seigneurial mill and he was the undisputed title-holder of his land. Land could not have been acquired much more reasonably.[51]

REVENUE FROM THE DOMAIN

The domain, the land which the seigneur had set aside with the intention of establishing a farm, a fishing station, or a sawmill for his own use, was an altogether different source of revenue. Domains were not always developed, or even set aside,[52] but by the end of the French regime there was at least one developed domain on almost every settled rural seigneurie in the colony. Some of these domains were no larger than the rotures on either side. More often they extended the entire depth of the seigneurie, usually five or ten miles or more, and were several hundred yards wide. A few domains were twenty or thirty arpents along the river by only a little more in depth. Although most seigneurs set aside only one domain, a few withheld three or four;[53] and, as has been shown, the division of a seigneurie among a number of coseigneurs led to the establishment of several domains in one seigneurie. Whatever their shape, size, or number, these domains were for the seigneur's use, and were exploited by him in a variety of ways.

In some cases, the seigneur farmed the domain himself. The seigneur of an arrière-fief on the Ile d'Orléans reported that the domain produced almost no grain when he acquired it in 1704, but that he had increased the output by his own labor to fifty minots of wheat and seven hundred bundles of hay a year.[54] In the early years the manor on such a domain was a small building of vertically placed split logs, roofed with thatch. Later it might be faced with heavy planks, or rebuilt of squared timbers interlocking at flush corners, a construction known as *pièce sur pièce,* which had been brought from France and which became very common in Canada. In the eighteenth century the seigneur might have built a small stone house. He had a kitchen garden, a few cows, a pair of oxen, some pigs, a horse, and a number of fowl. His principal crop was wheat or hay, and he grew some peas and oats. Such a seigneur usually had a special place in the church, and he collected a small amount in dues from a few censitaires, but he was an habitant in everything except title. He and others like him may have composed a third to a half of all the seigneurs in the colony.

Some seigneurs let their domains to tenants. The seigneur might have lived on the domain with his tenant, as was apparently the case in the 1730's in Vincelotte, where there was a stone manor house fifty feet long and twenty-two wide, and a small house of *pièce sur pièce* construction for the tenant.[55] Other seigneurs let the entire seigneurie, including the manor house, the power to grant rotures, and the revenue from the censitaires.[56] Whatever the agreement between the seigneur and his tenant, the rent was high. In 1675 the Jesuits let the domain, most of which must still have been bush, in their newly settled seigneurie of La Prairie de la Magdeleine for five hundred livres a year payable in wheat, plus an additional hundred and eighty livres a year for the support of each priest living in the seigneurie, and the obligation to feed any guests. The tenant was to cook for the priests, supply their firewood, and perform several smaller chores.[57] It was a hard bargain, and almost certainly he was unable to stick to it. When Aubert de la Chesnaye rented one of his seigneuries (Lachenaie) he charged six hundred livres for each of the first three years, one thousand for each of the second three, and twelve hundred for each of the last three years of the contract.[58] The tenant acquired a seigneur's rights, but as there were still very few censitaires, most of whatever he hoped to make out of the seigneurie had to come from the domain. In later years rents were even higher.

Rents such as these were the major part of a seigneur's revenue from his seigneurie until almost a hundred families were paying the annual dues for their rotures. However, because a seigneur's revenue from the domain increased if he operated it himself and, particularly, because few tenants were willing to assume the risks involved, rented domains were not as common as might be expected. At most the domain may have been rented at any given time in one-tenth of the seigneuries.

Usually a large domain was operated by the seigneur. He employed several farm hands, and may have done some of the manual labor himself unless he was a man of some importance in the colony, in which case his role was exclusively managerial. Such domains were the largest farms in Canada, and on a few of them there was also a sawmill or a fishing station. Although there was only one censitaire in the seigneurie of Ile Verte in 1735, a gristmill and a sawmill as well as the usual farm buildings were on the domain.[59] The two mills had been put up by the seigneur for his own use. Even more capital had been invested in the domains in Terrebonne where, as mentioned earlier, the gristmill was the largest in the colony—a stone building one hundred and twenty feet long, forty feet wide, and three stories high. The sawmill was only slightly smaller, and there were barns, stables, and cowsheds as well. Three hundred and fifty square arpents were cultivated, and over one hundred and fifty square arpents were meadow.[60] In 1745 Terrebonne was sold for 60,000 livres,[61] the highest price paid for a Canadian seigneurie during the French regime, and at least nine-tenths of this sum must have been for the buildings and cleared land on the domains.

The account books of the Séminaire de Québec afford the most complete record of the revenue from such domains. There were three domains in Beaupré, the Séminaire's largest seigneurie: one of them at Baie Saint-Paul, and two—La Grande and La Petite Ferme—in the parish of Saint-Joachim. In the early 1730's each of the domains in Saint-Joachim contained approximately two hundred arpents of cultivated land, another fifty arpents of meadow, a number of substantial farm buildings, and a lodging for the priests.[62] By Canadian standards they were large, well-managed domains. Table 5–2 indicates their net yearly profit from 1711 to 1722. The rapid increase in profits until 1718 reflects a shortage of wheat coupled with one of the many financial crises which attended the overissuing of card money. Wheat prices skyrocketed and pulled all other prices up as well. A good harvest and an order

TABLE 5-2

Net yearly profit from La Grande Ferme and La Petite Ferme, 1711-22

Year	Profit in livres	Year	Profit in livres
1711	1,022	1717	17,071
1712	2,102	1718	27,533
1713	(?)	1719	21,609
1714	3,840	1720	5,180
1715	5,968	1721	5,373
1716	9,611	1722	4,534

Source: Le Grand Livre, I (Archives du Séminaire de Québec).

withdrawing card money resulted in the precipitous drop. Table 5-3, comparing the produce and revenue from La Grande Ferme in 1718 and 1720, indicates clearly the change that had taken place. The productivity of the domains in 1718 and 1720 was roughly equivalent, but wheat, which was worth twelve livres a minot in 1718, brought two and one-

TABLE 5-3

Revenue from La Grande Ferme in Beaupré, 1718 and 1720

Item	1718			1720		
	Quantity	Livres per unit	Total value	Quantity	Livres per unit	Total value
Wheat	1,160 minots	12	13,920	1,053 minots	2.25	2,369
Oats	9 minots	6.3	57	...	...	...
Oxen in spring	2	400	800	2	120	240
Oxen for butcher	2	150	300	3	70	210
Cows	6	100	600	5	40	200
Calves	6.5[?]	25	162	8	10	80
Sheep	...	...	...	4	6	24
Horses	...	...	...	1	200	200
Beef	...	...	...	80 lbs.	0.25	16
Pork	6 barrels	200	1,200	6 barrels	60	360
Butter	1,068 lbs.	1.5	1,602	724 lbs.	0.5	362
Eggs	81 doz.	1	81	22 doz.	0.2	4
Hay	2,726 bundles	1	2,726	...	...	...
Game (bustards)	95	6	570	49	2.5	122
Miscellaneous	...	...	833	...	...	377
Total revenue			22,851			4,565 *
Total expenditure			4,705			2,299
Total profit			18,046			2,265 †

Source: Le Grand Livre (Archives du Séminaire de Québec).

* Total in source: 4,761
† Total in source: 2,462

quarter in 1720, and all other prices had also dropped two to four times. However, in 1722 when prices were as low as they ever were, the two domains still cleared more than 4,000 livres, a figure which was probably a minimum for the two domains during the last forty years of the French regime. A large domain could be decidedly profitable.

Table 5–3 indicates the type of products which came from these domains. Wheat was the principal crop, accounting for approximately half of the revenue. The other half came from a wide variety of products: oxen, beef cattle, cows and calves (all sold on the hoof), some beef, several barrels of pork, several hundred pounds of butter, eggs, and some game (bustards, according to the Séminaire's clerk, but more likely grouse or wild geese). Such a list could have come from any roture; the large domains produced more of the same things.

They may also have produced them more efficiently. Agricultural implements were primitive in early Canada,[63] as they were almost everywhere in North America at the same time, and the basic tenets of soil conservation were neglected. The Intendant de Meulles complained in 1685 that the Canadians never fertilized their land, and decided that if some of the best land did not appear to deteriorate it was only because the winter snows preserved a vapor in the soil which engendered an invigorating salt.[64] In the eighteenth century some farmers were manuring their land, and here and there instructions were given to *dessoller ny dessaisonner.* A *sole,* the root of the verb *dessoler,* was a field alternately planted in different crops during an *assolement* or rotation. The instruction to *dessoller ny dessaisonner* meant to rotate crops, usually wheat followed by peas or oats and a year of fallow.[65] This rotation, although not entirely satisfactory, was a vast improvement over no rotation at all. With very little evidence to go on, it seems a reasonable assumption that such improvements were likely to be introduced first and followed most carefully on the larger domains. Certainly the generally poor wheat crops which contributed to the high wheat prices after 1715 do not show up in the statistics for the domains in Beaupré. Perhaps the priests had enlarged their wheat acreage, perhaps they irrigated and fertilized their fields more regularly and rotated their crops, thus reducing the effects of a bad year. Whichever it was, and probably it was a combination of these factors, the seigneur operating a large domain was better able to take advantage of periods of high prices than the habitant. A period of privation for the latter could be a profitable time for the former.

In a few cases the domain was not a farm. A number of sedentary fisheries were established along the St. Lawrence well below Quebec, and seigneurs like Aubert de la Chesnaye who acquired land in this part of the colony had no intention of farming it. These fisheries have been carefully studied by Fauteux,[66] and there is no need to repeat his excellent work, except to point out that, although a good deal of time and money went into them, the sedentary fisheries were isolated from either the best fishing banks or the markets, and seldom lasted for more than a few years. Several seigneurs tried to manufacture wood tar or to cut masts. However, the market was a long way off, ships did not always arrive when they were expected, in which case the masts rotted, and when Canadian tar reached France it was seldom as good and as cheap as its competition from the Baltic. These industries fared no better than the sedentary fisheries.[67] More successful were the sawmills, which were operated in Terrebonne, Beaupré, Ile Verte, and half a dozen other seigneuries to supply a small but steady Canadian market for beams and planks.

Several points are finally clear. Because the dues an individual censitaire paid to his seigneur were fixed at a very low level, a seigneur lost money when he had only a few censitaires in his seigneurie, and was not solidly in the black until he had forty or fifty families. With five hundred his profits could be very large, although the Ile de Montréal was the only seigneurie in this class during the French regime. The revenue from the domain, on the other hand, could be sizable in the first years after a seigneurie was settled, and was likely to be the seigneur's principal source of revenue for many years, often making up what the seigneur was losing on his censitaires. When a seigneur had a hundred families or more in his seigneurie the revenue from the domain generally took a secondary place. However, because revenue from the domain tended to increase as the value of money decreased, profits from the domain on a large, well-settled seigneurie could be much larger than from the censitaires during periods of inflation. The seigneur who could save these profits until prices returned to a lower level would do very well indeed.

If a seigneur was interested in making money out of his seigneurie, energy and capital invested in the domain (as long as it did not go into the fishery or the mast business) was generally well spent. Profits were seldom as spectacular as they were during the price spiral after 1715, but there were profits. To be sure, the seigneur of Terrebonne went bankrupt building several large mills, but a more modest outlay like that of the Séminaire de Québec in Beaupré could have been expected to produce a steady return. Since censitaires were a source of profit only if they numbered forty or fifty families, a seigneur who could hope to establish this number in his seigneurie would be an active colonizer; if he could not, he would devote most of whatever energy and capital he put into his seigneurie into establishing the domain. The measures a seigneur could take to attract settlers, and the success he could expect are discussed in the next chapter.

6 : The Role of the Seigneurs
in Settling their Seigneuries

ALTHOUGH the assumption is inherent in most of the literature on early Canada that there was a cause and effect relationship between the seigneurial regime and colonization,[1] the mechanics of this relationship have not been explained. Beyond a general picture of riparian settlement in a double line between Montreal and Quebec, there is no information about settlement patterns in the colony or about the seigneur's role in shaping them. A cause which is not understood is thought to have produced an effect which has not been described.

In order to assess more accurately the importance of the seigneur as a colonizer, the distribution of population in the colony at different periods of time must be mapped carefully, and the patterns which appear on the maps must be explained. This explanation involves first an analysis of official policy towards settlement in Canada—and because much of this policy has been described by Munro it can be treated briefly here—and second a measure of the depth of the pool of potential settlers on which a seigneur could draw. Finally, information is needed about the inducements with which an individual seigneur could attract settlers to his seigneurie, and about the counterattractions of the fur trade and the town markets which also influenced the habitants' choice of location. When this evidence is added to that in previous chapters, it should be possible to make a more considered appraisal of the seigneur's role as a colonizer.

THE DISTRIBUTION OF POPULATION IN THE COLONY

The maps in this chapter, showing the distribution of population in Canada in 1667, 1692, 1712, 1739, and 1760, are based on the censuses for or near these dates, but they have been adjusted here and there to take into account data from old maps, from the *aveux et dénombrements*, from local parish histories, from modern topographic sheets, and occasionally from observations in the field. The censuses were not accurate. Groups of people were missed or lumped in such large divisions that, even with the supporting data, all of these maps are somewhat subjective. As they stand, some of their details are best approached with caution, although the major trends they show are almost certainly correct.

The distribution of population in 1667, four years after the arrival of the first shiploads of settlers sent by the king, is shown on Figure 6–1. There was a band of settlement along the north shore on either side of Quebec from ten miles above the town to twenty miles below it. Settlement had begun to push inland along the Saint-Charles River and towards the newly established village of Charlesbourg. Some 450 people were scattered around the Ile d'Orléans. Trois-Rivières was a village of 200, and there were another 350 people along the north shore within a dozen miles downstream. There were almost 800 people on the Ile de Montréal, all living in the village of Villemarie (Montreal) or close to it along the shore. The south shore of the St. Lawrence remained virtually empty; perhaps a few families were settled opposite Trois-Rivières or Quebec, but not enough to appear on the map.

In the next twenty-five years the population rose from 4,000 to 11,000, and settlement spread out from each of the older centers (Fig. 6–2). The north shore was settled for twenty miles on either side of Quebec, and there were patches of settlement from the seigneurie of Grondines (seigneurie No. 1 in the Government of Quebec*) to Baie Saint-Paul at the eastern end of Beaupré (No. 26, Government of Quebec). Farms extended several miles up the Saint-Charles River. The Ile d'Orléans was inhabited around its circumference, there were a few people on the small

---

* The colony was divided for administrative purposes into three governments—Montreal, Trois-Rivières, and Quebec. There is no indication that these administrative subdivisions had any bearing on settlement, but they are handy labels for a discussion of settlement patterns in Canada, and are utilized for this purpose only.

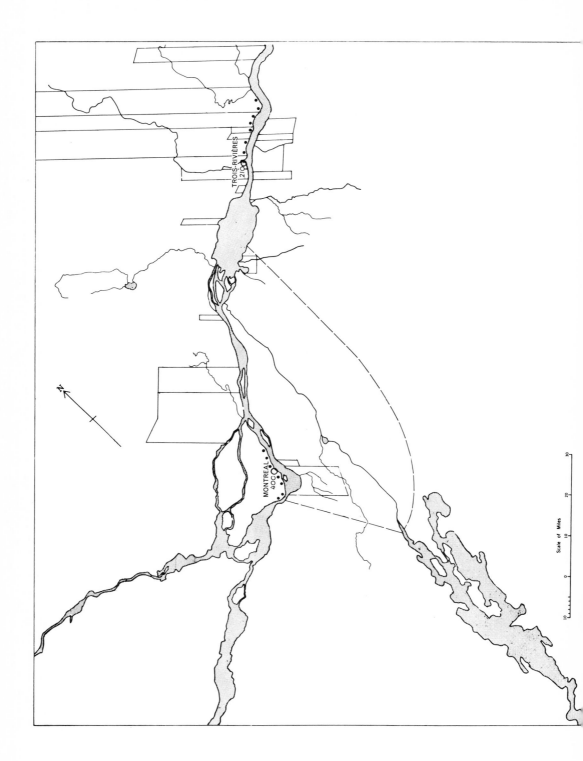

TROIS-RIVIÈRES
21,000

MONTREAL
400,000

N

Scale of Miles
10   0   10   20   30

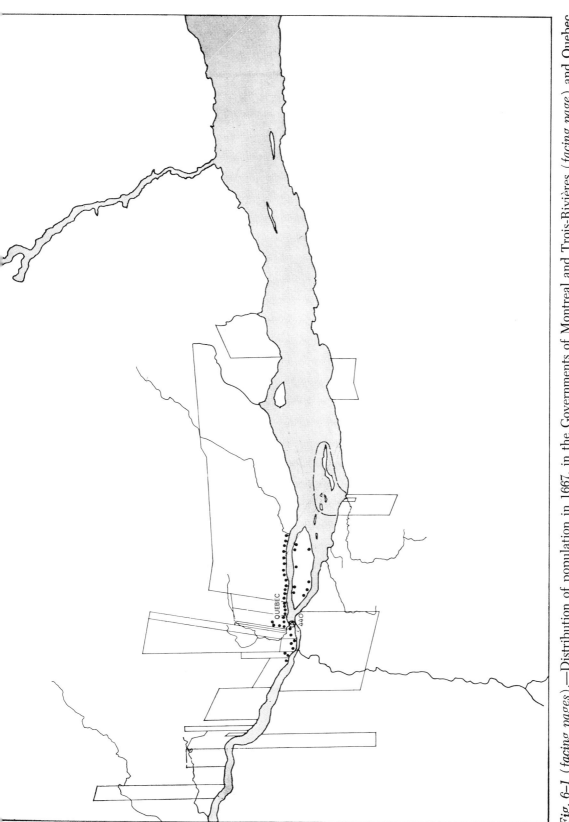

Fig. 6–1 (facing pages).—Distribution of population in 1667, in the Governments of Montreal and Trois-Rivières (*facing page*) and Quebec. Each dot represents 50 people.

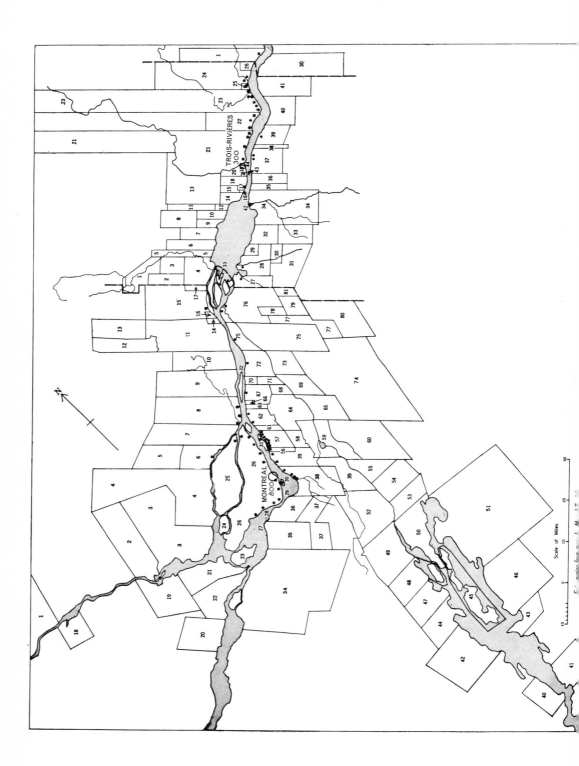

TROIS-RIVIÈRES

MONTREAL
800

Scale of Miles
10   0   10   20   30

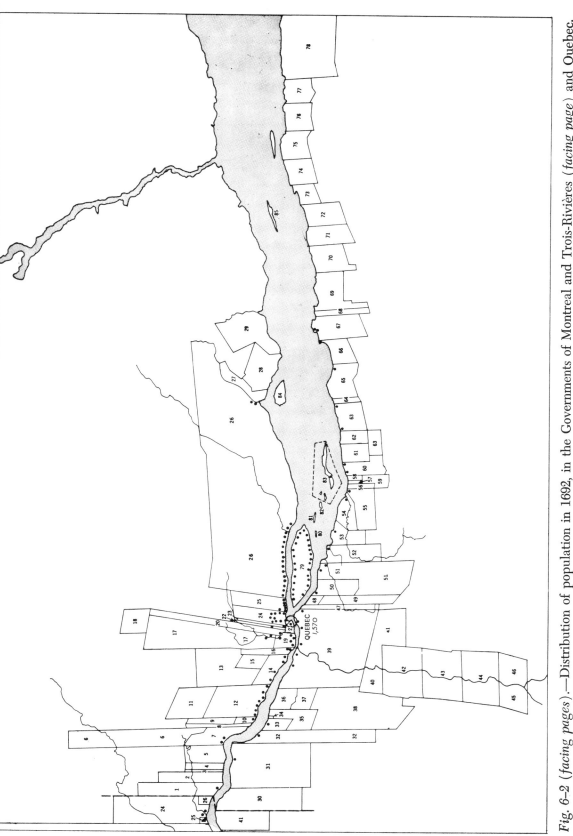

Fig. 6–2 (facing pages).—Distribution of population in 1692, in the Governments of Montreal and Trois-Rivières (*facing page*) and Quebec. Each dot represents 50 people; see appendix or back endpaper for key to numbered seigneuries.

islands immediately downstream, and in isolated settlements along the south shore. Settlement in the Government of Trois-Rivières had pushed a little farther along the north shore towards Quebec, and had begun on the south shore almost opposite the village of Trois-Rivières. Except for a few families at the mouths of the Yamaska and Saint-François rivers, there was still no settlement around Lake Saint-Pierre, and only a few families farther up the St. Lawrence until within a few miles of the Ile de Montréal. The south shore east of the island, particularly in the seigneuries of La Prairie de la Magdeleine and Boucherville (Nos. 38 and 57, Government of Montreal), was settled, as was the north shore in the seigneuries of L'Assomption and Lachenaie (Nos. 7 and 8, Government of Montreal). Ile Jésus contained a handful of settlers, and settlement had pushed farther away from Villemarie along the shore of the Ile de Montréal.

By 1712 the population of the colony was approaching 20,000, and many of the empty stretches along the river had been filled in (Fig. 6–3). A line of settlement extended with few interruptions along the north shore from Quebec to Trois-Rivières, and on the south shore from the mouth of the Chaudière to a point opposite Ile aux Oies. At the other end of the colony, settlement was contiguous for thirty miles downstream from La Prairie de la Magdeleine. There were still very few people around Lake Saint-Pierre or along the south shore between the seigneuries of Contrecœur and Deschaillon (No. 72, Government of Montreal; No. 30, Government of Quebec). The area of settlement north and west from Quebec had expanded, and elsewhere settlement was beginning to spread away from the river. A second range had opened up in Boucherville, and the banks of tributary streams were being settled in several seigneuries. There was also a small community on the Richelieu at Chambly.

Thus between 1692 and 1712 the population had risen slowly along the north shore from Beaupré to Trois-Rivières, although much of the increase in this strip was away from the river north and west of Quebec, or in gaps in earlier settlement along the shore. The population density on the settled coastal strip in Beaupré increased, but it remained virtually unchanged on the Ile d'Orléans. Along the south shore in the Government of Quebec, the population had risen slowly in Lauzon, the most densely settled seigneurie in 1692, and more quickly both up- and down-river. The most rapid growth was just below Quebec, the principal area in which young families moving out of the older seigneuries were settling. The only growth in the Government of Trois-Rivières was in several of the seigneuries around Lake Saint-Pierre. At the Montreal end of the colony growth was fairly even and more rapid than anywhere else except along the south shore below Quebec. Settlement had spread west along both shores of Ile Jésus, pushed farther around Ile de Montréal, and expanded along the opposite south shore as older areas were being more densely settled and new ones opened.

By 1739 (Fig. 6–4) the population of the colony had risen to over 40,000. Settlement along the north shore was contiguous from almost thirty miles below Quebec to a point opposite the middle of Ile Jésus except for a few empty patches between Trois-Rivières and the western end of Lake Saint-Pierre. Along the south shore there was still more empty than settled river-front land in the Government of Trois-Rivières, but otherwise settlement was contiguous for fifty miles in either direction from Quebec, and from the western end of Lake Saint-Pierre to La Prairie de la Magdeleine. Farms extended around the Ile de Montréal and half way around Ile Jésus. By 1739 a block of land several miles wide and twelve to fifteen miles long had been settled immediately north and west of Quebec. The second range in Boucherville had expanded, and settled second ranges had appeared nearby in the seigneuries of Verchères (No. 67, Government of Montreal), Varennes (No. 61, Government of Montreal), and Ile de Montréal. There had been a marked expansion up several tributaries. Settlement extended eight or ten miles up the Assomption River into the seigneurie of Saint-Sulpice (No. 9, Government of Montreal), three or four miles up the small river in La Prairie de la Magdeleine, an equal distance up the Yamaska and Saint-François rivers (which empty into the St. Lawrence at the southwest corner of Lake Saint-Pierre), the Sainte-Anne and Batiscan rivers (twenty miles east of Trois-Rivières), and the river at Baie Saint-Paul. There was settlement for a dozen miles up the Rivière du Sud, and a short distance up two smaller streams in La Durantaye and Beaumont (Nos. 51 and 50, Government of Quebec). Some settlers were scattered along the Richelieu from Chambly to its mouth, and others in two patches thirty miles up the Chaudière.

Between 1712 and 1739 the population had grown most rapidly in the Government of Montreal and least in the Government of Trois-Rivières. Almost all seigneuries in the Montreal area had grown in population,

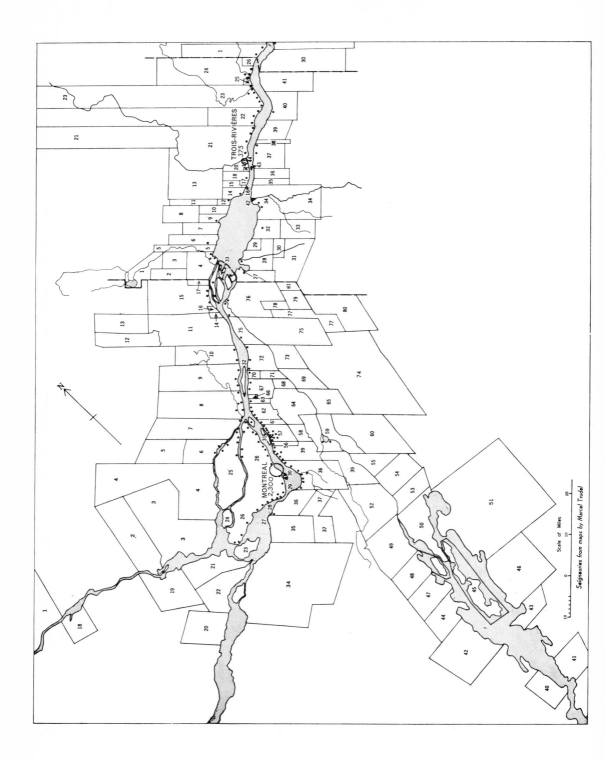

Seigneuries from maps by Marcel Trudel

Scale of Miles

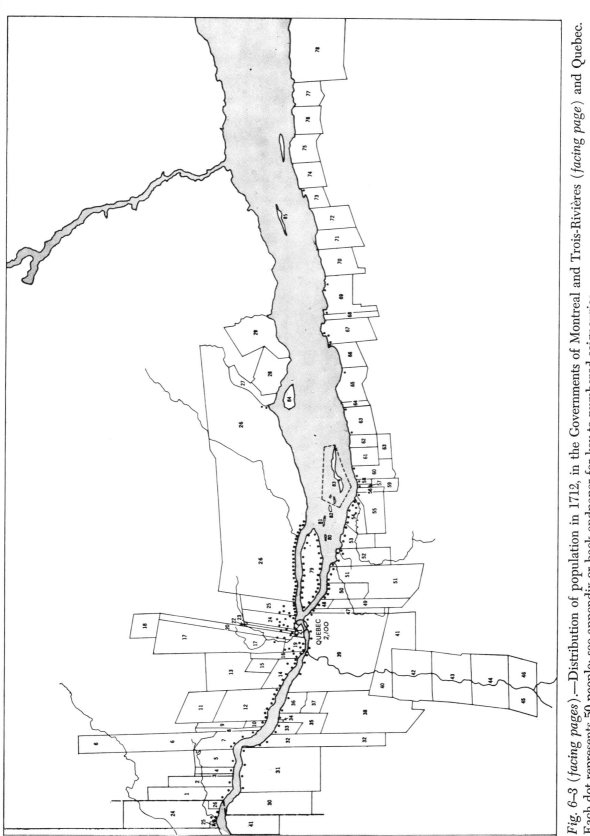

Fig. 6–3 (facing pages).—Distribution of population in 1712, in the Governments of Montreal and Trois-Rivières (*facing page*) and Quebec. Each dot represents 50 people; see appendix or back endpaper for key to numbered seigneuries.

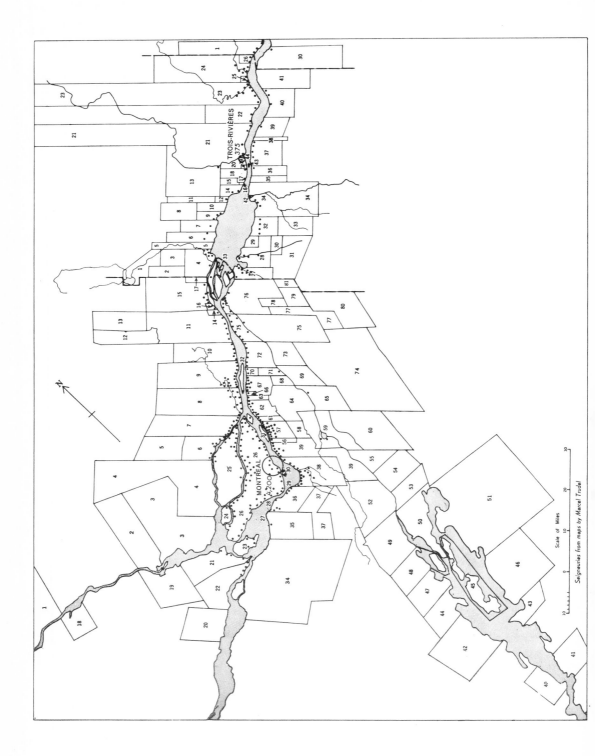

TROIS-RIVIÈRES

MONTRÉAL

Scale of Miles

Seigneuries from maps by Marcel Trudel

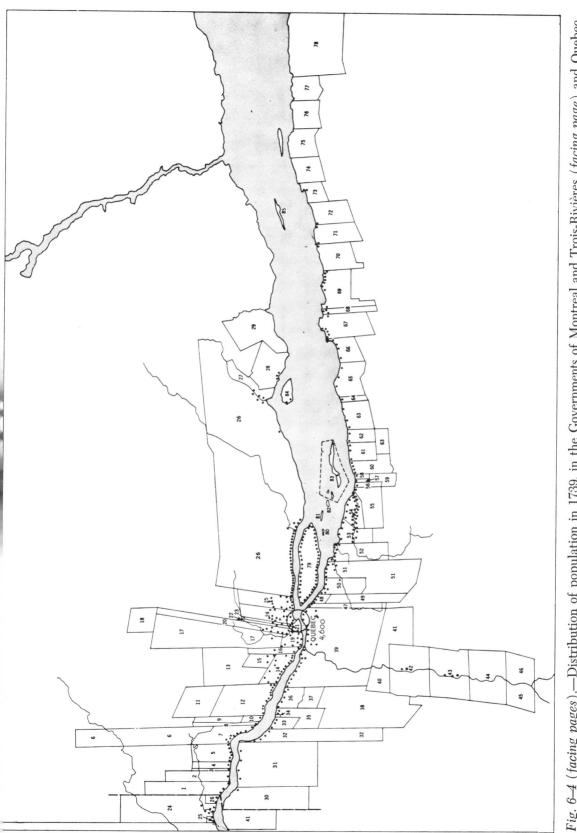

Fig. 6–4 (facing pages).—Distribution of population in 1739, in the Governments of Montreal and Trois-Rivières (*facing page*) and Quebec. Each dot represents 50 people; see appendix or back endpaper for key to numbered seigneuries.

particularly the island itself, which by 1739 was settled along its northwest shore and in several interior ranges. There was a new area of settlement west of the Ile de Montréal, and uninterrupted growth along both shores from points opposite the middle of the island to Lake Saint-Pierre. Some of this growth represented the increasing population densities of settled land along the shore, some a push back into second or third ranges or along tributary streams. Population growth was spotty in the Government of Trois-Rivières, which in 1739 had just been connected by road with Montreal and Quebec. The only two areas of substantial expansion were at the extremities of the government, that is, at the southwest end of Lake Saint-Pierre and, at the other end, in the seigneurie of Sainte-Anne (No. 24, Government of Trois-Rivières). In the Government of Quebec there was a slight increase in population density in the first range along the north shore, particularly in Deschambault and Portneuf (Nos. 5 and 7, Government of Quebec), and in the belt north and west of Quebec. The Ile d'Orléans, which had not increased in population from 1692 to 1712, had expanded by almost a thousand in the next two and one-half decades. As all the land on the island had been conceded well before 1712, farms there were undoubtedly being subdivided. Such subdivisions had not yet taken place on the more recently settled south shore opposite the Ile d'Orléans; hence the slight population growth there. However, the population had increased substantially along the south shore well below the Ile d'Orléans and above Quebec, and there had been a rapid push up the Rivière du Sud.

At the end of the French regime (Fig. 6–5) there were two ribbons of settlement, one extending for more than one hundred and fifty miles along the north shore of the St. Lawrence, the other for almost two hundred miles along the south. Although there were still a few gaps in the Government of Trois-Rivières, the river front was almost entirely settled, and expansion inland had continued fairly rapidly. Along four minor tributaries of the St. Lawrence—the Assomption, Batiscan, Boyer, and Rivière du Sud—settlement extended at least twelve to fifteen miles upriver, and five to six miles along some ten other tributaries. The Séminaire de Québec had opened a new *côte* (a short line of settlement not necessarily on the river) in Beaupré, which was two or three miles from the river and several hundred feet above it. In many seigneuries, particularly those along the south shore near Montreal and on the island itself, second or third ranges had been conceded and settled. Settlement was almost continuous along either shore of the Richelieu from its mouth to Chambly and slightly beyond, and there was a strip along the Chaudière thirty to fifty miles from the St. Lawrence.

There are striking regional variations in the patterns of population change from 1739 to 1760. Very little expansion occurred along the St. Lawrence in the Government of Quebec, except along the south shore below Ile aux Oies, and along a small section of the same shore towards the boundary of the Government of Trois-Rivières. The strip of new river-front settlement in La Durantaye may reflect an error in the census figures for 1739 or 1760. Two seigneuries, Beaupré and the Ile d'Orléans, had actually lost settlers. However, young people were emigrating from almost all the older parts of the government to the south shore well below Ile aux Oies, to three small tributaries on the south shore just below Quebec, and to the Chaudière. In the Government of Trois-Rivières, the population had increased quite rapidly around the north shore of Lake Saint-Pierre and up the Batiscan River, but elsewhere had remained virtually stagnant. There was even a slight decline in Champlain (No. 22, Government of Trois-Rivières) in part of a strip just east of Trois-Rivières which had not increased in population since 1667. The new settlement north of Lake Saint-Pierre was in an area which had been opened up in the late 1730's by the completion of the through road from Montreal to Quebec. Older settlements in the Government of Trois-Rivières had not grown, even though their population density was lower than that in comparable areas in either of the other two governments.

There was also relatively little growth in most of the older seigneuries in the Government of Montreal. The population of the Ile de Montréal had increased slightly, but two of the principal seigneuries on the south shore opposite, Boucherville and La Prairie de la Magdeleine, had lost inhabitants. Varennes and Verchères nearby, which grew as much as Boucherville declined, had been less densely settled in 1739, and continued growth gave them population densities roughly equivalent to that of Boucherville in 1760. It is clear, however, that there was a general movement of young families away from the south shore of the St. Lawrence to the Richelieu, and that this exodus was greatest from the most densely settled seigneuries. The rapid growth of Ile Jésus compared with the virtually static population on the Ile de Montréal is also striking and is, no doubt, explained by the fact that in 1739 river-front property on the latter was settled whereas much of this land on the Ile Jésus was

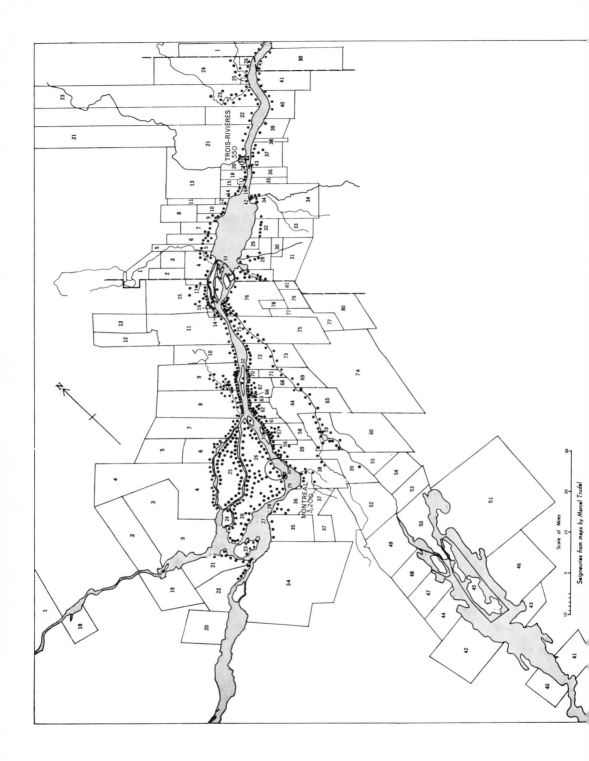

TROIS-RIVIÈRES
550

MONTREAL
5,200

Scale of Miles

Seigneuries from maps by Marcel Trudel

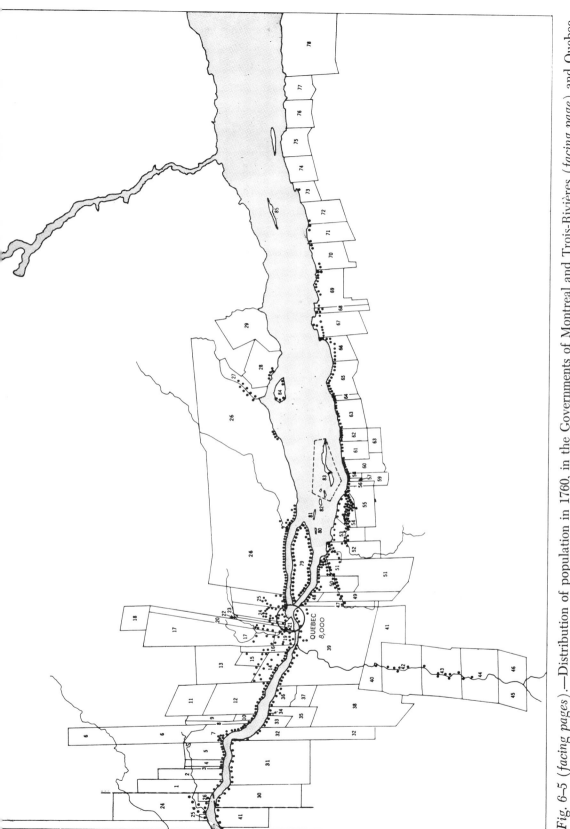

Fig. 6–5 (facing pages).—Distribution of population in 1760, in the Governments of Montreal and Trois-Rivières (*facing page*) and Quebec. Each dot represents 50 people; see appendix or back endpaper for key to numbered seigneuries.

not. Young families from the Ile de Montréal had moved across the channel to Ile Jésus, or a little farther to an expanding fringe of settlement on the mainland to the north.

If the maps are examined closely, a number of examples can be found of population densities changing across seigneurial boundaries. Boucherville grew more rapidly than the seigneuries on either side, although it was not better situated in relation to the legal market in Montreal and the illegal one in Albany and New York than its immediate neighbors. The high population in Boucherville reflects the interest of a seigneur who brought settlers there in the first place,* and the fact that, once in the seigneurie, these settlers and their children stayed because they were advantageously located. When the population rose to the point where farms were being divided into marginal units, the emigration began which is apparent from a comparison of Figures 6–4 and 6–5. (See Chap. 7 for a more detailed discussion.) Evidently the seigneurs were also responsible for the early settlement of Cap de la Madeleine (No. 21, Government of Trois-Rivières) and Champlain. By 1667 the river front in these seigneuries just east of Trois-Rivières had been settled, but the population did not increase in the next hundred years. It remained static because these seigneuries were isolated from the Montreal and Quebec markets, and because the river front was sandy and infertile. The fact that the population did not grow is not surprising, but the early settlement is difficult to explain if the seigneurs were not responsible. The Jesuits and the seigneur of Champlain had evidently brought settlers to the area in the 1660's but none thereafter, and because the area was not particularly attractive, the population did not grow.

A number of other patches on the distribution maps of 1667 and 1692 (Figs. 6–1 and 6–2) may reflect a seigneur's colonizing efforts. Then most seigneurs still controlled an entire seigneurie, and in this period they were under some pressure to develop their land. Moreover in 1692 the last round of the bitter commercial war between the French and the Iroquois had made a series of armed agricultural camps of much of the western half of the colony. The thought that if they strayed too far they might present a scalp to a wandering Iroquois may have led habitants to settle temporarily under a seigneur's fairly close direction. The fifty

---

* Pierre Boucher, the first seigneur of Boucherville, was probably the most energetic colonizer in all the ranks of Canadian seigneurs, but even his efforts, which included a trip to France, probably produced no more than fifty settlers for his seigneurie.

settlers in Grondines and the hundred in Deschambault in 1692 had perhaps been placed there by the seigneurs, or they may have come on their own, looked over the land, and requested concessions. There are almost no records on this phase of early settlement, and the maps do not clarify the matter.

Although seigneurs may have directed initial settlement in a few seigneuries, the maps do not suggest that they played a significant role thereafter. The fact that between 1712 and 1739 the population in Saint-Sulpice grew more rapidly than in bordering seigneuries, that the population density along the St. Lawrence shore in La Durantaye and L'Assomption apparently rose from 1739 to 1760 while remaining static in neighboring seigneuries, or that the population expansion up the Rivière du Sud in the same period by-passed Bellechasse (No. 53, Government of Quebec), might reflect the influence, one way or the other, of the seigneurs. There are other examples, although they are not easily found, but the dominant impression from the maps is that settlement spread along the waterways of the colony with little regard for seigneurial boundaries.

OFFICIAL POLICY TOWARDS THE SEIGNEUR AS A COLONIZER

Although the maps suggest that most Canadian seigneurs did not take an active part in settling their seigneuries, there is no doubt that the Company of New France and, later, the king intended that they should. The Company, required to bring 4,000 colonists during the first fifteen years after 1627 and three hundred more each year thereafter (see Chap. 3), included in almost all of its seigneurial title deeds the clause that settlers brought by the seigneur would be credited towards this charter obligation. The seigneur was not required to settle his land, but his seigneurie had been granted to him in the expectation that he would bring some settlers to Canada.

This system was tightened up shortly after the introduction of royal government. In 1672 the seigneurs were ordered to clear their land within a year or forfeit half of it,[2] and the ordinance of 1679 which stipulated that a quarter of the uncleared land would be withdrawn in a year and a twentieth every year thereafter[3] was a milder version of the same threat. These ordinances required the seigneur to clear land, although not necessarily to settle it.[4] However, in a colony where there was never enough manpower to form the woodcutting brigades needed to clear the seigneuries, and where, if there had been, the clearing would have cost the seigneur far more than he could dream of realizing from his seigneurie, the two were indistinguishable. After 1672 a seigneurie could be confiscated if its land were not developed, and land was developed in Canada only by established settlers.

Until 1711 the seigneur held his land in *dominium plenum,* and could dispose of it as he saw fit. That is, he could divide his land into many small rotures and rent or sell each, or into a number of arrière-fiefs, the seigneurs of which would have the responsibility for settlement. Almost all the land conceded by the seigneur was in rotures given in return for the small annual payments which have already been mentioned, but until 1711 there was no reason why a seigneur had to grant land this way. In that year the king issued an edict from Marly which ordered the Canadian seigneur to grant a roture without initial charge to anyone who asked for one.[5] If the seigneur refused a request, the intendant could make the grant and collect the annual charges in the king's name. The seigneur, forced to subgrant land to whoever asked for it, had become legally little more than the king's land agent.

This Edict of Marly was a decisive break with French customary law, and an attempt to adapt to New World conditions. As settlers were the chronic shortage in Canada, it seemed logical to make land as accessible as possible in the hope of attracting them. Moreover, the king had been convinced since the 1660's that the seigneurs would do nothing to promote settlement, a conclusion which seemed obvious enough from the results of the proprietary period,[6] and in 1711 evidently decided that by withholding land for sale the seigneurs were an actual stumbling block to settlement. However, as was often the case, the king and his advisors did not altogether understand the Canadian situation. Canada in 1711 was a sparsely settled colony of only 20,000 inhabitants; any prospective censitaire could always have obtained an undeveloped roture free, and if he paid for it, he was a dullard indeed. A cleared roture within a few miles of Quebec or Montreal always had to be bought, not from the seigneur, but from the censitaire who was already farming the land. A partly cleared roture on which there were several farm buildings could have brought 2,000 livres or more, but an undeveloped roture of the same size, however favorably located, sold at from ten to one hundred livres.[7] At such prices any seigneur who had attempted to speculate in uncleared land would simply have diverted settlers elsewhere.

Cleared land was a different matter. When a man abandoned a roture after clearing a few arpents, the seigneur could reunite it temporarily to his domain and, because the roture had some value, insist upon a cash payment when he reconceded it. Several seigneurs bought up partially cleared rotures and sold them again at a slight profit. Probably a few seigneurs near Quebec had withheld some cleared land, claiming that it had already been conceded once or that it was part of their domain, and the censitaires complained to the officials, who relayed their complaints to France.[8] The king, who was quite prepared to blame the seigneurs for lagging settlement, reacted with the Edict of Marly mentioned above. However, the edict changed very little; henceforth the seigneurs were required to subgrant in the way that most of them had always been distributing their land.

Nevertheless, this Edict of Marly did make a common Canadian practice the law of the land, and in later years intendants saw to its enforcement. The Intendant Bégon reported in 1719 that he was persuaded that all seigneurs were making the concessions requested of them because he had received no complaints on the matter[9] (a reasonable conclusion given the habitants' proclivity for disputation), but a year later there was one such case when the Sisters of the Hôtel-Dieu in Quebec refused a concession in Saint-Ignace.[10] The intendant ordered them to make the grant, and when they refused he made it himself in the king's name. A decade later the governor and intendant informed the minister that a number of seigneurs had set aside large domains with the intention of selling parts of them, and that some coseigneurs considered themselves censitaires and, therefore, exempt from the obligation to subgrant.[11] However, it was usually an easy matter to determine who was a seigneur and who was not, and not very many censitaires can have been deceived into paying for land they could have had for nothing. Officials in Canada argued that no action should be taken in the few cases in which censitaires had paid unnecessarily for land, because the censitaires had every reason to know better.[12] They did suggest that certain parts of the Edict of Marly might be reissued, and their suggestion was implemented in a royal decree of 1732 which forbade the sale of uncleared land, and ordered the seigneurs to clear their land and to establish settlers.[13]

However, responsibility for settlement did not rest solely with the seigneur, for both the Company and the king granted rotures and, as is pointed out in the next section of this chapter, sent far more settlers to Canada than all the seigneurs put together. Talon in the 1660's (see Chap. 9) and both Frontenac and Champigny some years later granted rotures in the king's name.[14] During the years of the royal ban on seigneurial concessions, the king intended to grant land in Canada *en roture* only, but as those who worked rotures could get them in established seigneuries, the king's officials received few if any requests for rotures during this period. There was one curious compromise. The king permitted an augmentation to the seigneurie of Sainte-Marie on condition that the seigneur pay a cens of twenty livres for each square league. The seigneur could subgrant land at the rate of one sol and one capon for each arpent of frontage.[15] Because of the annual cens, the augmentation was a roture which, in this case, was held from the king. Yet land could be granted in it as if it were a seigneurie. This was an extraordinary combination which broke several cardinal tenets of the coutume, and may have been unheard of anywhere in France. It marked the furthest that the king and his ministers ever went in reducing the authority of the Canadian seigneur without dispensing with him altogether. To take the final step, the king would have had to shoulder the entire responsibility for settlement. A move in this direction was proposed in 1730 by the Intendant Hocquart, who envisaged the establishment of a village under royal control on Lake Champlain,[16] but except for the period of royal interest in the 1660's and early 1670's, Canada did not seem to the king and his ministers in France to warrant this degree of involvement.

THE POOL OF AVAILABLE SETTLERS

The Canadian seigneur who was anxious to establish settlers in his seigneurie could bring colonists from France, or could attempt to attract those who were already in the colony. In the mid-1630's, shortly after the Company of New France began to grant large seigneuries, it appeared that the seigneurs might indeed recruit colonists in France. Robert Giffard, who had been granted Beauport in 1634, sent thirty or forty colonists to his seigneurie that year, and another contingent in 1635.[17] A small group of immigrants that arrived in 1636 had been recruited in part by the eight men who had acquired Beaupré,[18] and both the Sulpicians and the Jesuits sent a few settlers. However, these initial successes were not followed up. There were between 200 and 300 people in Canada in

1640, and barely 2,500 in 1663. Some had been sent by the queen or the Company, some had been born in the colony, and a handful had been brought by the seigneurs. Although not a total failure, the attempt to make the seigneur the key to colonization was hardly a resounding success, and the banks of the St. Lawrence were almost as empty at the end of the proprietary period as they had been in 1627.

This failure coupled with a young king's vision of a French empire in the New World led to the withdrawal of the Company charter and to a flurry of royal interest. Louis XIV, as he pointedly reminded Talon, considered each of his Canadian subjects as one of his children and urged the intendant to watch over them like "un bon père de famille," [19] the ideal relationship in French customary law between seigneurs and their vassals. Lending substance to these words were fairly frequent dips into the royal treasury, and several hundred settlers almost every year for a decade. While royal enthusiasm lasted, some three thousand new settlers were established in Canada, and as a result the population increased four times in twenty years.

In taking over the task of recruiting and transporting settlers to Canada, the king was nonetheless adamant that seigneurs settle their own holdings. There is, however, no indication that he expected them to bring settlers from France, or that the seigneurs considered themselves obligated to do so. The Company had cast the seigneurs in an important role in the hope that they would bring settlers, but the king steadily restricted their power. His was not the sort of treatment designed to stimulate the seigneurs to undertake the trouble and expense of colonization, and during the century of royal government very few of them did. M. de la Bouteillerie recruited a few settlers for his seigneurie of Rivière Ouelle; François Berthelot, who never came to Canada, sent supplies and probably some settlers for his seigneurie of the Ile d'Orléans; and there may have been a few others. If a seigneur had brought some settlers himself, the intendant would have responded warmly and probably would have written to France for a small *gratification;* but even when threatening a seigneur with the loss of his seigneurie, the intendant never insisted that he bring settlers from France if he could not find them in the colony. The king, in ordering seigneurs to settle their seigneuries or to give them up, hoped to ensure that undeveloped land would be returned to the royal domain, rather than to force seigneurs to recruit settlers in France.

Whatever the king's treatment of the Canadian seigneurs, it is unlikely that they would have brought many settlers to a colony which had very little drawing power. A few merchants were interested in the fur trade; and the religious orders, in savage souls to win, but Canada, for most who had heard of it, was indeed many *arpents de neige* where those fortunate enough to survive the rigors of winter faced the savages in summer. A difficult voyage to this destination was not an appealing prospect. There were rich men in Boston and Virginia, and the immigrant to either could dream that some day he would fare as well, but for anyone with visions of wealth, Canada was not the place. Money was made in the fur trade, most of it by merchants who stayed in France, while the grain trade with the West Indies produced small profits but no prospect of abundance.[20] Few of the upper middle class who came to Canada maintained their former level of income. The Canadian equivalent of the French peasant probably enjoyed a higher standard of living and certainly a much less fettered life than his French counterpart, but few French peasants had the means or the inclination to move to a distant land. Then as now, Frenchmen tended to stay in France, and a more attractive appeal than Canada's was needed to dislodge very many.

The seigneur who considered bringing settlers to the colony had to find recruits in France, and pay for their passage and support during the first weeks or years in the colony, a total cost in the order of one hundred livres for each settler he brought.[21] Very few seigneurs had that sort of money to spare, and if they did there was no reason to spend it transporting settlers to the New World when the revenue from them was as low as shown in the last chapter. This was the reason why seigneurs did not bring settlers and why, after 1663, no one really expected them to do so.

With the few exceptions mentioned above, the seigneur's role in settling his seigneurie was restricted to attracting settlers who were already in the colony. Of these there were two sources: newly arrived immigrants from France, and habitants or their offspring in other Canadian seigneuries. Approximately 10,000 immigrants came to Canada during the French regime.[22] Of this number, almost 4,000 were *engagés* who, much like the indentured servants in Virginia, were committed to several years of service for the seigneurs or censitaires who had engaged them. Some 3,500 were soldiers who had been released from service and induced to settle on seigneuries which had usually been acquired by their officers. Towards the end of the French regime, a thousand prisoners—salt-smugglers for the most part—were sent to Canada, and years before as many women had been sent to be brides. Roughly five hundred Frenchmen immigrated to Canada on their own.

Among these immigrants the only immediate prospects for rotures were some of those who had come on their own and the soldiers, after their release from formal military service—perhaps a settler a year for each five or ten seigneuries. As this trickle of immigration never produced a pool of potential settlers on which a seigneur could draw, his principal source of settlers was second or third generation Canadians who were moving off one or other of the older seigneuries. A seigneurie like the Ile d'Orléans, almost all of which had been conceded in rotures well before the eighteenth century, produced a steady outflow of grown sons and daughters; and an active seigneur might hope to divert some of this flow or, if he held good land along the river, expect requests for it sooner or later.

THE INDUCEMENTS WITH WHICH A SEIGNEUR COULD ATTRACT SETTLERS

Besides a persuasive tongue or particularly good land in his seigneurie, the seigneur had recourse to only two inducements to lure a prospective censitaire from another seigneurie to his own: he could reduce the annual dues below the common rate, or provide superior milling facilities. For example, the Jesuits, who in their seigneurie of Notre Dame des Anges, near Quebec, had a standard rente of one sol and one capon for each arpent of frontage, made only four concessions at this rate in La Prairie de la Magdeleine, their seigneurie at the other end of the colony, before reducing the rente to six deniers or one-half sol and one capon for each arpent of frontage. Within four years of this reduction, which can be explained only if it was needed to attract settlers, the Jesuits had conceded forty rotures in La Prairie de la Magdeleine.[23] When settlement was well established a few years later, the rente was again raised to the level in Notre Dame des Anges.[24] Years later Governor Beauharnois offered to exempt any prospective censitaire from all rentes and corvées in his large, new seigneurie if the censitaire lived on and improved his roture. Rentes and corvées would become due if the roture were abandoned.[25] These liberal terms apparently did not produce any settlers, but they were certainly designed to do so.

Because no one interested in farming would consider settling far from a gristmill, a seigneur had to have a mill, promise to build one soon, or be situated near a mill on another seigneurie if he were to have any hope of attracting settlers. Cases where a seigneur reneged on a promise to build a mill, or neglected an existing one so that it ground poor flour or was closed down, were common disputes between a seigneur and his censitaires, particularly after the beginning of the eighteenth century when wheat began to find a fairly regular market in the West Indies. The seigneur of Dautré, who was involved in 1720 in a suit over the ownership of the land on which he had built his mill, pointed out in his defense that there were no settlers in the seigneurie when he acquired it, that the first building he had put up was the mill because it was essential to attract settlers, and that, because of the mill, he had acquired a good number.[26] A decade later a prospective seigneur assured the minister in France that although there were empty seigneuries everywhere in the colony, he was told that it was because there were no mills in these seigneuries. He was willing to undertake all the expenses of a mill although he knew it would cost him more than he could expect from the seigneurie during his lifetime. As there were many poor in Trois-Rivières, the development of a seigneurie was, he concluded, a needed charity.[27] By building a good mill a seigneur could expect to attract some settlers, especially if he added a reduction in the rente as well. The latter inducement without a mill was not likely to have much effect.

If the seigneur reduced the dues he was undermining his future income, and if he built a mill he was involved in a heavy initial outlay and probably an operating deficit for years. Only a few seigneurs ever reduced their annual dues to attract settlers. On the other hand, while there were never nearly as many mills as seigneuries, a surprising number of mills were built. There were forty-one in 1685, seventy-six in 1719, and one hundred and eighteen in 1734, or almost half as many mills as there were seigneuries intended for agricultural development.[28] Some of these mills were built by censitaires after the seigneur had reneged on his responsibility. Others were built in the wake of periods of extremely high flour prices by seigneurs who were undoubtedly gambling on another price spiral. (See Tables 5–2 and 5–3, together with text discussion.) Still others, particularly the earlier ones, were built by the seigneurs in an effort to attract settlers and to fulfill their seigneurial obligations.

Beyond building a mill or lowering the rentes there was not a great deal that a seigneur could do to speed the settlement of his seigneurie. During the decade after 1663, when shiploads of immigrants arrived almost every year, a few energetic and persuasive seigneurs like Pierre Boucher were able to attract a number of settlers quickly,[29] but when the stream of immigrants dried, there was no one to attract except the habitant who lived on another man's seigneurie, and little enough with which to persuade him. Most of the seigneurs who lost their land along the upper Richelieu in 1741 claimed to have made determined efforts to attract settlers.[30] Whether they did or not, the problems they faced are clear enough. The holder of a seigneurie on Lake Champlain would have had to build a mill and he might have had to reduce his *cens et rentes* to induce settlers to move into a new area. Even so he could not have expected more than two or three families a year; there was still not enough population pressure on land along the St. Lawrence to push settlers up the Richelieu any faster. To be sure, in 1765 there were some eight hundred people in seven seigneuries which had been granted in the 1730's along the Chaudière, although this expansion, which has been contrasted in the literature with the failure along the Richelieu, was at an average rate of not more than a family per seigneurie per year.

In summary, settlers were scarce in Canada, seigneurs could do little to attract them, and unless they were concerned about the plight of the poor (like the seigneur in Trois-Rivières mentioned above), there was little reason to try. With but a handful of settlers a seigneurie was an economic liability, not an asset. Some seigneuries were too small, even if entirely settled, to produce a much larger revenue from the censitaires than the average habitant earned from his farm, and many others which were originally much larger were divided among a number of coseigneurs. The reasons why the seigneurs were not more dynamic colonizers are clear.

THE PRINCIPAL FACTORS INFLUENCING THE DISTRIBUTION OF POPULATION

The patterns of population distribution shown on the maps in this chapter cannot, therefore, be explained by the activity of the seigneurs. To understand these patterns, the physical and legal limits to settlement in the valley which are discussed in Chapter 2 must be kept in mind. Legal agricultural settlement ended just north and west of the Ile de Montréal, at the western boundary of contiguous seigneurial concessions.

At the other end of the colony, continuous settlement along the north shore ended where the hills of the Pre-Cambrian Shield and the St. Lawrence intersect thirty miles below Quebec, and faded out along the south shore as the coast become steeper and the summers cooler and shorter around the Gaspé arc. North of the river, the Shield was a few hundred yards to a few miles away, while on the south shore bogs and extensive patches of glacial sands and gravels often limited settlement to a narrow band along the river. The river banks along either shore for two hundred miles and more were usually cultivable; the river itself was the transportation artery which tied men to other settlements and to the world of commerce. To live some distance from the river was to be shut off from these connections when no one had any intention of living a self-sufficient existence. It remains only to explain why people settled where they did along this line of contact between the farm and the outside world.

The maps leave no doubt that Montreal and Quebec were foci on this line. Settlement was blocked in Beaupré and above Montreal, but elsewhere the expansion outward from the towns can be followed step by step on successive distribution maps. The major area of settlement away from any waterway was immediately north and west of Quebec, while the other important development of second and third ranges was on the Ile de Montréal, and along the south shore opposite. The village of Trois-Rivières, which was much smaller than either Quebec or Montreal during most of the French regime, was not a major attraction, and the pace of settlement in the middle of the line did not increase until a through road was completed between Montreal and Quebec in the 1730's. Thereafter the habitant in the middle was less isolated from the two principal towns, but was still distant enough so that expansion was more rapid elsewhere.

Both Montreal and Quebec held local markets several days a week to which the habitants brought agricultural produce—as they still do today in Quebec City.[31] Both towns were markets for firewood and timber; they were bases for merchants and peddlers who toured the countryside in the fall to buy up the habitants' surplus wheat and peas; and they furnished such manufactures as iron tools, nails, pots, power and shot, guns, and cloth which were almost always part of the habitant's life. Although some habitants may have had no need to visit a town for years on end, town and country were not independent. Each supplied goods and services to the other, and this interdependence is shown quite clearly on the maps of population distribution.

It is equally apparent that there were centrifugal forces at work in the colony. A very few seigneurs had established censitaires in isolated seigneuries, and many more censitaires undoubtedly moved outward to avoid the restricting influence of royal officials, churchmen, or, in some cases, seigneurs. A move away from the older areas of settlement meant more independence, and more independence made it easier to partici-pate in the fur trade. Governor Denonville complained in 1685 that too many habitants were settling in isolated areas along the river, and suggested that "The principal cause . . . of this separation of dwellings is the desire of each one [of the habitants] to be ahead of the others in order to obtain more furs, and this is so true that if we are not careful, I am sure they will extend their dwellings as far as the Ottawa tribes. . . ."[32] Although Denonville may have exaggerated, it is clear that the fur trade and agglomerated settlement often did not go well to-gether (see Chap. 9), that the trade shifted settlement towards the Montreal end of the colony much more rapidly than would otherwise have been the case, and that it created some of the patches of settlement ahead of the regular expansion outward from the towns.

Shortage of land near the towns was a much more inexorable centrifu-gal force than the fur trade, especially as the relative importance of the trade declined in the eighteenth century. Because of the riparian nature of settlement in the colony, land in a seigneurie measuring one league along the river by five in depth—that is some twenty-five square miles— was often effectively barred to additional settlers when fifteen or twenty families controlled the range along the river (as could easily happen, particularly in the early years when one habitant often owned several rotures). Except near Quebec and Montreal habitants would not take rotures in second ranges if there was unconceded river frontage not too far away, preferring, for example, to be sixty miles from Quebec and on the river, rather than forty or fifty miles from the town and two or three miles from navigable water. Eventually the original holdings were divided among offspring and the population density in the first range doubled or tripled, but this occurred after a generation or more. Meanwhile the settlement wave, such as it was in Canada, had moved on.

It was primarily this interaction between the centripetal attraction of the towns and the centrifugal pull of the fur trade and of new agricultural land that was moving people about in the colony. For the most part the seigneurs' involvement in the settlement process was only to grant land to anyone who requested it. Although a few seigneurs brought settlers to their seigneuries, it is difficult to see how as a group the seigneurs influenced the pattern of population distribution in Canada in any significant way, and the conclusion is unavoidable that if there had been no Canadian seigneurs, that is, if all the land in Canada had been held *en roture* from the king, the settlement pattern would not have been different.

The assumption that there was a cause-and-effect relationship between the seigneurial system and colonization is certainly misleading. All land was to have a seigneur; no one disputed this basic tenet. Landholding was largely regulated by the Coutume de Paris, which had evolved within the seigneurial system and gave legal expression to many of its basic attitudes. In this sense, however, there was a parallel cause-and-effect relationship between English common law and settlement in Upper Canada. The seigneur was the agent by which the seigneurial system might have stimulated and directed settlement, but because settlement usually involved him in more expense than revenue, his role was notably passive.

7 : The Roture

BECAUSE many aspects of the seigneurial geography of early Canada reflected less the influence of the seigneurs and seigneuries, a subject which has been discussed in Chapters 3 to 6, than that of the censitaires and their rotures, it is now necessary to narrow the focus of this study and examine some of the patterns which developed within seigneuries. The point of departure for this large-scale geography of the seigneurial system is the roture, the concession of land which a censitaire received from his seigneur. Most of the cleared land in the colony was on rotures, most of the colony's agricultural produce came from them, and most of the people in the colony lived on them. The size and shape of rotures, the location of them within a seigneurie, and the number held by individual censitaires—considerations of much relevance to an understanding of the economic as well as of the seigneurial geography of the colony—are discussed in this chapter.

THE SIZE OF ROTURES

The many thousands of rotures conceded in Canada were remarkably uniform in size. Although there were areal extremes ranging from a fraction of a square arpent in one of the villages to several square leagues,[1] at least 95 per cent of all rotures were between forty and two hundred square arpents in size, and probably 80 per cent of these contained a hundred and twenty square arpents or less. Concessions smaller than two by twenty arpents were usually bits and pieces fitted into interstices between older rotures or into the corners of the seigneu-

117

rie: censitaires seldom placed much value on a roture of fewer than forty square arpents. A concession of more than two hundred square arpents may have been made to one of the seigneur's offspring, or to a censitaire of more than average means, but there were no concessions of this size in many seigneuries and only a few in most of the others.

There is no evidence that the size of rotures varied consistently from one part of the colony to another or even within individual seigneuries, so that a censitaire could neither expect more or less land if he settled on a Church seigneurie, nor choose among lay seigneuries on this basis.[2] There were slight variations in different periods. During the proprietary years concessions tended to be a little larger; some seigneurs were not averse to concessions of six, eight, or ten arpents in frontage by several leagues in depth (e.g., 1.5 in Beaupré and 4 in Notre Dame des Anges, in a few rotures), although even in this period most rotures contained well under two hundred square arpents. Later, Talon decided that a concession of forty square arpents was enough land for each censitaire,[3] and intended his villages of 1,600 square arpents to be divided forty ways. Some of the seigneurs to whom Talon had granted land began making concessions of a similar size.[4] After Talon's departure, newly granted rotures tended to be a little larger again, but generally the size of concessions *en roture* varied remarkably little. There was no protracted trend towards larger or smaller concessions; if a prospective censitaire applied for a roture in any seigneurie at any time during the French regime, he usually obtained approximately eighty square arpents of land.

Despite the small range in the size of rotures, it is probably incorrect to assume either that seigneurs had agreed on an optimum operational size for their rotures, or that official policy dictated the limits. Louis XIV had been convinced in 1663 that rotures in Canada were so large that censitaires could neither protect themselves from the Iroquois nor clear very much of their land,[5] and his insistence on this point was undoubtedly reflected in Talon's smaller rotures. However, within a few years the king's attention was directed to the seigneuries, and very little was said about the size of rotures in the voluminous correspondence crossing the Atlantic during the rest of the French regime. Probably their minimum size was determined by a tacit consensus among seigneurs and censitaires about the area needed to make a profitable farm; the maximum, by what censitaires were willing to pay in dues, or by what the seigneurs thought they could collect. The amount of cleared land on rotures of forty or four hundred arpents might have been the same for many years, although the annual dues for the latter size could have been ten times as great. Common sense suggested the smaller size to the censitaires. And the seigneur hesitated to concede unusually large rotures, knowing that his censitaires often abandoned their concessions after three or four years if they could not meet the payments, that if censitaires stayed on large rotures less land in the seigneurie would be cleared than if the rotures were smaller and that less grain would be ground at the banal gristmill.

THE SHAPE OF ROTURES

Except where rotures abutted on a shoreline they were bounded by straight lines, and these lines almost invariably formed approximate rectangles. Probably the oldest extant roture contract was the concession in 1637 by Robert Giffard, seigneur of Beauport, of three hundred square arpents to Noel Langlois. This roture, which was to front on the St. Lawrence and extend into the interior between two parallel lines, was roughly rectangular.[6] In the next decade, all concessions for which record has been preserved were for parcels of land with the river-front dimension a small fraction of the depth. In most cases the ratio was approximately 1:10, although ratios of nearly 1:100 were known.

As fields were extremely irregular in shape throughout much of France, the straight line boundary and characteristic proportion of field breadth to length of 1:10 were not automatically introduced to Canada as part of the settlers' French heritage. To be sure, the open field of the early Middle Ages was divided into long, thin strips, and later, during the period of agricultural prosperity and expansion throughout the last half of the twelfth and thirteenth centuries, street or dike villages (*Waldhu-fendörfer, terroir en arête de poisson*) with elongated farms extending at right angles from them, appeared in the Netherlands, in Germany, and in northwestern France. In North America sections of the New England proprietary townships were subdivided in long, thin strips, and the strip farm appeared in areas of French settlement in Illinois, Wisconsin, and Louisiana. Whether the Canadian strip farm was copied from those in Europe or in New England (the latter connection is extremely unlikely) or developed independently in a Canadian context is unknown. Certainly there is a connection between the strip farm and an organized approach to agricultural settlement, whether organization was provided by the lord or overseer of a medieval manor, by the director of a colonization scheme in East Germany in the thirteenth century, by the proprietors of a New England township, or by seigneurs and royal officials in Canada. In each case, individuals were not completely free to select and to demarcate their own agricultural land; when they were, a hodge-podge of field shapes such as that in colonial Virginia was the result.

Whatever the importance of these considerations, the elongated rectangle with its long axis at right angles to the river and with a width-to-length ratio of approximately 1:10 offered many advantages which help to explain why the rectangular strip appeared so quickly and was modified so little in Canada. These are summarized in the following list.

1. A strip pattern gave frontage on a major transportation artery, whether river or road, to a maximum number of rotures. A censitaire living along the St. Lawrence was on the colony's main street, and was connected to the town markets or to the furs of the interior. When access to the river was complicated by particularly steep banks or by marshes along the shore, settlement lagged until a road was built away from the river, and then the line of attachment became the road. When all the river front had been conceded, rotures lined the roads for the same reason as they had lined the river front. Sometimes the road marked the boundary between ranges, sometimes it cut through the middle of a range (see Fig. 7–4), but in either case the ribbon-like rotures gave all censitaires direct access to it.

2. The rectangle with a low ratio of width to length permitted families to live on their own farms but close to their neighbors. If the rectangle were two arpents in width, a censitaire could have neighbors on either side almost within a hundred yards, and he could enjoy the convenience and comradeship of close neighbors, without a daily trek to his land.

3. The rectangular shape permitted rapid and cheap surveying. A seigneur could divide his seigneurie into rotures in an afternoon by walking along the shore and driving a stake every so many paces. A chain established the shore dimension precisely. If a censitaire had acquired a roture adjacent to a previously surveyed concession, and if the back line for the range had been determined, he needed to survey only one straight line to know exactly what land he held. No system could have been easier to employ.

4. The strip pattern, as applied to riverside locations, permitted maximum access to the river for fishing. Throughout the French regime

fish taken from the St. Lawrence were an important source of food, and in the years of initial settlement or of poor harvests, life would have been even leaner without them. The narrowness of the rotures placed this food source at as many doorsteps as possible.

5. Because the strips cut across the grain of the land, they often included a variety of soil types and vegetation associations. Some concessions began in the natural grassland along the shore of the river, ended a mile or more away and several hundred feet higher in the rocks of the Shield, and in between crossed several slopes and terraces with different soils and plant associations. Not many rotures included such a range, but where they did the variety may have commended the strip to its holders; on the other hand, if they wanted a little more of the pasture along the shore and less of the rocks behind, it may have been annoying.

Against these advantages was the fact that a ribbon of land a hundred yards wide and a mile deep was often an awkward unit to farm. The cows might have been pastured in a field a mile or more from the house and the pigs let loose in a woodlot even farther away. A milking might have involved a two-mile walk, an attempt to round up the pigs, even more. Yet most farmers were closer to their livestock than if they walked to their farm every day from a compact agricultural village, and with numerous progeny they should not have lacked for cow- or swineherds. Although service roads on strip farms were longer and took up a larger percentage of the farm area than if the roture had been more nearly square, land was seldom scarce during the French regime. If the standard roture had been square, the river front would have been quickly conceded, settlement would have been forced away from the river, and an elaborate network of roads would have been required. Censitaires would have lived in compact agricultural villages or in isolated farmsteads rather than in the straggling linear villages which became common. Canada would have been a different colony, and probably one that was less well adapted to the valley. It is arguable that strip farms in contemporary Quebec are inefficient anachronisms, but in early Canada probably no other shape would have provided so much net advantage.

THE DISTRIBUTION OF ROTURES WITHIN A SEIGNEURIE

In theory rotures were conceded along the river until all the shoreline in a seigneurie had been taken, and then behind these concessions in a series of ranges (*rangs*). Had this system been followed precisely,

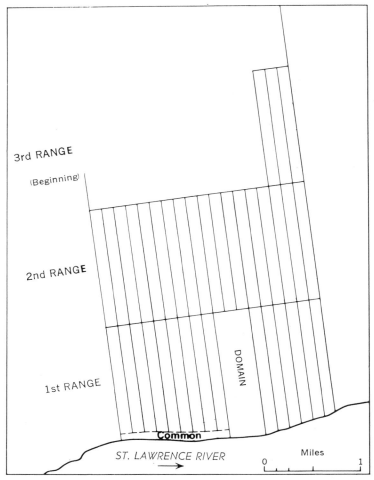

Fig. 7–1.—Rotures in a hypothetical seigneurie.

cadastral patterns within Canadian seigneuries would have looked like those shown in Figure 7–1. In fact few were nearly this regular, and some of the variations warrant brief mention.

Usually rotures were conceded in contiguous strips away from the domain or the seigneurial boundary until the first range was filled. Then concessions were made in a second range. Temporary gaps within a range developed when censitaires avoided marshy land which made access to the river difficult, or sought out strips of natural grassland along the shore. If isolated patches of rotures were settled before the intervening land, each patch may have developed some awareness of itself as a distinct community. (See Chap. 9 for discussion of community organization within seigneuries.)

In some seigneuries the St. Lawrence shore remained unconceded while rotures extended several miles inland along navigable tributaries (see Fig. 7–2). Such interruptions in the usual pattern were common around Lake Saint-Pierre where a low, marshy shoreline made direct access to the river difficult. The censitaires' determination to settle on a transportation route had not changed, but because of the marshy shoreline along the St. Lawrence access to the main river was easier by way of the tributary. If a river crossed a seigneurie some distance from the St. Lawrence, rotures often jumped back to the interior river after a single range had been conceded along the St. Lawrence. There were at least two almost parallel but unconnected lines of rotures, one along the St. Lawrence, the other along one of several small tributaries in all the seigneuries along the south shore below Quebec between Lauzon and Rivière du Sud. At the other end of the colony rotures were conceded along the Assomption River and its tributaries after a first range had been filled along the St. Lawrence (see Fig. 7–3). The two rivers were distinct lines of attachment with a band of unconceded land between. Censitaires in such seigneuries would rather settle some distance from the St. Lawrence along a tributary which gave easy access to the main river through another seigneurie, than closer to the St. Lawrence in a second or third range.

Even when ranges were conceded contiguously, rotures within them were not always the same length, or oriented along the same *rhumb de vent*. Figure 7–4 shows the ranges in the Jesuits' seigneurie of Sillery, where they were probably as regular as anywhere in the colony. Note, however, the adjustments around an irregularly shaped domain, around Chemin Saint-Augustin which focused rotures in the eastern part of the second and third ranges, and along the Saint-Charles River in the northeast, as well as the several small rotures inside the fourth range. Each of these variations had a marked effect on settlement patterns within the seigneurie.

Second ranges began to be conceded near Quebec in the 1660's and 1670's, but elsewhere they seldom appeared before the beginning of the eighteenth century. By the end of the French regime there were second ranges in almost all riparian seigneuries except those nearly midway

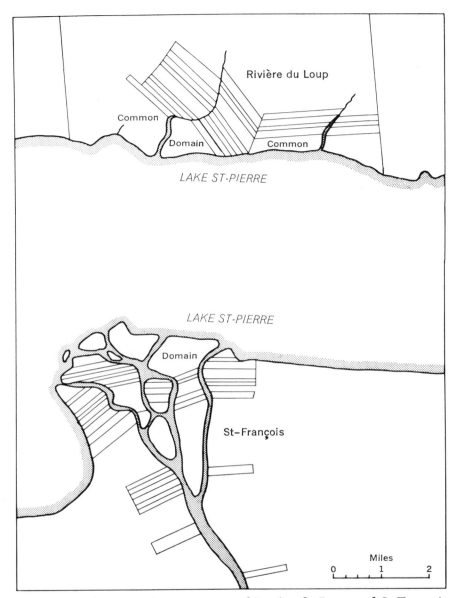

Fig. 7–2.—Rotures in the seigneuries of Rivière du Loup and St-François in 1709.

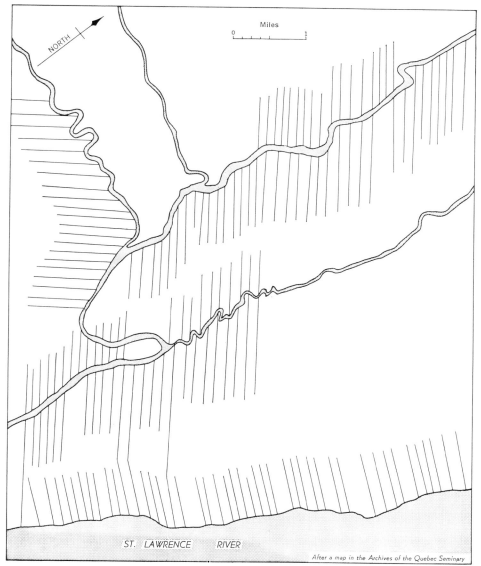

Fig. 7–3.—Rotures in St-Sulpice near the end of the French regime.

between Montreal and Quebec or well below Quebec on the south shore, although only near Montreal and Quebec were second ranges well settled in 1760.

It may be questioned whether any of the variations from the hypothetical model in Figure 7–1 were related to soil quality. Rotures were not

Fig. 7–4.—Rotures in Sillery, 1754. After map in National Archives, Canada.

conceded in the acidic podzols which had developed on the thin layer of rocky till covering the slopes of the Shield (although part of a roture might extend into these soils), but the question is really whether on the off-the-Shield portions of individual seigneuries soil conditions affected the distribution of rotures.

A map of cadastral boundaries during the French regime and a soil map are required to answer this question, and the two are available for the seigneuries of Ile Jésus and Saint-Sulpice. Soils on the island are generally fair to good, but there are two extremely poor soils—the Sainte-Philomène sandy loam and the Farmington clay loam—in a patch of several square miles along the north shore near the island's eastern end. Today the area of the Sainte-Philomène sandy loam is used primarily for its underlying gravel; the Farmington clay loam, a shallow soil which dries out rapidly, is usually left in bush. A cadastral map of the island prepared in 1749 by the Séminaire de Québec [7] shows rotures extending across the Farmington and Sainte-Philomène series without a break, although several rotures contained almost no land fit for cultivation. In Saint-Sulpice there is a broad band along the St. Lawrence of aeolian sands, peat bogs, and partially decomposed mucks. Of the three, only the aeolian sands can be cultivated, but they are not particularly fertile. This coastal strip was conceded without a break before settlement jumped to the banks of the Assomption River where soils are a great deal better. However, it is clear the attraction was the Assomption River rather than the superior soils because no attempt was made to avoid areas along the river where soils were poor. Had there been no interior river, ranges almost certainly would have been added behind the one along the St. Lawrence.

It is clear that the location of rotures was affected less by soil quality than by the tributaries of the St. Lawrence. Patches of bad land may have been jumped temporarily, but the gaps were always filled. Here and there a man may have moved off a roture because the soils were unproductive, but the rotures themselves were conceded across all the soils of the St. Lawrence lowland.

THE NUMBER OF ROTURES WHICH A CENSITAIRE
COULD LEGALLY ACQUIRE

In theory a censitaire who worked his own land was entitled to one roture. As almost all seigneurs required their censitaires to *tenir ou faire* *tenir feu et lieu* (to live on or have someone else live on their land), a censitaire could not have two concessions unless he found a tenant for one whenever this rule was enforced. Occasionally censitaires attempted to by-pass this restriction by applying for rotures from different seigneurs.[8] These censitaires hoped to sell the rotures quickly to incoming settlers,* and let them revert to the seigneur if no buyer appeared. From the seigneurs' point of view this speculation was extremely disadvantageous. Although he could withdraw rotures either for the nonpayment of dues or because the obligation to *tenir feu et lieu* was neglected, he had to apply to the intendant for permission to do so. When the original contract was only a year or two old, the intendant usually ordered the seigneur to postpone the take-over for at least another year. If the contract obligations still had not been fulfilled at the end of this time, the seigneur regained possession of a forest tract which would have to be reconceded and settled before he would begin to profit from it.

The intendant, in an attempt to prevent this speculation in land, issued an ordinance in 1682 which required all censitaires to *tenir ou faire tenir feu et lieu,* and forbade any of them to hold more than two rotures.[9] During the next twenty-five years there were a number of ordinances directing censitaires in one seigneurie or another to live on their land,[10] and in 1711 the matter was reviewed in one of the Edicts of Marly.[11] The king pointed out that he had been informed that many rotures were neither cleared nor inhabited, that the economic development of the colony was being threatened thereby, and that an undue burden was placed on the censitaires who did *tenir feu et lieu* because they had to shoulder the entire burden of the public works program. † He stated that rotures were granted only with a view to developing the colony, and ordered all censitaires to settle on and improve their holdings. If the curé and local militia captain agreed that these conditions had not been met within a year of the publication of the Edict, the neglected rotures could be confiscated by the seigneur.

---

* Uncleared rotures had a market value in only a few seigneuries near the towns during most of the French regime, and even there were seldom worth more than 15 to 30 livres. The frequency of roture sales and the reasons for them are discussed in more detail in Chapter 8.

† Censitaires were required by the central government to contribute to the construction and maintenance of roads and bridges, and often to assist in the construction of the church. A censitaire who did not live on his holding and did nothing about the public road which crossed it could be a great nuisance to the others, and probably increased the work which they would have to do.

This Edict of Marly contained little that was new, for the roture contracts requiring censitaires to *tenir feu et lieu* plus the ordinance of 1682 gave ample authority for withdrawing undeveloped concessions. The Edict set a time limit, and it gave direct royal sanction for the reunion of rotures to the seigneurial domain; it was, therefore, a more impressive document than its predecessors, and to impress was probably its function. When rotures were withdrawn after 1711 this Edict of Marly was inevitably cited as authority.

After 1711 there were many ordinances which required censitaires to *tenir feu et lieu* within a year or lose their rotures, or which permitted seigneurs to reunite undeveloped rotures to the seigneurial domain. A few rotures were withdrawn somewhere in the colony every year, and well over a thousand rotures must have reverted to the seigneurs during the last forty years of the French regime.[12] On the other hand, there is no doubt that a number of censitaires continued to hold rotures in two or more seigneuries,[13] and it is clear from the *aveux et dénombrements* and *papiers terriers* that there were many more rotures than able-bodied men in most seigneuries. In these seigneuries it was impossible for the censitaires to *tenir feu et lieu* on all concessions, and yet the seigneurs showed no inclination to withdraw most of the undeveloped rotures.

In fact, neither seigneurs nor royal officials ever took the requirement to *tenir feu et lieu* at face value. It had been inserted in roture contracts to insure that land was developed and to protect seigneurs from censitaires who held rotures without improving them or paying the dues, by giving the seigneur a convenient handle for withdrawing the land. Usually a seigneur attempted to withdraw a roture only if the dues had not been paid, and would reinforce his representations to the intendant with the observation that no one had kept *feu et lieu*. Thus the Jesuits requested the return of an abandoned roture in Cap de la Madeleine because there was no record that the *cens et rentes* had ever been paid, or that anyone had maintained *feu et lieu*.[14] Another seigneur wanted to repossess a roture because the censitaire had left for Louisiana thirteen years before, and was presumed to be dead. When a negligent censitaire was located, he was ordered to pay the back dues and to *tenir feu et lieu* within a year or face the confiscation of his land. The crucial part of the order was that he pay the outstanding dues. Ordinarily, the seigneur would never have complained if the dues had been paid, and was satisfied when they were.

Occasionally the seigneur took action against a censitaire who had paid his dues regularly but had not developed his land. Such a roture contributed nothing to the banal gristmill, and the seigneur who was managing his seigneurie carefully, and had a prospective censitaire in mind who could be counted on to develop the concession, would apply to the intendant for permission to withdraw the roture on the grounds that no one had kept *feu et lieu*. Neighboring censitaires might also complain about an uncleared concession. In many roture contracts the censitaires were required to "donner jour" or to "donner du Decouvers à ses voisins," that is, to clear enough land so that neighboring fields would not be shaded; because of the shape of fields in Canada, an uncleared roture could shade a large part of an adjacent field for several hours a day. There may also have been complaints about absentee censitaires who avoided the government corvées for road and bridge construction, or the repairs to their section of the fence around the common.

These considerations were in a seigneur's mind if he applied to the intendant for permission to withdraw an undeveloped roture for which the dues had been paid. The censitaire in question characteristically would put up a stout defense, perhaps claiming, as did Jean Boutin in Bellechasse in 1723, that he had told the seigneur when he applied for the roture that it was intended for his boy. The lad was only now of an age to farm, and would be settling on the roture within the year.[15] In the face of such an argument the seigneur was not likely to regain possession. The usual upshot was an order requiring the censitaire to *tenir feu et lieu* before a specified date, and he lost the roture only when that time limit, and perhaps an extension of it, had passed.

In summary, if a censitaire in a carefully supervised seigneurie refused to pay the *cens et rentes* he would lose his roture fairly quickly; if a censitaire paid the dues without developing the land he ran a slight risk of losing it; if he paid the dues and cleared the land, it was absolutely safe, and the fact that neither he nor a tenant lived on the roture was immaterial. There is no indication that such a roture was ever withdrawn. The seigneur was earning all he could expect, neighboring fields were not being shaded, and if the censitaire was avoiding his just share of the public works projects, this would be worked out in court. The seigneur would not withdraw a roture for this reason as long as he received the maximum revenue from it.

From time to time the intendants ruled in effect that censitaires were required neither to stick to the letter of the *feu et lieu* clause in their roture contracts nor to limit their holdings to two rotures. In 1720 censitaires living near the village of La Prairie de la Magdeleine complained that their common was used by censitaires who lived in Saint-Lambert (another part of the same seigneurie), but who held rotures near the village. The censitaires from Saint-Lambert were not paying for the right to use the common, they were not contributing to its maintenance, and they did not *tenir feu et lieu* on the rotures which they held near the common. To this the Saint-Lambert censitaires replied that they were ready to pay the charges for the common and to aid in its upkeep, but that one censitaire could not *tenir feu et lieu* on several rotures. They or their children had cleared and cultivated the rotures near the village of La Prairie, but as their homes were on rotures in Saint-Lambert, no more could be expected. The intendant agreed, and ruled that they were entitled to use the common as long as they continued to "faire valoire" their rotures near the village of La Prairie.[16] He saw nothing irregular in the fact that no one was living on these rotures.

Certain practical considerations played a more important part than did ordinances and edicts in limiting the number of rotures a censitaire was likely to own. The annual dues for three or four undeveloped rotures were fifteen to twenty livres a year, and there was not a great deal that the censitaire could do with the land. Sooner or later he would be able to sell, but if many years passed the sale price would not cover the dues which he had paid. Consequently few censitaires held more than one or two undeveloped rotures, which they generally kept for their children. The most prosperous censitaires held four or five developed rotures, but this was near the ceiling. Labor was expensive, agricultural profits modest and the children, who had provided much of the labor, were likely to marry and move away or to divide the rotures between them.

THE FRAGMENTATION OF ROTURES

Because a censitaire's land was divided equally among his children, many rotures were broken up into several farms after the death of the original censitaire. If he left five arpents of frontage to ten children, a strip half an arpent in width became the property of each, although because of the legal contracts between a man and his wife, inheritance was seldom this simple. Usually all property belonging to man or wife other than that acquired in the line of direct succession was held conjointly by both parties (the *communauté des biens*). When the husband died, his widow retained half the estate; the other half was divided among her progeny. If she remarried and had several children by her second husband, half of the new *communauté* (which included the wife's half from the earlier marriage) passed on her death to her second husband, and the other half was divided among the offspring of both matches. In a few cases, the *communauté des biens* was replaced by a *douaire,* an agreement by which the wife received a sum of money (the *douaire préfix*) or half the land her husband had inherited (the *douaire coutumier*) although this land was held in usufruct and eventually passed to her husband's heirs.[17] The *communauté des biens* or the *douaire* were designed to protect the widow, but in no way altered the basic tenet that all children had the right to inherit property, and no one more than any of the others.

However, rotures were not inevitably divided among all offspring. Some parents gave their land to one child who agreed to care for his parents until their deaths and, in some cases, to make a cash payment to each of his coinheritors. Such an arrangement was a common way of ensuring that the elderly would be cared for and that the family land would not be divided.[18] When no such agreement had been reached the family land was subdivided when the father or mother died.

Figure 7–5 shows the periods of divided control of each of seventy-one rotures along the river in the parish of Sainte-Famille on the Ile d'Orléans. Undoubtedly there were more periods of divided control than the figure shows, and the duration of many of the periods indicated is not known. This latter uncertainty is indicated by question marks which are common enough to keep the reader properly wary.

Figure 7–5 does indicate that, at least until 1725, a subdivided roture was likely to revert eventually to one owner. A sale price could be agreed upon for the entire roture and one of the coinheritors (or anyone else) could contract to pay each of the others his share; an auction could be arranged similar to those by which seigneuries were often bought and sold, and the roture sold to the highest bidder;[19] or one of the coinheritors could deal individually with each of the others and acquire all the rotures in a succession of deals spread over a number of years. Almost as frequent were the exchanges or donations by which parcels of land shunted back and forth, tending in the process to crystallize in larger units which usually corresponded to the rotures before division.

The censitaire who had inherited part of his father's land usually faced a choice between farming the fraction or selling it and moving to a new area. As long as good land was available along the river within a reasonable distance of Quebec or Montreal, the latter alternative was usually the more attractive, especially if the censitaire had established his own farm before his parents died. However, the family property was permanently subdivided if the deceased censitaire, by hard work, a judicious marriage, and some shrewd sales or trades during his lifetime, had acquired several developed rotures. Such holdings could be divided into two or more farms of average size, and because such a farm was much more attractive than the prospect of clearing a new roture, two or more of the offspring inevitably stayed on the family land. There was, therefore, no continuity of large holdings from generation to generation. When a larger-than-average concentration appeared, one man's effort had put it together, and the unit he had created disappeared at his death. A son might re-establish the family farm in its original proportions, but it was more difficult for him than it had been for his father because partially cleared land in favored areas became more expensive.

Usually only one censitaire lived on a single roture which was divided among several coinheritors. None of the seventy-one rotures in Sainte-Famille in 1725 contained more than one farmhouse, although the ownership of most of these rotures had been divided at one time or another. When a roture was divided, some of the inheritors usually sold their shares at once and left for another part of the colony, others settled nearby and cultivated their sections of the family farm as additional fields; and one lived in the family home, farmed his fraction of the roture, and hoped to acquire the rest. In most parts of the colony his was a reasonable expectation at any time during the French regime.

However, rotures in a few seigneuries near Quebec were being subdivided well before the conquest into two or more inhabited farms. These seigneuries had been settled for several generations, they were located near a town market, and they contained a limited amount of cultivable land. Land had become scarce: a young man could marry a local girl and acquire some land thereby, or could buy bits and pieces here and there, but not so easily as before. In this situation the family farm attracted more of the offspring. Most still sold their fractions and moved to a new area many miles away, but as early as 1733 there were two or more houses on more than a quarter of the rotures in Beaupré,[20] a

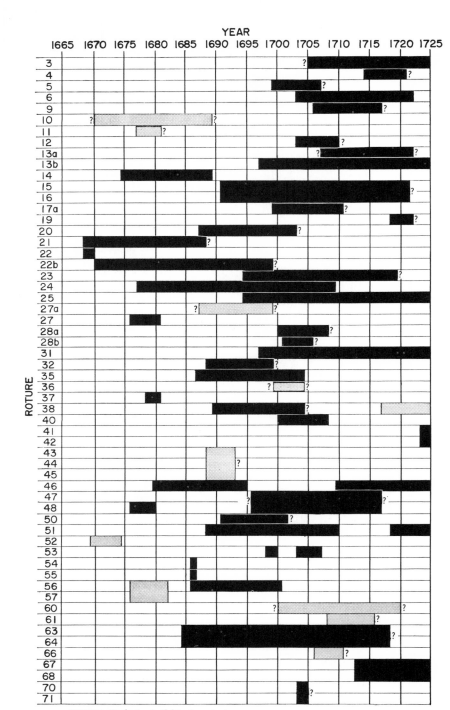

YEAR

ROTURE

	Period of divided control
	Period of divided control, nature of division uncertain
?	Beginning or end of period uncertain

sure indication that the original rotures were being permanently subdivided among coinheritors. There were four houses on one of the rotures, each fifty yards from its neighbor on a strip of land fifty yards wide and almost four miles deep (though the actual farms were perhaps only half a mile deep, the rest of the land extending into the Shield).

By 1745 reports of this fragmentation of rotures had reached the king, who issued an ordinance on the subject. He suggested that agriculture was languishing in Canada because

> most habitants cultivate only the portions of land which have fallen due to them by the partition of their father's property, and usually find themselves reduced to such a small area that the said habitants cannot provide for themselves; . . . the same habitants could, however, undertake other establishments more useful for them and their families and more advantageous for the general welfare of the colony. . . .[21]

The ordinance forbade anyone to build a house or a barn on a plot smaller than one and one-half by thirty or forty arpents unless the plot was in a village or town. If the order were broken, a hundred-livre fine would be imposed on the guilty party and his buildings demolished. This was not an idle threat; during the next few years several stone buildings were razed because the royal ordinance had been contravened.[22]

As was often the case, the king and his ministers in France did not really understand the Canadian situation. Few habitants were content to farm their fraction of the family roture. None of the rotures in La Prairie de la Magdeleine, the Jesuits' seigneurie near Montreal, had more than one house on it in 1733; [23] nor was there any sign of divided rotures on the Ile de Montréal two years before.[24] In those seigneuries good land was still available in many undeveloped rotures and in the seigneurial domain, and in this situation, rotures were not broken up into permanently separated farms. These small farms had appeared only where land had become scarce, as in Beaupré, Notre Dame des Anges, the Ile d'Orléans, and in a few other seigneuries near Quebec. The ordinance

Fig. 7–5 (*facing page*).—Periods of divided ownership of rotures in Ste-Famille before 1725. Of the 71 rotures (which with subdivisions totaled 87 parcels of land) only those which were divided are listed here; the other one-third are not shown. Based on the inventory of land records prepared by Léon Roy, "Les Terres de l'Ile d'Orléans; les Terres de la Sainte-Famille," *RAPQ* (1949–51), pp. 147–260.

aiming to forestall the extreme fragmentation of Canadian farms was sound, but it was not as pressingly needed as the king had been led to believe.

THE NUMBER OF ROTURES HELD BY A CENSITAIRE

The assumption made in Chapter 5 that each censitaire in a well-established seigneurie owned two rotures is obviously based on an average of several landholding situations. These are well illustrated in the parish of Sainte-Famille on the Ile d'Orléans. Sixty-five rotures had been conceded in the parish by 1667. Three of these rotures were subdivided into separate farms, and five censitaires owned two concessions each; there were, therefore, sixty-three farmers in the parish.[25] In 1689 there were seventy rotures, five of which were divided into smaller farms. However, six censitaires owned two rotures each; two owned three; and one, five. In the process of many exchanges and sales, these censitaires had been able to enlarge their holdings, and although there were five more rotures in the parish than in 1667 there was one fewer censitaire. By 1709 the trend towards larger farms had become more apparent. In that year thirteen habitants held two or more rotures, and one of them held five. The number of landholders had dropped to fifty-nine. By 1725, the effects of the inheritance system were appearing, for only eight men held more than one roture, and the number of landholders had risen to sixty-one. There were no *aveux et dénombrements* or nominal censuses of the island during the next thirty years, but because its population almost doubled from 1712 to 1739 although there was no new land to concede, it can be safely assumed that many farms were subdivided shortly after 1725. From 1739 to 1760 the population of the island declined slightly, an indication that no further fragmentation of farms was taking place.

Clearly the amount of land controlled by a censitaire on the Ile d'Orléans, and probably in other seigneuries as well, fluctuated in a definite cycle. This cycle can be summarized as follows: (1) There was a period of initial settlement during which most censitaires held one roture. (2) There followed a period during which many of the original settlers or their offspring acquired two or more rotures. As long as free land was available nearby, there was little population pressure within settled areas. Many censitaires applied to the seigneur for an additional roture in the second range, and bought two or three others along the river. (On the Ile d'Orléans the amount of agricultural land was always limited, and consequently fewer censitaires held several rotures than was the case in larger, more isolated seigneuries.) (3) There was a period during which the larger holdings were broken up, and many individual rotures were permanently subdivided—a period which began as soon as all the good land nearby had been conceded. Fragmentation was often completed in a generation. (4) Finally, there was a period of equilibrium during which the amount of land a man held changed very little. Rotures could not be further subdivided into economical farms, and a few of the smallest holdings may have been amalgamated into larger units.

Although the stages of this cycle were probably never as sharply defined as thus outlined, the change in population density which was one corollary of the cycle is apparent in the maps of population distribution in Chapter 6. If the size of holdings in a given area followed the several stages closely, the population density would remain constant for a period after initial settlement, would then rise abruptly, and would eventually stabilize at a new and higher level. The maps clearly show, for example, that between 1712 and 1739 the population density increased rapidly on the Ile d'Orléans, and this change undoubtedly reflected a rapid subdivision of rotures in the intervening years.

Similar changes in population density took place along the south shore below Quebec. This shore was unsettled in 1667, and was still sparsely inhabited in 1692. During the next twenty years, however, the first range filled in solidly for thirty miles below Quebec. From 1712 to 1739 settlement spread another forty miles downstream and up the Rivière du Sud, while the population density increased as rotures were subdivided in the area of older settlement immediately below Quebec. The distinction between this area where rotures had been divided and newer areas where they had not is clearly reflected in a comparison of Figures 6–4 and 6–5, showing population distribution in 1739 and in 1760. The population density had not increased along the shore immediately below Quebec because rotures there had already been divided and were in the fourth stage of the cycle. Farther down the St. Lawrence and along the Rivière du Sud the population density increased rapidly because rotures were being divided for the first time. The population density along the Rivière du Sud was higher than along the two small rivers between it and the Chaudière because the Rivière du Sud had been settled before the other two and was, therefore, at a more advanced stage of the cycle.

Except near Quebec, the last two stages of the cycle were seldom reached until after the conquest. As a general rule, the size of holdings varied directly with the distance from the town, and the population density varied inversely. In 1762 fourteen out of the twenty-four censitaires in Petite Rivière, a seigneurie on the south shore a hundred miles below Quebec, held four arpents of frontage or more,[26] that is to say, lived on holdings which were probably larger than the original rotures. Not far away in Kamouraska the number of habitants holding more than four arpents was almost double the number holding two arpents or less.[27] On the other hand, of one hundred and forty-two holdings in Beauport, a seigneurie on the north shore a few miles northeast of Quebec, one hundred and twenty were two arpents or less in frontage, and of these, seventy were no more than one arpent.[28] Only six habitants owned as many as four arpents of frontage. It remains to be seen whether these differences in the amount of land which a man held led to similar differences in rural standards of living.

8 : The Habitants' Use of the Land

ALMOST all Canadian censitaires were farmers who would have been described as peasants in France, and in Canada were known as habitants. Today this epithet suggests rurality, small scale agriculture, and the frame of mind associated with both. Its meaning was roughly the same during the French regime, although the distinction between urban and rural people was not so sharp as it is today, and the man who could put *Sieur* in front of his name was not thought of as an habitant however well he fitted the other criteria.

Until recently the few references to the habitants in the correspondence of officials in Canada during the French regime have furnished most of the information about this largest segment of the population of the colony, and as these references are frequently contradictory, they have permitted a wide latitude of interpretation. Additional evidence has been forthcoming only recently in the form of careful inventories of farm tools and household belongings, descriptions of farm buildings, and analyses of the habitants' legacy of folk songs and tales. However, little enough is known about many aspects of the habitants' daily lives, while their attitudes towards those traditional authorities, the king's officials, the Church, and the seigneurs, have remained subjects for conjecture. Yet an evaluation of the habitants' attitudes towards their seigneurs, and towards the seigneurial system in general, appears essential to an understanding of that system. The habitants formed the largest class in Canada, and in a land where the unpopular demands of authority often were by-passed, the seigneurial system largely became what they fashioned it to be.

This chapter, which treats the uses the habitants made of the land they acquired, and the next chapter, which examines the patterns of settlement within seigneuries, attempt to outline some of the evidence relevant to an understanding of the habitants' feelings about seigneurs and the seigneurial system. Some of this evidence can be found in more detail in studies by Marcel Trudel, Robert-Lionel Séguin, Luc Lacourcière, and several others,[1] but that dealing with land sales, crop and livestock distributions, income levels, and settlement patterns is presented here for the first time.

SALES OF ROTURES

It cannot be assumed that all or even most habitants acquired their rotures with the intention of establishing farms. Land sales were common in spite of the fact that the inherently protective coutume and a scarcity of money militated strongly against them. A man might buy a roture only to discover that the sale had interfered with someone's *légitime* and was, therefore, illegal; or he might be forced by the provisions of the *retrait lignager* to give up the land to a relative of the seller who was willing to refund the sale price. To buy a single roture he would often have to deal separately with several coinheritors plus the widow for her half of the *communauté*. Moreover the seigneur's *lods et ventes* constituted a sales tax on rotures of 8.5 per cent.[2] Protecting the *lods et ventes* was the seigneur's *droit de retrait* which, although not in the Coutume de Paris, was stipulated in most roture contracts in Canada, and gave the seigneur the right to take over a roture within forty days of its sale by paying the purchase price to the first buyer.[3] The scarcity of money may have been a less serious check on land sales, for although habitants rarely had the thousand livres or more which it took to buy an established farm, they could usually make a down payment, and afford a 5 per cent interest on a debt which they retired in a number of installments. Sometimes they paid in kind—in furs when they could get them, or with a number of chickens and minots of grain per year.[4] Creditors were generally lenient, and most habitants were chronically in debt, for the money shortage resulted in a type of installment plan buying which covered most of the habitants' purchases.[5]

Figure 8–1, which shows the sales in the parish of Sainte-Famille on the Ile d'Orléans before 1725, gives some indication of the frequency of land sales during the French regime. The figure is based on Léon Roy's inventory of landholders in the parish which, in turn, was drawn from the maps by Villeneuve (1689) and Catalogne (1709), an *aveu et dénombrement* (1725), and a variety of other documents pertaining to land ownership. The inventory is a remarkable description of the ownership of rotures, but inevitably there were years for which the ownership of a roture is not clear, and transactions for which there is no record. Nevertheless, it is the most nearly complete record of its kind. Not included in Figure 8–1 are alienations within the family—the sale of a fraction of a roture by one coinheritor to another or by a coinheritor to his stepfather, for example—a type of alienation which was at least as common as those shown.

The most striking feature of Figure 8–1 is the number of sales during the first years of settlement on the island. To take the evidence from one parish, a third of all the rotures on the Ile d'Orléans had been sold within ten years of their concession, and there is evidence that land sales were equally rapid in many other areas. In 1678 only half of the ninety-two rotures in the Jesuits' seigneurie of Notre Dame des Anges were in the hands of their original owners.[6] In some cases the rotures were thirty years old and the original owner had died, but the percentage of second owners was just as high among the newer concessions. Of the twenty-three rotures in Charlesbourg, one of the three villages which Talon had laid out in 1666, only ten had not changed hands within twelve years. Five of the twenty-three rotures had had three owners, and three had had five. Not all of these alienations were sales. Censitaires frequently exchanged rotures and sometimes they gave them away, but without a doubt the immigrant who had just acquired a roture was almost as likely to sell it within two or three years as to settle down and farm.

This was not what the king expected of the colonists he had sent out, and his Intendant Talon issued a stern ordinance on the subject.[7] Habitants were forbidden to sell their concessions before putting up a building and clearing at least two arpents suitable for *culture de la pioche* (a *pioche* being a mattock which could be used around stumps and roots). In a few cases the seigneur inserted a clause in his contracts requiring the habitant to hold his land for several years, a provision which was probably seldom more effective than when, in 1708, the Jesuits added it to a contract for the Ile aux Ruaux.[8] The habitant was to hold the land for twenty years; he sold it, notwithstanding, in 1710.

The turnover of land was most rapid during the 1660's and 1670's. New

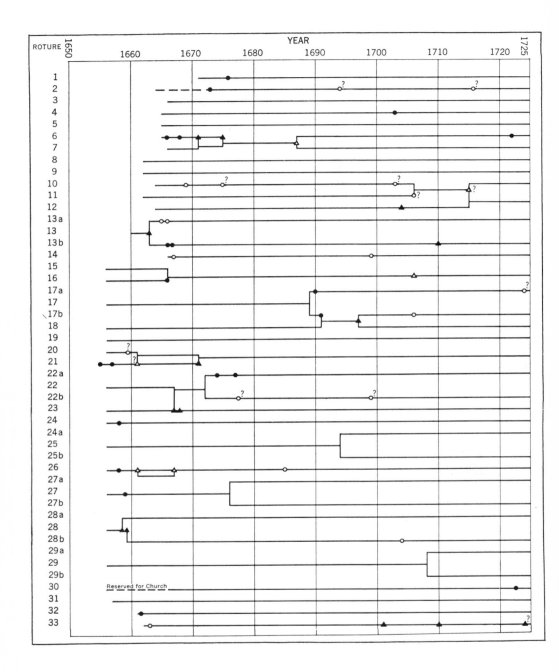

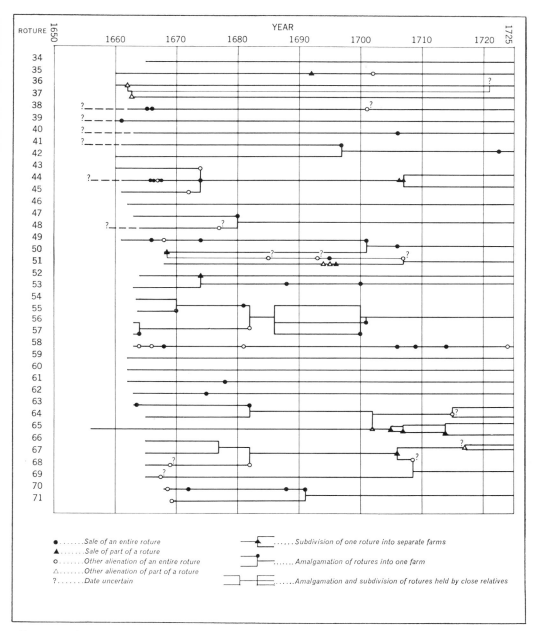

Fig. 8–1 (facing pages).—Sales and other alienations of land outside the family in the parish of Ste-Famille from the concession of the rotures to 1725. Based on the inventory of land records prepared by Léon Roy, "Les Terres de l'Ile d'Orléans; les Terres de la Sainte-Famille," *RAPQ* (1949–51), pp. 147–260.

settlers were arriving almost every year, and after a man had spent a year or two in one spot he often left it for another. As land was available almost anywhere, he had ample choice. Often an habitant cleared a little land on his first roture and then sold it to a newcomer for perhaps a hundred livres, while an entirely neglected roture would fetch ten or twenty livres if it was located near Quebec or Montreal. Through several such transactions in two or three years he earned enough to keep body and soul together, and perhaps a little more which could go towards some improvements on a permanent farm. Moreover, immigrants who had not been farmers in France may have preferred trading land to farming it, at least until they had gained some experience in a new environment. Later on habitants occasionally took rotures for the timber, and when they had cut the best of it, sold the roture or abandoned it to a seigneur who, in return, may have complained about "ceux qui après avoir depouillé, depargney, et denué une terre du meilleur bois l'abandonnent et delaissent." [9]

The spree of land trading slowed in the late 1670's and then virtually stopped, not to resume until the turn of the century. The pace of the 1660's and early 1670's was bound to taper off when immigrants were no longer sent to Canada, but it was the Second Iroquois War which almost stopped sales altogether. From Montreal to Trois-Rivières the colony became a series of fortified camps. This war, which the Canadians had largely brought on themselves, shook the colony to its roots, and the outcome was uncertain almost until the end of the century. In such an atmosphere little land was changing hands; even below Quebec on the Ile d'Orléans the war resulted in the hiatus in land sales which is clearly revealed in Figure 8–1.

Land sales resumed when victory over the Iroquois was assured. Some new rotures were sold again within a short time of their concession, and others which were several decades old changed hands from time to time. Of the seventy-one concessions in Sainte-Famille, part or all of fifteen were sold out of the family between 1700 and 1725, and another twelve were alienated in other ways. The frequency of land sales was probably similar in other well-established seigneuries, and more rapid where settlement was recent. In the older areas the checks on sales which were built into the coutume were becoming effective, and the family farm was appearing steadily more attractive as good land nearby was becoming scarce. Nevertheless, as a third of the rotures in Sainte-Famille passed in part or entirely from one family to another between 1700 and 1725 landholding was certainly not rigid. Land in France in the early eighteenth century, and in parts of French Canada in the present century probably changed hands less rapidly. On Ile Verte, an island near the south shore more than a hundred miles below Quebec, just over a fifth of ninety-one holdings were alienated out of the family between 1913 and 1948.[10] Although Ile Verte is an isolated corner of Quebec and its inhabitants probably form as stable a community as any in the province,

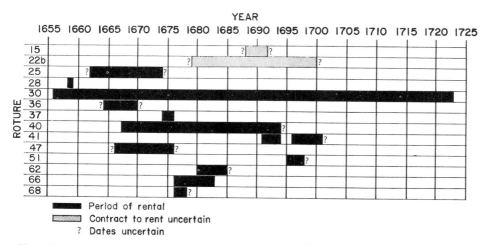

Fig. 8–2.—Rented land in the parish of Ste-Famille from the concession of the rotures to 1725. Of the 71 rotures only those which were rented at some time before 1725 are shown here.

it is entirely possible that there have been rural societies in Quebec in the twentieth century in which landholding has been much more stable than in any rural society in Canada during the French regime.

Figure 8–2 indicates the periods during which rotures in the parish of Sainte-Famille were rented before 1725. Few habitants in the parish rented land, and there is no reason to suspect that tenancy was more important elsewhere. An elderly and childless habitant might rent a roture to a tenant who contracted to look after his landlord.[11] A guardian who administered a roture for several coinheritors who were minors might rent it until his charges were of age. The announcement of the intention to rent would be made in front of the church after mass, and the inheritance let to the highest bidder.[12] However, as long as free land was available nearby, tenants were bound to be scarce; in those areas where land was becoming scarce, few censitaires had extra rotures to rent.

Whether or not rotures were developed by the original grantees, some land was cleared sooner or later in most of them. Trees were felled and burned, or were girdled and left to blow over. In 1636 a Jesuit reported that a man could clear two arpents of trees, if not of stumps, in a year,[13] but it is apparent from Figure 8–3 that the rate and amount of clearing varied enormously in different parts of the colony, and even within individual seigneuries. Except in Ile Dupas et Chicot, where the farms were small, and in the parish of Sainte-Famille, where the farms were relatively large, there were wide variations in the amount of cleared land per roture in each of the seven seigneuries or parishes shown in the figure. Even more striking are the differences in the amount of cleared land per roture in different seigneuries. Three decades before the conquest approximately 75 per cent of the rotures in the parish of Sainte-Famille contained more than sixty arpents of arable and pasture, whereas in Notre Dame des Anges, La Prairie de la Magdeleine, and Saint-Sulpice, most clearings were patches of twenty-five arpents or less. In Beaupré and on the Ile de Montréal, the majority of rotures contained thirty to sixty arpents of cleared land, while in Ile Dupas et Chicot the largest clearing on a roture was less than twenty arpents.

The average number of cleared arpents per family in each of the census divisions of 1739 is shown cartographically in Figure 8–4. Farms tended to be largest near Quebec and Montreal, where, by 1739, the land had been settled for several generations. As rotures near the towns were beginning to be divided by this date, the rapid extension of clearing rather than the appearance of small, submarginal farms appears to have been the first corollary of the subdivision of rotures. However, even in the areas of extensive clearing, few habitants owned more than one hundred arpents of arable and pasture. The high price of farm labor, the small market in the colony and abroad for its agricultural products, the absence of primogeniture at the *en censive* level, the checks on sales inherent in the coutume and, near the towns, the growing population pressure which made it steadily more difficult for the ambitious habitant to buy additional rotures—all militated against these larger farms. In many seigneuries, even a few of those near the towns, no farms were larger than

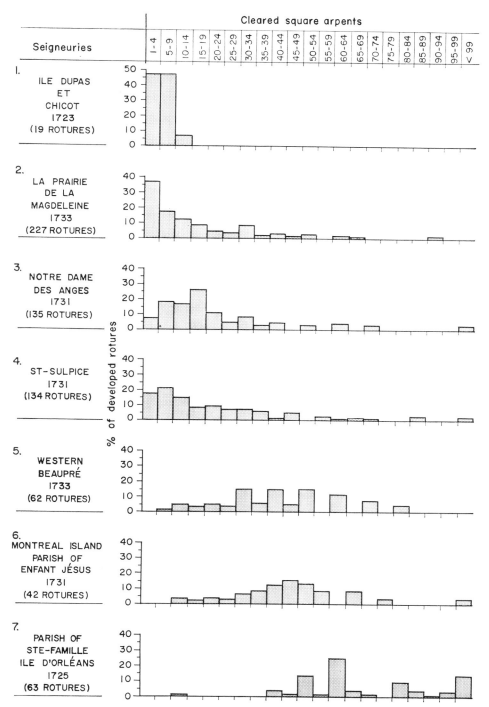

Fig. 8–3.—Cleared land on developed rotures in seven seigneuries, 1723–33.

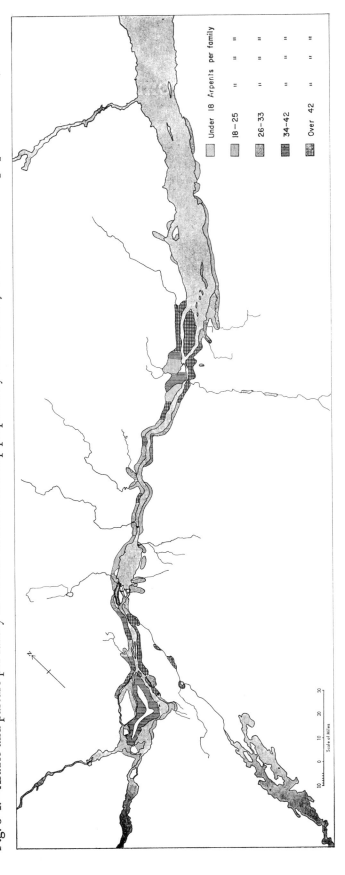

Fig. 8-4.—Arable and pasture per family in Canada in 1739. Base map prepared by the University of Wisconsin Cartographic Laboratory.

Under 18 Arpents per family
18 − 25 " " "
26 − 33 " " "
34 − 42 " " "
Over 42 " " "

Scale of Miles

forty or fifty arpents, while probably no habitant during the French regime ever controlled as much as two hundred arpents of cleared land.

The amount of cleared land per family was generally smallest in the Government of Trois-Rivières or well below Quebec, both areas in which settlement was relatively recent in 1739. Recency of settlement is undoubtedly the principal explanation of the small farms in Ile Dupas et Chicot and of the many farms of a similar size in Saint-Sulpice where, in 1731, settlement along the Assomption River was beginning (see Fig. 8–3). On the other hand, in 1739 almost all the settlement along the Richelieu below Chambly was less than fifteen years old, while that along the Chaudière was scarcely five. Settlers were apparently optimistic about the agricultural potential of land in these southward projections of settlement which occupied areas of generally fertile soils and which were connected by road to points on the south shore near Montreal or Quebec. There was apparently less optimism about the future of agriculture and hence less clearing in the Government of Trois-Rivières, where even after the completion in the late 1730's of a through road from Quebec to Montreal, markets for agricultural produce were remote; and along the lower St. Lawrence, where the handicaps of a cool summer and short growing season were added to the problems of marketing.

The small amount of cleared land per family in some of the seigneuries near Quebec or Montreal can be explained neither by recency of settlement nor by problems of marketing. La Prairie de la Magdeleine, the Jesuits' seigneurie opposite Montreal, had been settled in the 1670's, but clearings were still small and patchy sixty years later (see Fig. 8–3). The difficulty of draining the low, flat land in the seigneurie may account for these small farms, but the fact remains that few habitants in the seigneurie can have sold agricultural produce in the nearby Montreal market. As La Prairie de la Magdeleine lay across the busy fur route from the upper St. Lawrence and Ottawa rivers to the Richelieu River, Lake Champlain, and Albany, it is a fair guess that the fur trade, rather than agriculture, was the principal interest of most of its population. In Portneuf, fishing is known to have been the first occupation of many habitants (see Chap. 5), as may have been the case in De Maure, a seigneurie controlled in 1739 by the Sisters of the Hôtel-Dieu in Quebec, and operated in part as a haven for indigent families. The low ratios of arable and pasture per family in the seigneuries immediately north of

Quebec reflect the small rotures, most of them no larger than forty square arpents, which were originally conceded there. An error in the census data may account for the low ratio in Bellechasse, on the south shore opposite the eastern tip of the Ile d'Orléans.

Although an average figure for the amount of cleared land per family in Canada during the later years of the French regime is only misleading, it can be said that in those areas near the towns where agriculture was the prime economic activity, most farms contained more than thirty and less than one hundred arpents of cleared land. Elsewhere farms were generally much smaller, a reflection of recency of settlement, of relatively low assessments of the agricultural potential of the areas and, in some cases, of conflicting economic interests.

THE FARM OPERATION

The habitant in Canada, like most farmers in North America in the seventeenth and early eighteenth centuries, was not abreast of many agricultural practices which were common in the Europe of his day. No attempts were made in Canada to improve stock by selective breeding, and in the long run the quality of stock in the colony undoubtedly deteriorated. Crop rotation was unknown during the early years when high seed-to-yield ratios—commonly 1:10, and sometimes even 1:25—were obtained from virgin soils. Later, although there were occasional reports of crop rotation, probably neither the three-course rotation (wheat or rye followed by barley, oats, or peas, and then by a year of fallow) which was common in northern France, nor the two-course rotation (wheat followed by one or two years of fallow) which was more characteristic of the Midi, became standard practice in Canada. Moreover, there were many reports that the habitants did not know what it was to fertilize their land,[14] although there are indications here and there in the documents that manure was occasionally put on the land and that fodder crops were sometimes plowed under.[15] With such slight care soils were soon overworked; reports of soil exhaustion appeared in the 1660's, and continued throughout the French regime. Probably habitants in Canada planted grains or pulse in a field until the seed-to-yield ratio dropped to approximately 1:3, and then either neglected the field or converted it to meadow. Peter Kalm noted that most Canadian meadows had once been cultivated land,[16] and presumably they were destined to be cultivated again when the soil had regained some of its original fertility.

The abandonment in North America of several fundamental techniques of European agriculture stemmed less from the facts that many of the immigrants had been urban poor in Europe and that, at the level of individual farmers, contacts with Europe ended when the Atlantic was crossed, than from the discovery that land was as plentiful in North America as it was scarce in Europe. In France a peasant with eight or ten arpents of land could feed his family and his livestock and produce a modest surplus for sale only if he tended his land carefully. To neglect manuring or to shift a rotation from three to two courses was to court disaster. If an advance in technique resulted in the short run in improved living standards, in the long run it usually led to a smaller farm, and when this contraction took place the peasant could not abandon the innovation.[17] North American agriculture, on the other hand, quickly became extensive. It mattered relatively little if soils in one field were worn out as long as there was empty land nearby. Because agricultural production per man almost certainly rose in North America the change was not necessarily atavistic, but rather a change from one agricultural system to another which lasted as long as land remained plentiful.

Whatever the size of an habitant's farm or the methods by which he worked it, wheat was almost invariably his staple crop. Grains and pulse (peas were a field crop in Canada) were planted on at least nine-tenths of the planted arable in the colony, and wheat on approximately three-quarters of it. There was a slight tendency to diversify agricultural production in the eighteenth century, but the percentage of wheat in the total grain and pulse harvest was only a few points lower in 1739 than it had been forty and more years before. Some of this crop was winter wheat, although most was planted in late April or early May soon after the snow left the ground.[18] In either case the harvest came in the first weeks of September, and the level of prosperity in Canada usually varied directly with its size.

In 1739 most of the wheat grown in the colony was produced within a thirty-mile radius of Montreal or Quebec (see Fig. 8–5), principally because the population was low and settlement relatively recent farther from the two principal towns. Wheat production per family was between 80 and 130 minots in most census units, although there was a concentration of higher yields per family immediately north and east of the Ile de Montréal in an area of generally fertile soils close to the Montreal market, and a concentration of lower yields per family around Lake Saint-Pierre, and in a few seigneuries near Quebec. Yields per arpent and seed-to-

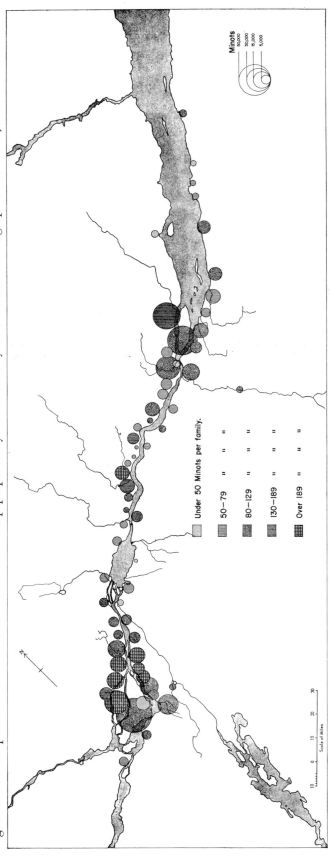

Fig. 8–5.—Wheat production in Canada in 1739. Base map prepared by the University of Wisconsin Cartographic Laboratory.

yield ratios are more difficult to calculate because they must be based on precise estimates which are not available in the documents of the amount of seed sown per arpent, and of the percentage of cleared land planted in wheat each year. In France in the late Middle Ages approximately two bushels of wheat were sown per acre (1.55 minots per arpent);[19] and for want of any other, this figure may be assumed in Canada. The fraction of cleared land in Canada which was planted in wheat varied from place to place, but an average of three-eighths is suggested by the many reports that approximately half of the cleared land (excluding natural prairie) was planted in any given year,[20] and by the census totals for the principal crops which indicate that approximately three-quarters of this half was planted in wheat. If the total wheat crop in 1739 is divided by three-eighths of the cleared arpents in that year, an average yield per arpent of 9.08 bushels is obtained. This figure divided by 1.55 gives an average seed-to-yield ratio of 1:5.8. Table 8–1 applies this same calculation to several seigneuries in the colony. Although the estimates on which the figures in Table 8–1 are based are open to question, it is certain that

TABLE 8–1

Wheat yields from sample seigneuries for the year 1739

Seigneurie	Minots per arpent	Seed/yield ratio
Les Eboulements and Baie St-Paul	14.75	1:9.5
Beaupré	7.28	1:4.6
Ile d'Orléans	7.63	1:4.9
Notre Dame des Anges	14.38	1:9.2
Portneuf	14.47	1:9.3
Les Grondines	5.88	1:3.7
Rivière Ouelle	6.96	1:4.4
La Durantaye	10.37	1:6.4
Lauzon	5.07	1:3.2
Lotbinière	6.66	1:4.2
Champlain	6.79	1:4.3
Maskinongé	7.50	1:4.8
Gentilly	13.92	1:8.9
Lanoraie	8.66	1:5.5
Lachenaie	12.11	1:7.8
Ile de Montréal	6.93	1:4.4
La Prairie de la Magdeleine	12.18	1:7.8
Contrecœur	5.71	1:3.6
Varennes	14.58	1:9.4
Châteauguay	15.67	1:10.1

yields per acre and seed-to-yield ratios in Canada during the French regime compare very unfavorably with contemporary standards, and probably were little if any better than those in medieval Europe when seed-to-yield ratios of 1:3 or 1:4 were characteristic.[21] That early Canadian ratios were not still lower is a reflection less of the quality of agricultural techniques than of the fact that some of the arable was fertile virgin land on which seed-to-yield ratios may have been as high as 1:24.

Almost every habitant raised peas, oats, and barley. Peas were always a dietary staple, and in the eighteenth century a surplus was exported almost every year to the French West Indies and occasionally to France. Oats was raised for feed, as was the small quantity of barley grown on most farms, although whenever the wheat harvest failed, barley bread appeared on many tables. Some habitants planted a little rye. Corn, the mainstay of agriculture in the Indian villages in the colony, was not popular with the habitants, who apparently were little more fond of it than of potatoes, with which they were familiar, but which they would not grow.[22] By 1739 many habitants in almost every seigneurie raised some flax. On the other hand, hemp, which had been in vogue during the first decades of the century when the king had intermittently subsidized its production, had all but disappeared.

Almost every farmhouse had a kitchen garden nearby. Onions, cabbage, lettuce, several varieties of beans, carrots, cucumbers, red beets, common radish and horse-radish, parsnips, thyme, and marjoram were all grown in Canada, and probably any habitant had planted most of them in his kitchen garden at one time or another. Pumpkins and melons could be raised during the longer summers near Montreal, and were common there. Usually there was a patch of tobacco in a corner of the garden. Most adults smoked, as often did boys of ten or twelve years of age.[23] The prosperous in the towns could afford Virginian tobacco; the habitants smoked a coarser leaf which they had grown, or which had come from those areas of sandy soils in the Government of Trois-Rivières, where in the eighteenth century some specialization in tobacco production had developed.*

Most habitants had several fruit trees somewhere on their rotures.

---

* Tobacco production shifted frequently because of soil exhaustion, but throughout the eighteenth century the censuses indicate a tendency for production to center in different parts of the Government of Trois-Rivières.

Apple trees were most common, and much of the crop was converted into a cider which was reported to be the equal of that in Normandy.[24] Plum trees thrived everywhere in the colony. Pears could be grown near Montreal but farther downstream the winters were too severe, as they were everywhere for peaches and apricots.[25] Cherry trees may have been grown here and there, and a few vineyards were planted on sunny southern exposures near Montreal.[26]

Of the approximate half of their cleared land which the habitants did not plant in any one year, some was plowed fallow, but most was meadow and pasture. Although there were commons in many seigneuries, and although habitants often turned their cattle, sheep, and particularly their swine out to graze in the forests behind their farms, the need to put up a lot of hay to tide livestock over a long winter, and to provide a pasture from which they could not stray into neighboring fields, led habitants to supplement these meadows and pastures with their own. Initially natural meadow along the river was used for both hay and grazing, but when it became insufficient a sizable field in another part of the farm was allocated for these purposes. Other than Peter Kalm's remarks that grass and white clover were planted in the meadows, and that he considered them better than those in the English colonies,[27] there is little information about the quality and carrying capacity of the Canadian meadows.

From the earliest years of the colony, cattle were its most important livestock. In the 1660's most habitants owned two or three cows and perhaps an ox, and by the eighteenth century there were five or six cows and one or two oxen on most well-established farms, while the most prosperous habitants owned as many as eighteen or twenty head. Cattle were raised primarily for domestic use, and provided milk, butter, cheese, and meat for the habitant's table, and power for his farm operation. There were small surpluses on many farms, and milk, butter, cheese, and occasionally a cow or an ox found their way to the town markets. Most of the cattle in the colony were concentrated near the towns (see Fig. 8–6), although this concentration was not as marked as in the case of wheat (compare Fig. 8–5) because livestock could be walked to market. Consequently the average number of cattle per family was not necessarily highest near the towns. In the Government of Quebec the ratios were highest towards the westward margin of the government, and in Beaupré, on the Ile d'Orléans, and well below Quebec along the south

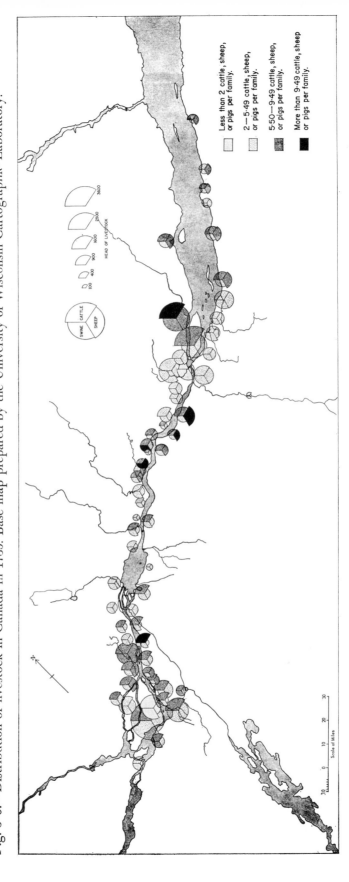

Fig. 8-6.—Distribution of livestock in Canada in 1739. Base map prepared by the University of Wisconsin Cartographic Laboratory.

shore; in the Government of Montreal similar ratios were on the mainland north and south of the Ile de Montréal, and for some miles to the east towards Lake Saint-Pierre. Areas in which there was a good deal of low, wet land, such as Baie Saint-Paul and Rivière du Sud in the Government of Quebec, or Saint-Sulpice and La Prairie de la Magdeleine in the Government of Montreal, in which wheat production per family was low, were not anomalous in terms of numbers of cattle.

The first horses came to Canada during Talon's intendancy,[28] and before long they were being bought from the New Englanders in such numbers that the Intendant Champigny complained about the money which was draining to the English in return for unneeded horses.[29] But the habitants loved hard, fast rides, and at first kept horses for this pleasure more than for work. Pedestrians were soon protected by an ordinance which fined a rider ten livres plus costs for each man he knocked down, and churchgoers were ordered to walk their horses when within ten arpents of the church to prevent tangles of carriages or sleighs in the churchyard. As the number of horses increased, some officials became concerned that horses were consuming feed which could be better used for cattle, and for this reason Jacques Raudot ordered in 1709 that no habitant was to keep more than two horses and a foal. Because horses had become work animals, Raudot could not ban them altogether. In 1710 he forbade habitants to borrow their neighbors' horses for midnight gallops because the horses had to rest after the labor of the day.[30] Later the same year he admitted to the minister in France that horses were needed in Canada for the many farm tasks which they performed more efficiently than oxen.[31] Nevertheless, officials were worried that there was too much riding. The habitants were becoming *efféminés;* they were forgetting how to snowshoe, and were losing the advantage in winter warfare which they had always held over the English.[32] Probably, however, few habitants needed or could maintain more than two horses and a foal, and certainly after the excitement of their arrival had worn off, these horses saw much more service as draft animals on the farm than they did for pleasure riding.

Some sheep were sent to Canada in the first years of royal government, but twenty years later Governor Denonville reported that few habitants kept even two or three.[33] Sheep had to be sheltered and fed throughout the winter, and as long as feed was scarce the habitants saved whatever they had for their cattle. In 1705 Raudot explained to the minister that the habitants did not keep more sheep for this reason, but pointed out that six sheep ate no more than one cow, and were certainly more profitable.[34] Before long many habitants had decided as much, and the sheep population rose steadily. In 1739 there were sheep in all developed seigneuries in the colony, although Figure 8–6 suggests that they were not as inevitably present on Canadian farms as either cattle or swine. Areas in which the ratios of wheat and cattle per family were high, such as the south shore near Montreal, contained notably few sheep. On the other hand, in several seigneuries, particularly a number along the south shore in the Government of Quebec, there was some specialization in sheep, although it is uncertain whether the relatively high figures for sheep in these seigneuries reflect several large or many small flocks. Certainly in some parts of the colony few habitants owned any sheep; in other areas many habitants may have owned four or five, and a few may have had flocks of twenty or thirty.

Because pigs were usually turned out in the forest behind a man's farm or in the streets of one of the towns at night, travelers in Canada seldom saw them. The censuses indicate, however, that pigs were common in all parts of the colony, and that in the eighteenth century most habitants had three or four. The only clue in the census of 1739 that there was any specialization in pigs is in the figures for the seigneurie of Deschambault, in the Government of Quebec. (On Fig. 8–6, see the north shore, ten miles from the west end of the government.)

Almost all habitants kept some poultry. Poultry were not counted in any of the censuses, but the single fact that rentes were often paid in part in capons is proof that there were chickens on almost all farms. Turkeys, ducks, and geese were not uncommon.

With the possible exception of the pigs, livestock were quartered indoors from mid-December to late March or early April. In a few cases habitants had all-purpose barns in which they kept both hay and livestock, but much more frequently they built three separate structures: a barn in which grain was threshed and hay stored, a stable for cattle (*étable*), and another for horses (*écurie*). Robert-Lionel Séguin has described these buildings carefully,[35] and there is no need to repeat his description here, except to point out that although construction materials were usually planks or squared logs and thatch, they were often purchased by the habitant, who frequently hired a carpenter to put up the buildings. Community barn raisings were rare until the nineteenth century.[36] During the French regime an average barn was approximately thirty feet long and twenty feet wide, and construction costs may have been as much as three to four hundred livres in years when money was relatively valuable.[37] The stables were smaller buildings which cost substantially less.

After the few tools which had been shipped from France were broken or lost, the habitant made most of his own.[38] He fashioned rakes, picks, and forks entirely from wood, but had to buy a saw, an axe, and the blades for his sickle, scythe, and hooking bill (*serape*) which he used to harvest peas. A forge was established in Montreal in 1674 to manufacture these blades, and soon there were blacksmiths and forges scattered through rural Canada. Plows, which were in common use by the 1670's, usually had an iron cutting edge, and the heavy wheel in front of the Canadian plow was often made by a wheelwright. In the eighteenth century a winnowing screen (*crible*) replaced the simpler basket, and had to be purchased. Other tools were usually made by the habitant, and by the North American standards of the day they were not unduly crude.

Although the labor on the great majority of farms in Canada towards the end of the French regime was supplied entirely by the habitant and his family, many habitants, perhaps 10 or 15 per cent of them, employed additional help.[39] A few took *engagés* who, like the indentured servants in Virginia, were bound to several years of service in return for their Atlantic passage. Others, although these habitants were never very common, owned Negro or Indian slaves.[40] Much more frequently an habitant agreed to provide food, clothing, and shelter for the young son or daughter of a neighbor in return for several years of service from the child. A girl would usually stay in the habitant's family until she married, a boy until he was old enough to establish his own farm, and to this end the habitant with whom he had lived usually agreed to give him a cow when he left.[41] Nor were day laborers or hired hands uncommon, especially towards the end of the French regime when an increasing population reduced the value of labor to the point where a man could be hired for an average yearly wage of approximately one hundred and fifty livres.[42] A prosperous habitant was likely to have one or two girls from the neighborhood living with the family and working about the house with his wife, a boy who performed some household chores and assisted with planting and harvesting, and one or two hired hands.

It is clear from the above pages that there was a wide range in the income which different habitants received from their land. At one extreme some habitants owned a hundred or more arpents of cleared land and hired one or two farm hands; at the other, they lived on a very few cleared arpents and, if agriculture was their only livelihood, walked a narrow line between a meagre living and starvation. It may be possible to suggest the amount of cleared land which an habitant needed before he could begin to market a surplus, and the income which he might have obtained from a large farm.

Consider a farm of fifteen cleared arpents. Approximately three-eighths of the land (between five and six arpents) was planted in wheat. Two arpents were devoted to grains grown primarily as feed for livestock, to peas, and to a kitchen garden. Most of the remaining land was in meadow; for the livestock—the horse, the ox, the two or three cows, and one or two pigs—had to be tided over a long winter. Assuming an average yield of nine minots per arpent, the farm produced approximately fifty minots of wheat. Of this, one-sixth was reserved for the next year's seed, one-fourteenth went to pay milling charges, one twenty-sixth went to the Church, and two or three minots may have been used to pay the *cens et rentes*. Approximately thirty-four minots were left for domestic consumption and sale. An average habitant had six people to feed, counting himself, his wife, and four children, and if each of them consumed four hundred pounds of flour a year, or just over a pound a day,* then the thirty-four minots would be consumed on the farm. The few eggs, the small quantity of milk, and the vegetables from the kitchen garden were probably consumed by the family as well, although Peter Kalm remarked that the poorer people were content with meals of dried bread and water, and took "all other provisions such as butter, cheese, meat, poultry, eggs, etc., to town to get money for them . . . to buy clothes and brandy for themselves and finery for their women." [43] Even if this were true, the sales from such a farm must have been small and intermittent.

---

* An exact figure for the average flour consumption per person in Canada during the French regime cannot be calculated; but the estimate seems conservative in view of the fact that bread was as much the staple of Canadian diet as wheat was the staple of the colony's agriculture. In other bread-eating societies (prerevolutionary Russia, for example) average flour consumption has been at least this high. Laborers in Canada were occasionally allocated two pounds of flour per day, but their consumption would have been higher than the average for men, women, and children.

Although there were farms of this size in most parts of the colony, their size was not static unless their owners were more interested in fishing, lumbering, or the fur trade than they were in agriculture. Otherwise land clearing proceeded steadily. When the farm reached thirty arpents of cleared land, roughly a hundred minots of wheat were produced on it, some sixty of which were available for domestic consumption or sale. There were probably one or two horses and as many oxen, five or six cows, three or four pigs and perhaps a small flock of sheep on such a farm. A fraction of the farm produce—ten or fifteen minots of wheat, a pig or a calf, some butter and perhaps some fruit and vegetables—was sold almost every year. In good years there may have been an income from sales of 200–300 livres (assuming average wheat prices); in other years no sales at all.

Those few habitants who owned as much as a hundred arpents of cleared land were distinctly more prosperous. Such a farm produced just over three hundred minots of wheat, more than two hundred of which remained after the several charges and reserves. There may have been ten or fifteen cows, three or four oxen, three or four horses, half a dozen swine, and perhaps ten sheep. The farm produced a marketable surplus of at least one hundred minots of grain, a calf or two, as many lambs, a pig, some dairy products, and some fruit and vegetables. The average yearly income from the farm may have been 500 livres (again assuming average wheat prices), and it is not difficult to imagine years when the income might have approached 1,000 livres. If the owner of the farm was not wealthy, by the standards of the day he was comfortable. Perhaps the habitants desired no more and, unlike some of the Puritans, relaxed their labors when they had reached this standard. Be that as it may, there were hurdles in Canada which made it extremely difficult for an habitant to farm enough land to become wealthy, however hard he worked or however shrewdly he bargained.

Inevitably the habitant began with an uncleared roture or, at most, with a farm of average size, for the inheritance system at the *en censive* level insured that larger holdings should be subdivided. He could, of course, purchase additional land, and hire men to farm it. However, labor was always expensive, as was cleared land (its price reflected the labor costs for clearing), and the only justification for these expenditures was a buoyant market for agricultural produce. Herein lay the overriding dilemma of Canadian agriculture. The lower St. Lawrence did not produce an agricultural staple for which there was a French market. Throughout the seventeenth century the only market for the surplus from Canadian farms was the sixth of the population who lived in Quebec, Trois-Rivières, and Montreal, and although by the end of the French regime this market had expanded to 16,000 people, many townsmen still raised most of their own food. In the eighteenth century Canadian wheat, peas, pork, and beef were shipped to Louisbourg or to the French West Indies, but this trade was never large, and in some years it was interrupted altogether. The few seigneurs who, with more capital and better credit than the habitants, attempted to establish large, commercial farms bankrupted themselves unless they had an assured market in the members of a religious order.[44] An industrious habitant might build up a farm of approximately a hundred cleared arpents, he might employ one or two hired hands, and live comfortably, but he could hardly become wealthy by either French or colonial British standards.

NONFARMING OCCUPATIONS

A number of habitants were artisans who supplemented their income by doing odd jobs for their neighbors. Blacksmiths, carpenters, wheelwrights, harness-makers, and masons were scattered through rural Canada. These men were usually farmers who practiced their trades on the side, and although the ordinary habitant was a jack-of-all-trades, he would seek out their special skills from time to time.

Most habitants were woodcutters, and many were fishermen. In the early years a man had to clear his land before he could farm it, and later he needed wood for buildings, fences, and fuel. By the beginning of the eighteenth century, wood was scarce in some of the oldest seigneuries, so that for the first time in Canada standing timber had some value.[45] Many habitants near Quebec and Montreal began to supplement their incomes by regular sales of firewood,[46] and throughout the eighteenth century there were a very few habitants who owned and operated small, water-powered sawmills (mentioned from time to time in the *aveux et dénombrements*) as adjuncts to their principal occupation of farming.

All habitants who held rotures on the river fished now and then. In the 1650's eels were reported to be so abundant that during September and October two men could take five or six thousand each night.[47] If such quantities were not constant, nevertheless eels were caught throughout the French regime. Between Montreal and Quebec habitants also fished for salmon, catfish, bar, chad, carp, sturgeon, and many other species.[48] Below Quebec, herring, cod, and porpoises were important. Most habitants built fish traps of reeds or branches in shallow water close to the shore,[49] a few fished with lines from canoes or rowboats, and in winter they took large quantities of fish in nets stretched under the ice.[50] Some habitants applied for rotures only to acquire fishing sites, and every spring others left the banks of the St. Lawrence for the cod fishery in the Gulf, or to take up permanent residence in one of the sedentary fishing stations which merchants from Quebec or the mother country had established around the Gaspé shore.

It was the fur trade rather than the fishery which drew the largest number of habitants away from the agricultural fringes along the lower St. Lawrence. A season in the woods was an adventure which might be profitable, and throughout the French regime the lure of furs along the upper Ottawa and around the Grand Lac beyond attracted many of Canada's most vigorous youths. From the official point of view, these coureurs de bois were an endless headache. They enormously complicated the policing of the fur trade: the value of monopoly privileges in the trade was often seriously reduced by illegal competition, royal taxes were avoided, and a large volume of furs was regularly siphoned off to the English along the Hudson River, who paid more for beaver than any merchants in Quebec.[51] Because many able-bodied men were absent from Canada, the forest was cleared more slowly, and women and children as well as farms were neglected. Several officials reported that with many husbands away the morals of Canadian women had deteriorated almost as far as those of the coureurs de bois who changed Indian girls every week.[52]

All officials disapproved of the coureurs de bois, but to stop them was another matter. Many ordinances forbade habitants to leave their farms without permission. Even a man hunting in the woods could be breaking the law unless he had a pass, and the officials had discovered that hunting passes were likely foils for activities in the fur trade.[53] Fines of as much as 1,500 to 2,000 livres were listed for a first offense, the stocks or a whipping for a second, and Frontenac ordered the death penalty for a third offense.[54] At least one man was hanged. These measures, stern as they were, had almost no effect. Canada was a straggling colony spread out for two hundred miles along the St. Lawrence; the wilderness was at almost every back door, the river at the front. The routes out of Canada could not be policed, and the vast majority of the habitants who left for the fur country did so with impunity.

In 1679 the Intendant Duchesneau reported that the coureurs de bois earned little enough,[55] and a few years later Champigny described their life as one of "une misère extraordinaire."[56] If these comments were accurate—and because similar observations were made repeatedly there must have been some truth in them—the attraction of the fur trade for so many habitants is not easily explained. Perhaps immigrants who had not been farmers in France accustomed themselves slowly to the routine of a farm. Perhaps the complete independence which a man found in the forest, not to mention the charms of willing Indian girls, was compensation enough for many discomforts. Perhaps the fur trade was simply an adventure. But certainly the fur trade was the principal source of most of such wealth as there was in Canada, and if little of it filtered down to the coureurs de bois, they could at least hope that it would. Farming presented no better prospects than a full larder and a few luxuries from France; the fur trade appeared to offer more, and the habitants were neither the first nor the last in North America to be enticed into the wilderness by this hope.

The attractions of the fur trade were clearest in the seventeenth century when almost no markets existed outside Canada for Canadian agricultural produce, and it was then that officialdom was most exasperated by the coureurs de bois. Half or more of the able-bodied men in the colony before 1700 may have spent at least one season along the upper Ottawa. In the eighteenth century, as markets for agricultural produce expanded and the price of furs declined, the fur trade diminished in relative importance. Men still left the lower St. Lawrence for the fur country, perhaps in greater numbers than during the seventeenth century, but they were a much smaller percentage of the Canadian population.[57]

THE HABITANT'S STANDARD OF LIVING

With a farm of thirty cleared arpents or more and perhaps some additional revenue from nonfarming occupations, an habitant and his family were able to live comfortably. To be sure, winter was frequently a time of privation and occasionally in the early years a time of scurvy and death. Although acute shortages could occur whenever shipments of salt did not arrive, or a thaw ruined the meat which had been frozen for the winter, or drought reduced the harvest, these periods of hardship were exceptional in the eighteenth century. "Il n'y en a pas un seul qui ne mange pas de bon pain de froment," wrote the king's engineer Gideon de Catalogne in 1712.[58] Curds were eaten by young and old.[59] Beef, pork, and later mutton were also standard fare for at least part of the year, although it was not true, as Peter Kalm remarked, that "excepting the soup, the salads, and the desserts, all their dishes consist of meat variously prepared."[60] Eggs, poultry, and fish appeared regularly on the habitant's table. Vegetables of many varieties, particularly cabbages and onions, were eaten in season. "The common people in Canada," said Peter Kalm, "may be smelled when one passes by them on account of their frequent use of onions."[61] Apples, plums, and pears were plentiful in the fall. The forest yielded berries and nuts as well as some game.[62] A few habitants could afford French wines; many more drank Canadian beer or cider, or Canadian bouillon, a decoction brewed from spruce tips which was used from time to time in the fur trade.[63] The habitants were usually described as tall, strong, and vigorous, attributes which were as much the reflection of diet as of an invigorating climate and an out-of-doors existence.

In the seventeenth century, the habitants' clothes were usually made of material imported from France rather than of furs or skins.[64] Several governors and intendants urged the king's ministers to send hemp and flax seed and many more sheep to Canada, because Canadians were forced to buy French cloth and thread at exorbitant prices.[65] By the beginning of the eighteenth century some habitants were making "quelques mauvaises étoffes," and when French officials complained that this manufacture was detrimental to French interests, the Intendant Jacques Raudot retorted that "la moitié des habitants seroient sans chemises" if weaving in Canada were forbidden.[66] Domestic weaving was principally hampered by a shortage of wool or flax. When Madame de Repentigny attempted to establish a small weaving industry in 1709, she experimented with nettles, bark, buffalo hair, and even with the fluff from cottonwood flowers.[67] Clothing in those days can hardly have been elegant. Most habitants had one much-patched outfit made of imported cloth, some wore skins or furs, and a few wore cloth which had been woven in Canada. In summer, children were usually very scantily clad, even virtually naked.[68] Later in the eighteenth century when sheep and flax became common, much more cloth was made in Canada. There were spinning wheels in most farmhouses, while a loom, which was much more expensive, was usually shared by several neighbors.[69] The habitant bought only some bright cloth and a bonnet for his wife, and perhaps an outfit for himself which he wore to mass or to any other event which required some display.

Most of the first farmhouses in Canada were built of posts driven in the ground (*poteaux en terre*) to make a palisade-like structure which was chinked with clay and eventually covered with boards.[70] The roof was thatch or bark, and the floor was dirt. Very soon, however, farmhouses began to be built of roughly squared logs laid horizontally to meet at rebated corners. Some farmhouses of this French *pièce sur pièce* construction were covered with planks and others were plastered. Inside, floor and ceiling were usually planks. Towards the end of the seventeenth and throughout the eighteenth century, many farmhouses were built of beams and stone (*en colombage*), a type of architecture which resembled Tudor in construction if seldom in finish or elegance. Other houses were made entirely of stone. Their walls were two feet thick, windows were deeply inset and usually covered with paper or parchment,[71] floor and ceiling were planks, and the roof was thatch or boards. Whatever the construction, these farmhouses were rarely more than thirty-five to forty feet long and twenty-five to thirty feet wide. There was always an attic above the ground floor and often a cellar below.

Inside the farmhouse there were usually one or two bedrooms and a kitchen which opened into a dining and sitting room. The habitant, his wife, and the baby had a bedroom to themselves. The other children slept in two large beds in the other bedroom or upstairs in the attic, which on a cold winter night was the warmest part of the house. There was at least one large stone or clay fireplace and bake oven and, by the eighteenth century, often a heavy iron stove as well.[72] The habitant had purchased the stove, a few pots and pans, and some cutlery, but he made almost all the furniture himself.

In clearing and cultivating his land, in putting up a house, barn, and stable, in making tools and furniture, in fishing and fur trading, the habitant was both resourceful and industrious. There can be little doubt that his standard of living was substantially higher than that of most peasants in France, or that it compared favorably with living standards in rural New England. Indeed, however different they may have thought themselves to be, the habitant in Canada and the farmer in eighteenth-century New England had much in common. At one level similarities can be found in the facts that they were both small-scale, independent farmers, that with the exception of wheat they raised much the same crops, that they manured their land and rotated their crops equally little, that their buildings were similar in size and comforts if distinct in architecture, that in the older areas they faced increasing population pressures on the land and the contraction of farms. At another level there was a common zest for profit. If the conclusions from the study of one frontier township in mid-eighteenth-century Connecticut can be taken as representative, pioneer farmers in eighteenth-century New England appear to have been inveterate speculators who were involved both on and off the farm in an "almost frantic pursuit of a wide variety of projects or schemes." [73] Much the same can be said of the habitant, who was often trading land and developing a farm, who was involved in one way or another with the fur trade, who was fishing and occasionally cutting timber. The comparison of the habitant and the New England farmer can be pushed too far, but it cannot be too strongly emphasized that the habitant in Canada during the French regime was anything but a member of a docile and unenterprising peasantry. If he was not rich the explanation lies less in a lack of drive than in the absence of a large, accessible market for his agricultural produce, and in a legal system which stressed the common good over individual initiative.

Throughout the seventeenth century and into the eighteenth, the habitant's way of life was in a state of flux. Land changed hands rapidly: farming held little more attraction than fishing, and often a good deal less than the fur trade. A man was a farmer one year, a trader the next, and often a fisherman on the side. He moved freely within the colony, often selling a roture in one area to take up land in another, and he left the colony just as easily, although participation in the fur trade was almost as active along the lower St. Lawrence as in the Ottawa country. Denonville complained that every house in Canada had become a cabaret, and implied that their owners were selling alcohol to Indians who came to the colony; [74] and some officials denounced the immorality and lawlessness of the habitants almost as frequently as they attacked the coureurs de bois. Later in the eighteenth century, to be sure, most habitants settled into an agricultural routine. A moderately prosperous rural society was emerging, and as land became scarce in older areas near the towns, an attachment to the family land was developing. By this time the fur trade had spread far into the interior, and probably most of its practitioners had forsaken an agricultural life for good. If two social groups were emerging,[75] it is nonetheless clear that the habitants remained a vigorous, independent people who differed in occupation but probably little in temperament from the coureurs de bois.

9 : The Seigneurie as an Economic and Social Unit

ONE of the most persistent claims made for the seigneurial system in Canada is that it constituted an important unit of social and economic organization. "It served," wrote William Bennett Munro, in agreeing with Benjamin Sulte on the point, "as no other social organization could have served to give the colony a defensive strength against her encircling enemies." Guy Frégault suggests that the system was introduced into Canada "en vue de doter le pays de l'organisation économico-sociale," and that this was what distinguished it from the system in France. Thomas Gérin refers to the seigneurie as "the social unit of New France," while Gérard Filteau and Lionel Groulx, among others, have pictured the curé and the seigneur walking side by side as the kindly shepherds of their flock.[1]

Statements such as these have been based on a conception of seigneurialism in France in the late Middle Ages or in Canada in the early nineteenth century, rather than on the analysis of evidence from the French regime. Beyond the X's or Christian names at the bottom of roture contracts or deeds of sale, almost nothing was written by the habitants, and without this documentary evidence it is arguable that an understanding of the habitant's attitudes towards his seigneur can only be approached deductively. There is, however, some slight evidence in the previous chapters, which have shown that in approximately half of the lay seigneuries in the colony seigneurial control was divided, that absenteeism was fairly common, that until thirty or forty families were settled in a seigneurie the seigneur was likely to lose money, and that because the seigneur could do little to speed the flow of settlers to his seigneurie he seldom bothered to try. His role in the process of colonization was to grant land to those who applied for it. If Munro, Frégault, and the others are right, the seigneurs apparently came to life once settlers were on their land, and organized the habitants in sturdy, interdependent communities which could have provided Canada with that "defensive strength against her encircling enemies." None of the evidence about the seigneurs which has been presented in earlier chapters suggests that this sudden change took place, but the evidence is fragmentary. Furthermore, a conception of a seigneurie as a unit of social and economic organization may have crossed the Atlantic in the minds of immigrants and survived in Canada in spite of the seigneurs' indifference.

More evidence is certainly required in order to develop an inductive analysis of some of the habitants' attitudes, and without the record of diaries and letters, it may be helpful to turn to that provided by rural settlement patterns. Many have pointed out that settlement patterns reflect and influence the social and economic structure of society, and if this is valid, then these patterns must constitute to some degree a visible shell of social and economic organization. On the basis of information in the censuses, *aveux et dénombrements, papiers terriers,* and on many old maps, it is possible to depict in considerable detail the spatial patterns of rural settlement in Canada during the French regime. This chapter is an attempt to outline the geographical evidence, and to demonstrate its relevance to an understanding of the relationship between the habitant and his seigneur.

The principal problem in inferring the habitants' attitudes through an analysis of settlement patterns is that these patterns may not have been created by the habitants. If, for example, villages were established by the Crown, the habitants could have been forced into settlements which did not reflect their attitudes, and it would be risky to conclude that, because of the villages, the habitants' relationship with their seigneurs tended to be of one type or another. Moreover, the size, shape, and distribution of rotures influenced settlement patterns directly. In studying the relationship between settlement patterns and the degree of economic and social organization at the seigneurial level it is necessary, therefore, to examine first the official policy towards settlement within seigneuries, and then the influence of the rotures on settlement patterns. Against this background it should be possible to come to some conclusion about the degree to which the seigneuries coincided with the economic and social units which are suggested by the patterns on the land.

OFFICIAL POLICY TOWARDS SETTLEMENT WITHIN SEIGNEURIES

The Company of New France had no definite policy regarding the establishment of settlers in seigneuries. The Company was little interested in its charter obligation to bring settlers from France, and even less in what happened to them when they arrived. In 1662 or 1663 someone associated with the Company suggested that it bring settlers every year from French poorhouses, divide them into communities of ten or twelve people, supply each community with provisions and tools, and make each responsible for clearing a specified amount of land,[2] a plan which by-passed the seigneurs altogether, but which was not put forward until the Company's charter was about to be revoked.

Canada had been in royal hands for only a month when the king issued a decree which required all habitants in Canada either to clear their lands within six months of the publication of his order or to give them up.[3] The king and his ministers in France were convinced that concessions were much too large, that they could not possibly be cleared, and that they left the settlers isolated in the middle of their land so that it was easy for the Iroquois "à leur couper la gorge," as the king put it. He told the special commissioner whom he sent to Canada two months later that the colony could not be solidly established until its habitants were collected in *bourgades* and that to this end he was prepared to begin settlement over again by withdrawing all the land that had been conceded in rotures and reconceding it around a number of villages. The commissioner was to persuade the principal men in the colony that this was the best course and, if need be, to inform them that His Majesty was considering an order revoking all earlier concessions.[4]

This drastic order was never issued. However the decree requiring habitants either to clear all their land within six months or to forfeit it created sufficient stir, for the habitants who were already in the colony would lose all their cleared land and farm buildings if the decree were strictly enforced. The governor and bishop agreed to make sure, as far as they could, that the king's instructions were followed in the future, but declared that they had no intention of forcing habitants to give up their holdings.[5] The king, who probably realized that his ruling had been hasty, did not press the point; nor did he forget it. In 1665 he advised Talon that the colony would not be safe until the habitants were regrouped in villages, and instructed Talon to devise some means to bring about this salutary change.[6]

Talon reported shortly after arriving in the colony that he planned to establish a village, and before the end of 1666 he had three under way on land which he had appropriated from the Jesuits.[7] Charlesbourg and Bourg Royal were laid out as squares of approximately forty arpents a side with a small common in the center, and Petit Auvergne was a similar square sliced in half. Land was divided so that each habitant received forty square arpents and frontage on the common. With buildings grouped around the common such a settlement would be relatively compact, and yet each man would live on his own farm. Talon planned to supply his settlers with provisions for a year, to give each settler two cleared arpents when he arrived and require him to clear two more for a later settler. He also proposed to sprinkle older habitants among the newcomers who would quickly learn from the experience of the old. For Talon the advantages of grouping settlement in such villages were obvious: the habitants would be safer from the Iroquois, the ministrations of curé, judge, and doctor would be more easily provided, and the common would be near at hand. When blacksmiths, carpenters, masons, and other artisans were established in the villages, the habitants would not have to go to the towns in search of their services.[8]

Talon's villages were intended to be models of a type of settlement, and he was probably confident that once the advantages of village life had been demonstrated, seigneurs would quickly follow his lead. There is no doubt of his and the king's position—they were solidly in favor of villages—but the potentially disruptive decree of 1663 was allowed to lapse in favor of persuasion and example. Probably all the seigneurs in the colony knew that Talon was experimenting with villages near Quebec, and that the village was the type of settlement he favored. In granting new seigneuries Talon may well have offered their recipients some remarks on the subject, but nothing was formalized. The seigneurs remained as free as before to concede land as they wished.

Although Talon was the only royal official to concede land for the establishment of villages, the village question troubled many of the king's ministers. Soon after Talon left the colony, Frontenac reported that most of the houses in Beaupré, Beauport, and the Ile d'Orléans were at least four arpents apart, and urged that the colony would not be solidly established until land was set aside for villages.[9] Urgency was lent to the matter by the Second Iroquois War. In 1688 Denonville and Champigny told the minister that it was "indispensablement nécessaire" to gather settlers into villages because otherwise they were exposed to the smallest war parties.[10] Three years later Champigny wrote that the formation of villages was critical for the well-being of the colony,[11] and a report by an unknown author recommended ordering the habitants into villages and razing their buildings if they did not comply.[12] To such statements the minister in France would reply that the king had always considered the matter of the utmost importance, but that it was necessary to act "avec une extrême prudence," and convince the habitants that it was to their own advantage to settle in villages. No one was to be forced into a village against his will,[13] and in general this attitude prevailed throughout the Second Iroquois War. Although the western half of the colony became a series of armed camps in the face of the desperate military situation, the habitants never thought of these camps as more than temporary.

Most of the ministers' concern to establish habitants in villages had been generated by the Iroquois, and with this threat largely diminished by 1700, the matter disappeared from the official correspondence. Concessions continued to be made in some of the few sites set aside for villages in the colony, but apart from the ordinance of 1745 which forbade buildings on holdings smaller than one and one-half arpents in frontage [14] there is no record that the king's officials made any more attempts to influence the pattern of settlement within seigneuries. It has been suggested by Marcel Trudel that the ordinance of 1745 made village agglomerations impossible,[15] but this was neither its purpose nor, for the most part, its result. The ordinance was designed to prevent rotures from being divided rather than to prevent villages from being formed, and all established villages were declared exempt from its provisions. The governor and intendant had to approve new villages, and they would certainly have turned down an application to give village status to a row of houses along the front of several fragmented rotures, but they had no objection to a compact village in which each villager would have a small plot of approximately one square arpent and his fields somewhere else in the seigneurie. Eight such applications were received before the end of the French regime and passed automatically.[16] The ordinance of 1745 did prevent the straggling line of houses along the river or road from tightening beyond a certain point; but, as long as proper application was made, a seigneur would have encountered no opposition from the officials if he had set aside ten, twenty, or fifty square arpents, divided the land into plots, and established a village.

ROTURES AND SETTLEMENT PATTERNS

Habitants usually settled near the river or road which was the line of attachment for the rotures on which they lived. The distance between farmhouses depended on the width of the rotures. If all rotures were the same width and if each was inhabited, the settlement pattern in a seigneurie consisted of a row of nearly evenly spaced houses along the river, and successive rows along the fronts of successive ranges. Figure 9–1, in which the farmhouses have been added to the map of rotures in a hypothetical seigneurie, shows the degree of regularity of which the system was theoretically capable.

Settlement patterns in rural Canada were never as regular as depicted in Figure 9–1. Rotures were not always the same width, nor equally suitable for farming, nor the property of one man; some ranges were quite irregular; and the river or road was not an inevitable magnet. There were gaps in the lines where the land was uncultivable, where one man held two or three rotures of frontage, or where more rotures had been conceded than there were people to settle them. In some places the spacing between farmhouses narrowed when a number of rotures in succession were inhabited and a few of them, perhaps, were subdivided into two or three inhabited slices (as long as each slice contained one and one-half arpents of frontage). These shortened distances between houses, depending largely on whether the inheritors settled down to farm or sold their fractions, did not reflect a desire either to be closer to neighbors or to be near a certain service; the habitant living on a fraction of a roture would have been delighted to acquire the rest. Smaller slices of land were being settled, and consequently farm buildings were closer together.

The long, thin roture did not prevent the habitants from living in villages, but a cadastral pattern which suited linear settlement made compact villages awkward. Where land had been conceded in rotures the lines of settlement may have thickened in places, but the formation of a compact village was impossible unless the seigneur bought up several rotures and subdivided twenty or thirty arpents along the front, or

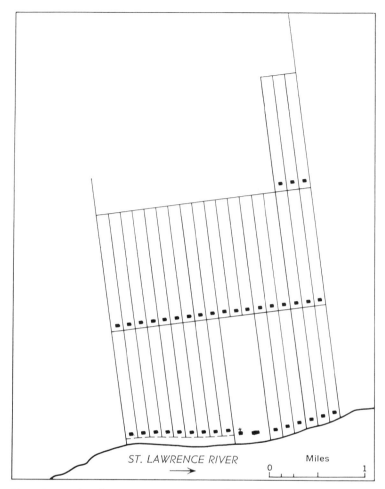

Fig. 9–1.—Settlement pattern in a hypothetical seigneurie.

subdivided a portion of the common or domain. Without the assurance that villagers would be forthcoming he was unlikely to do this. The establishment of a village in a settled area involved, therefore, a representation by the habitants to the seigneur, his approval of their request for a village, and then the acquisition of an appropriate piece of land. When in the 1750's eight seigneurs applied for permission to establish villages, they pointed out that villages were necessary "pour la commodité des habitants," [17] who likely had approached their seigneurs on the matter beforehand. Fifty years earlier in Chambly the habitants had requested that land be set aside as a common in a spot where they might eventually have a village, although theirs was the only instance of such foresight.[18] The difficulty of finding land for villages after rotures had been conceded had been foreseen in 1672 by Frontenac, who pointed out then that it would be necessary to buy up land which had already been granted, and recommended setting land aside every league and a half for future villages.[19] His advice was not taken, and although villages could still be formed, a fairly strong initial push directed by the seigneur was needed to launch them.

SETTLEMENT PATTERNS IN RURAL CANADA

Rural settlements in Canada can be divided for convenience into four types: villages and hamlets, isolated farmsteads, straggling villages (line or shoestring villages), and *côtes*. *Village* as used here refers to a compact settlement of not more than five hundred people in which there were several commercial and service functions. A *hamlet* was also a compact agglomeration but one with a smaller population (usually under a hundred) and fewer functions. The distinction between hamlets and villages is one of size; the precise categorical boundary is inconsequential. A farmstead is considered isolated when more than a quarter of a mile separates it from its nearest neighbor. The *straggling village* refers to a long line of closely spaced farmhouses, each located on an individual farm. During the French regime *côte* meant a line of settlement along the St. Lawrence, a tributary, or a road. As used here the word is given a sharper focus to mean a line of settlement which was short and isolated enough so that its inhabitants thought of the settlement as a distinct community.

There were six villages—Charlesbourg, La Prairie de la Magdeleine, Terrebonne, Boucherville, Pointe aux Trembles, and Verchères—in Canada at the end of the French regime. Talon laid out Charlesbourg near Quebec in 1665 and 1666; the Jesuits set aside land for La Prairie de la Magdeleine in the early 1670's; Pierre Boucher founded Boucherville at the same time; Terrebonne appeared sometime after 1710; Pointe aux Trembles and Verchères may have existed as early as the 1670's although there is no record of either until the eighteenth century. Five of these six villages were near Montreal. La Prairie de la Magdeleine, Boucherville, and Verchères were on the south shore opposite the Ile de Montréal;

Pointe aux Trembles was on the island a few miles northeast of the city; and Terrebonne was on the mainland to the north.

These six villages are shown in Figure 9–2. Boucherville, Verchères, and Pointe aux Trembles were compact agglomerations each of which had grown up in an area set aside by the seigneur for the purpose. The villagers held small plots which had been conceded along a grid of streets. Their fields, if they had any, were not contiguous with their village residences. La Prairie de la Magdeleine was also on land set aside for a compact village, but it had spread out along the road to Chambly, and the houses in a crescent east of the church may have been located on individual farms. Charlesbourg had been laid out around a central common, and the villagers were originally intended to live on their own farms around its perimeter. Well before 1760, however, the common had been divided up into lots and two streets had been added to the east. At the conquest most of the villagers lived on small plots, although the buildings around the village periphery were all on individual farms. Terrebonne spread along the river-front road and a short branch road leading to the church. Settlement north of the principal road was probably along the front of ordinary rotures, whereas the area between road and church was divided into small plots.

Each of the villages was the center of a parish, and the three villages in lay seigneuries were the places of residence of the seigneurs. A church was prominent in each village. As Charlesbourg and La Prairie de la Magdeleine belonged to the Jesuits and Pointe aux Trembles to the Sulpicians, these villages did not contain seigneurial manors, but the manor in Boucherville was fifty-two feet long, thirty feet wide, and two stories high, and was easily the most impressive house in the village. The manors in Verchères and Terrebonne were smaller.

Each village was a small service center for the surrounding agricultural population, as well as the abode of a number of farmers. The *aveu et dénombrement* for Boucherville in 1723 lists five bakeries, a general store, a store selling wheat, four storage sheds for grain, and a forge.[20] The store probably supplied most of the goods which the habitants in the seigneurie purchased. Their surplus grain apparently passed through the village, and their tools were repaired at the forge. Probably there were a harness-maker, a mason, and a carpenter as well, artisans whose trade did not require special buildings, and who would likely be missed by the *aveu et*

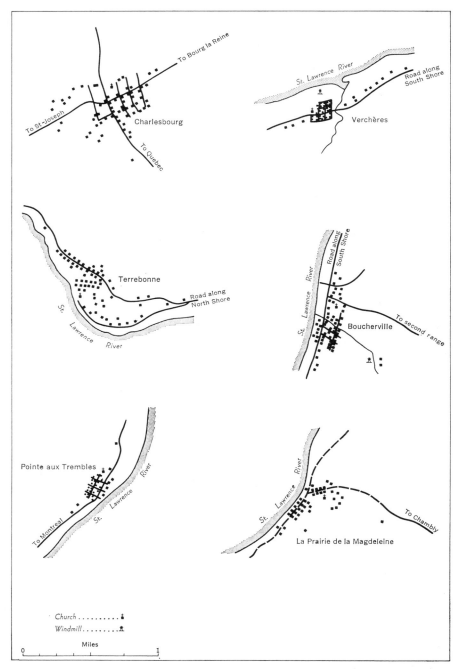

Fig. 9–2.—Villages in Canada in 1760. Based on map prepared for Governor Murray, 1760–62 (National Archives of Canada).

dénombrement. The role of five bakeries in the village is something of a mystery, for bread was usually homemade. Each of the bakeries may have been very small or, more likely, have been engaged primarily in buying and selling grain and flour. As there were thirty-two houses in the village—more, even with the addition of several artisans, than were needed for the nonfarming population—some villagers undoubtedly worked fields nearby. With twenty-five kitchen gardens, two barns, six horse stables, and five cow stables in the village, the functions of village and countryside clearly overlapped. The village was integrated into the structure of a rural economy which was based on wheat, and apparently made certain indispensable services more accessible than they would otherwise have been. Even if the seigneur's influence had been negligible, the life of the seigneurie would move around the village because so many of its important ingredients were provided there. Of the other villages, Pointe aux Trembles was the service center for a small fraction of the Ile de Montréal; Charlesbourg, for perhaps half of Notre Dame des Anges; and the other three, for the seigneuries in which they were located. That each of these villages appears to have been a useful service center makes the fact that there were only six villages in Canada in 1760 even more curious.

The scarcity of villages cannot be attributed to a system of land-granting which did not provide for village sites, because well before 1700 land had been set aside for a number of villages which never developed as such. There were two village sites in Beaupré,[21] one in Beauport,[22] Talon's three in Notre Dame des Anges, several near Montreal and, in a slightly different class, the camps between Trois-Rivières and Montreal which served as temporary villages during the worst of the Iroquois attacks. The village sites in Beaupré and Beauport had not been settled before the conquest, while most of the settlers whom Talon placed in his village sites moved on within a year. Although the rotures within Charlesbourg, Bourg Royal, and Petit Auvergne were eventually cleared, Charlesbourg, the only village in Notre Dame des Anges during the French regime, did not appear until the eighteenth century. Little is known about the early development of the village sites near Montreal, although with the possible exception of Boucherville where more than twenty concessions in the village were granted in 1673, there were no villages in the Government of Montreal before 1700. All the camps disappeared as soon as the Iroquois threat was gone. In short, village sites were available; and the king, his officials, and many seigneurs in the colony were eager that they be settled. Undoubtedly villages did not appear in the seventeenth century because the habitants would not live in them.

In 1689 a report was sent to France in which its anonymous author remarked wistfully that "There is no doubt that . . . the people of this country, neither docile nor easy to govern, are very difficult to constrain, for they like freedom and no domination at all. . . ."[23] Herein lies the principal explanation for the habitants' aversion to the village. In their eyes, the village meant supervision by the seigneur, the curé, or even the intendant. They may have remembered villages and seigneurs in France, and concluded, on the basis of their French experience, that it was wise to put some distance between themselves and both.[24] Certainly Canada was a new and empty land which offered freedom and at first not a great deal more, and the habitants quickly sized up the potential of their new environment. The Intendant de Meulles put the matter most unflatteringly in claiming that immigrants had come to Canada to "se mettre à couvert de leurs crimes," and betook themselves to isolated spots to indulge in their "habitudes vícieuses."[25] For the most part this was nonsense, but the fondness for the freedom which a new land offered was real enough.

Among other things, independence from the traditional channels of authority made it much easier for the habitants to participate in the fur trade, which, it must be remembered, was the principal commercial activity in the colony until the turn of the century, if not until the conquest. Unauthorized expeditions into the woods were forbidden many times over, and there were strict regulations dealing with the conduct of the trade along the St. Lawrence. These regulations seldom bothered the habitants who might have listened at the front of the church on Sunday to another denunciation of the coureurs de bois, and have been well on the way to the fur country Monday morning—but it was just as well not to live too close to the authorities. Others traded illegally with Indians who came to the colony. Frontenac, who could be as perspicacious as anyone in the colony, saw the problem clearly. It was desirable, he told the minister, to unite everyone in villages, but this would never be done until the habitants were prevented from trading with the Indians except in certain supervised places.[26] However neither he nor his successors were able to enforce such a reform.

After 1700 the relative importance of the fur trade declined, and as Canadian seigneurs proved to be anything but domineering, the habitants' suspicion of the village waned. Some of the few sites that had been set aside for villages began to be developed, and shortly after the turn of the century there was a request from the habitants in Chambly for land for a future village. Fifty years later there were the eight applications for villages mentioned earlier, an indication of the habitants' increasing interest in this type of settlement. The arguments were similar in each application: artisans could be established in the village so that the habitants would not have to go to the nearest town to find them, merchandise of all sorts could be sold in the village, and grain could be collected there so that the village would serve as an entrepôt between farm and town.[27] The proposed villages were to assume the role that, for several decades, Boucherville had been filling in its seigneurie.

As none of these eight villages was established before the conquest, it cannot be said that the declining hostility towards the village was replaced by any real enthusiasm for its creation. Most habitants were quite content living on their own farms, had never considered living anywhere else, nor apparently had been very inconvenienced by occasional trips to town for supplies and services. Once the long, thin rotures had been conceded, a certain push was needed to create villages, but if the habitants had been determined to have them, villages would have appeared quickly. Another difficulty was pointed out in 1694 by Frontenac and Champigny, who told the minister that if the habitants were grouped in villages they would be isolated from their farms by the many small tributaries of the St. Lawrence which carts could not cross.[28] In the eighteenth century roads improved and there were ferries charging small tolls at all the major river crossings, although before these improvements transportation across the grain of the rotures was rarely as difficult as Frontenac and Champigny suggested. Moreover, the villages which were proposed in the 1750's were to be service centers rather than domiciles for farmers, and whatever the transportation problem, the habitant would have had less difficulty travelling to a nearby village to buy or to sell than to a town many miles away.

That such service centers did not become more common is a reflection of the fact that, however useful they would have been, they were certainly not indispensable. The habitant's purchases were few—salt, molasses, perhaps a little wine, cloth, a few tools, nails, the metal parts for his cart, kitchen pots, powder and shot for his gun, and occasionally some livestock. Otherwise he was self-sufficient. He may have enjoyed occasional trips to Quebec, Trois-Rivières, or Montreal; if he did not, peddlers in the eighteenth century could supply most of his needs. The town markets for agricultural produce were strong attractions, but the village itself was less a market than a collecting point. Without it the habitant had to take his produce to town, or sell it to a merchant who came to his farm. One way or the other he always managed, for there is no indication that grain ever piled up because the habitants could not market it. Because settlement spread out along the transportation routes, it was relatively easy for the habitant to keep in contact with the town. Moreover, there was undoubtedly some specialization of function within his line of settlement. If he could not repair a broken cart wheel, one of his neighbors probably could. Another had a forge and did odd jobs for the habitants nearby. The straggling line of farmhouses, neither tightly agglomerated nor very dispersed, made this type of loose association easy, and to the degree that the straggling line included some of the characteristics of agglomerated settlement, villages were redundant.

Hamlets were even more rare. The four hamlets in Canada in 1760—Saint-Joachim in Beaupré, Longueuil in the seigneurie of Longueuil opposite Montreal, Chambly on the Richelieu, and Pointe Claire on the south shore of the Ile de Montréal—are shown in Figure 9–3. Saint-Joachim was one of the two sites which the Séminaire de Québec had set aside for villages in Beaupré, but it had never grown larger than a marginal hamlet. The other three, which were also on land allocated for villages, were larger than Saint-Joachim, but cannot be considered true villages. Three of the hamlets were close to a church; Chambly, which was not, probably had some special relationship with the neighboring fort. The Séminaire de Québec operated a store in Saint-Joachim, and there may have been a carpenter or blacksmith, or some other artisans in each hamlet. Although these four hamlets were small service centers for a few habitants, the hamlet as a settlement type in Canada was altogether insignificant.

The habitant did not turn to the most dispersed type of agricultural settlement, the isolated farmstead, as an alternative to the village or hamlet. There were some isolated farmsteads, not the "méchantes cabanes" in the woods which Governor Denonville suspected of sheltering debauchers,[29] but farmhouses which were set apart because they were

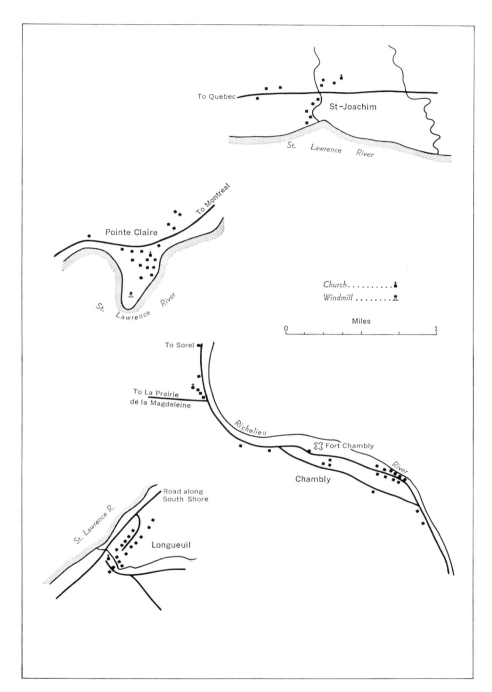

Fig. 9–3.—Hamlets in Canada in 1760.

the first in a new area, or because the land in adjacent rotures was unfit for cultivation. If of the former type, their isolation was short-lived, while there were never many of the latter.

Instead the habitants settled along the transportation routes in those lines of settlement which many have described as continuous straggling villages. While the concept of the continuous straggling village has been somewhat overdrawn, often there were houses every hundred or two hundred yards for a number of miles along the river. Figure 9–4 shows two such lines, one along the shore of the St. Lawrence in the seigneuries of L'Assomption and Saint-Sulpice, the other in the seigneuries of Terrebonne and Lachenaie. There were others on the Ile Jésus, the Ile de Montréal, the Ile d'Orléans, and in many other seigneuries.

The straggling village ended where it abutted on a stretch of unproductive land, a number of undeveloped rotures, or a tributary of the St. Lawrence, but rarely at the point of intersection with a seigneurial boundary. Each of the lines of houses shown in Figure 9–4 was crossed by a seigneurial boundary, but the lines offer no indication of the location of these boundaries. The Ile d'Orléans had been divided in the proprietary years into a number of arrière-fiefs each of which from the habitants' point of view constituted a separate seigneurie. As early as 1689 settlement ringed the island with only a few interruptions, none of which was the obvious corollary of a boundary between arrière-fiefs.

Unless the lines were interrupted by villages or hamlets, there were no obvious foci or divisions within the line where, as far as it is possible to judge from scanty evidence, one community ended and another began. Occasionally church, mill, and manor were all located on the seigneur's domain, although usually they were well separated. Churches were located at central points in the parishes, gristmills along streams or on promontories (if they were windmills) and spaced roughly forty to fifty families apart, and manors wherever the original seigneurs had set aside their domains. The part-time farmers who operated forges or did some carpentry on the side were scattered here and there along the lines. Thus in a straggling village several miles long, services usually spread out along the line, and each commanded a distinctive service area. The church served the parish, which was perhaps two seigneuries in extent; the manor received dues from the inhabitants of one—or a fraction of one—seigneurie; the gristmill received grain from forty or fifty habitants living, perhaps, in half a seigneurie; and the part-time farmer who was also a blacksmith or a carpenter did odd jobs for his immediate neighbors.

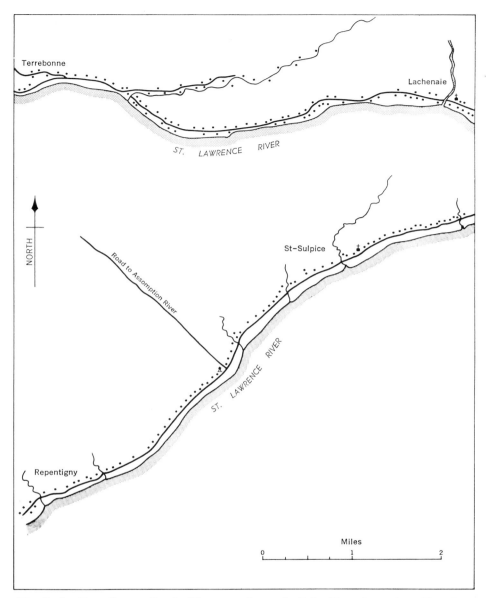

Fig. 9–4.—Two "straggling" villages at the end of the French regime. Based on map prepared for Governor Murray, 1760–62 (National Archives of Canada).

The côte was shorter than these extended lines, and was a distinct community set apart by breaks in the line of settlement. A large côte such as Sainte-Anne (Fig. 9–5) resembled a loosely knit village except for the fact that probably all the inhabitants of Sainte-Anne other than the curé were farmers who lived on their own farms. Saint-Joseph, a sprawling settlement a mile west of Charlesbourg, was a more dispersed côte which in the eighteenth century was known as a village. However it did not contain a church, a gristmill, or a manor, and probably not a store; it was simply a loose grouping of farmers each living close to this neighbors because of the shape of the Canadian roture. In the 1740's the Séminaire de Québec conceded a second range behind Saint-Joachim, and by 1760 there was a cluster of houses there. The settlement was isolated from any other, it had a distinctive name, and its inhabitants undoubtedly identified themselves with it. If asked where they were from, they would have replied that they came from Saint-Féréol in Beaupré, or from Saint-Féréol behind Saint-Joachim. There were dozens of similar settlements in Canada.

Côtes were usually created by irregularities in the size, shape, or orientation of rotures and ranges. Whenever a second range was settled a distinct côte usually emerged. In time it might have become part of a long line of settlement, but if the second range in the adjacent seigneurie began at a different distance from the St. Lawrence because concessions in the first range of the two seigneuries had not been of the same length, there was a line of discontinuity at the seigneurial boundary which would preserve distinct côtes in the second ranges of small, adjacent seigneuries. Short rotures like those within the fourth range of the seigneurie of Sillery (Fig. 7–4) could also lead to the development of a côte. And when the orientation of a line of rotures suddenly changed, as for example at a tributary of the St. Lawrence, the line of settlement was broken and the limit of a côte was often fixed.

Frequently there were a number of côtes within one seigneurie. At the end of the French regime there were five in Notre Dame des Anges, and at least three in Longueuil (Fig. 9–6) each just as clear a unit on the land as the village of Charlesbourg or the hamlet of Longueuil. Each of the côtes in Notre Dame des Anges was referred to in the seventeenth and eighteenth centuries as a village with a distinctive name, and those in Longueuil must have been similarly designated. The habitant might have had to leave the côte to market his grain, to attend mass, or to pay the

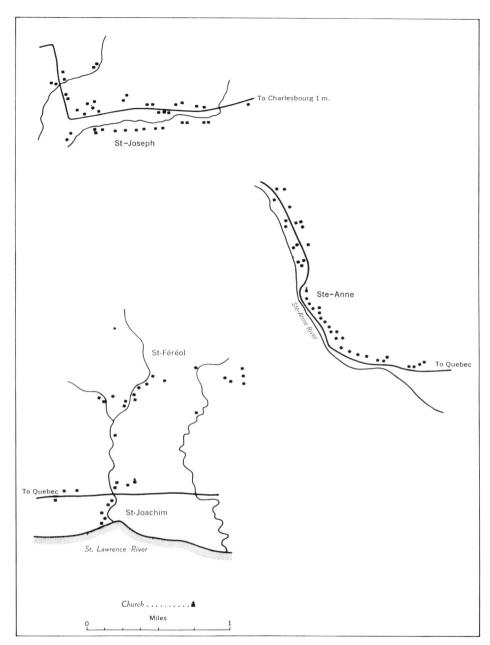

Fig. 9–5.—Three côtes in 1760.

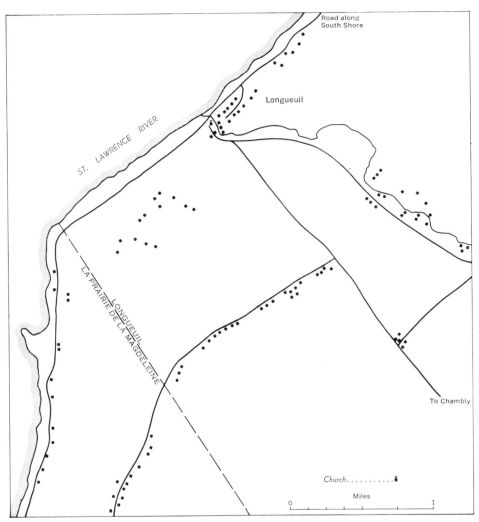

Fig. 9–6.—Settlement in parts of the seigneuries of Longueuil and La Prairie de la Magdeleine in 1760.

seigneurial dues, but the côte was his home or, perhaps more accurately, his neighborhood. He knew each of the inhabitants, and may have relied on some of them for skills which he did not possess.

ROADS, PARISHES, AND SEIGNEURIAL COURTS

Before summing up the evidence about the seigneuries as social units, it is necessary to consider briefly the spatial arrangement of roads, parishes, and seigneurial courts. Although the river was probably the principal transportation route in Canada throughout the French regime, roads in settled areas were quickly built. There were inevitable altercations over the route these roads were to follow and over the division of responsibility for their construction, but they were built.[30] Carts bogged down on rainy days, bridges washed out now and then, and the habitant who took exception to a road which crossed his roture may have felled some trees across the right of way. However, not long after a seigneurie had been settled, any habitant within it could usually have travelled by ox-cart from his own farm to the gristmill, and consequently to any other farm in the seigneurie, including the seigneurial domain.

If roads be taken as a unifying element for the seigneurie, it must be noted that long before the end of the French regime the road along the front of a range always continued into the adjacent seigneurie. Within each seigneurie, it is true, at least one road perpendicular to the axis of settlement connected interior ranges with settlements along the St. Lawrence. When there were several ranges an irregular grid appeared; the main roads ran parallel to the river and followed the lines of settlement, and smaller seigneurial roads crossed them at right angles. It was possible to travel with equal ease from one range or from one seigneurie to another. Certainly the first roads built in a seigneurie led to the gristmill, and the connections with roads in adjacent seigneuries may have been filled in a few years later. Nevertheless, long before a through road connected Montreal and Quebec in the 1730's, there were easy road connections between most adjacent seigneuries. Neither churches nor manors were obvious foci in the rural road network.

In the social organization of Canada the parish church played a special role. The church was the one place where many habitants came regularly together. Friends exchanged gossip after the mass, young people met, and an habitant who had some land or even a cow to sell might have made an announcement. Official edicts and ordinances were read and posted. The members of a parish attended mass every week, and this steady contact undoubtedly created a bond which made the parish a larger unit of social organization than most côtes.

Because attendance at mass was insisted upon, it was important that the church should be accessible to everyone in the parish. Often there were complaints that the church was too far away, and in 1721 an inquiry was conducted into the matter.[31] Representations were heard in each parish, and habitants were assigned to one or another on the basis of the findings. Ideally the church was to be located in the center of a parish of 200 to 500 souls, and new parishes were established or old ones divided roughly according to these criteria.[32] Consequently in large seigneuries like the Ile d'Orléans, Beaupré, or the Ile de Montréal, there were a number of parishes, while several seigneuries with small populations were grouped in one. A clearly differentiated line of settlement along a tributary was usually organized into one parish even if it crossed two or three seigneuries. Where there were no obvious groups, the seigneurial boundary often served as the boundary of a parish, and if the seigneurie contained roughly 200 to 500 people, seigneurie and parish might coincide. In most cases, however, parish and seigneurie were not identical areas; when they were, the social fibre of the latter was inadvertently strengthened. Much more usually the seigneurie was divided into several parishes, or became a fraction of one parish. It is incorrect to assume that the social cohesion of the parish was shared by the seigneurie because parishes fitted into the seigneurial framework.

By the terms of their seigneurial contracts, many seigneurs were entitled to dispense *haute, moyenne, et basse justice* within their seigneuries, that is, to judge all offenses except those committed against the royal person or property.[33] To discharge this role the seigneur was expected to provide a courtroom in or adjacent to his manor house, as well as those other accoutrements of justice, a bailiff, court clerk, crier, and prison. However, Canadian seigneurs never provided all of these men and facilities, and only a few exercised any of their judicial prerogatives. Because there were relatively few habitants in any Canadian seigneurie, the administration of justice was an expense for the seigneur rather than the source of revenue which it was in France. None of the judgments handed down by Canadian seigneurs were irrevocable. By the 1680's there were royal courts in Quebec, Trois-Rivières, and Montreal, and habitants could appeal to these courts, to the Conseil Supérieur in Quebec, or to the intendant. That appeals of seigneurial judgments rarely reached these higher courts is indication of the fact that very few seigneurs bothered to give them. All habitants could take their cases without charge directly to the intendant, and he or the royal courts handled almost all disputes. Here and there seigneurs exercised their right to dispense *basse justice* (i.e., the right to judge petty civil and criminal cases which could be fined no more than sixty and ten sols respectively) in order to enforce the collection of seigneurial dues, but almost all Canadian seigneurs allowed the administration of justice, which was a buttress of seigneurial strength in France, to pass out of their hands because this right was an expensive nuisance in an underpopulated land.

THE SEIGNEURIE AS AN ECONOMIC UNIT

The lines of settlement which grew up during the French regime along the banks of the lower St. Lawrence reflected little, if at all, the seigneuries through which they extended. The seigneurs' manors were not foci on the lines; seigneurial boundaries seldom interrupted them. Services were spread out in such a way that each usually had a distinctive service area which rarely was coterminous with seigneurial boundaries. There were only six villages in the colony, of which three probably were service centers for their seigneuries. The Séminaire de Québec operated a general store in its seigneurie of Beaupré, but this store may have been the only one of its kind (as it is not clear whether the general store in Boucherville was operated by the seigneur). Seigneuries in Canada were certainly not cohesive economic units, and probably few if any seigneurs had ever tried to make them that.

This is not to say that those seigneurs who granted exceptionally large or small rotures, who induced their censitaires to experiment with new crops, or who provided exceptional milling facilities did not influence the living standards of their censitaires. In 1739 average living standards in Beaupré appear to have been higher than in nearby Notre Dame des Anges, principally because most of the rotures in Notre Dame des Anges were exceptionally small.[34] The censuses picture a very uneven distribution of hemp, a commercial crop which, for a time, the king and his ministers were eager to establish in Canada, and some seigneurs may have introduced their censitaires to such a crop. Those seigneurs who maintained their gristmills carefully, or who relaxed their demands for the annual dues when times were hard, undoubtedly made life easier for their censitaires. Otherwise there was probably nothing the most kindly and conscientious seigneur could do in this regard.

THE SEIGNEURIE AS A SOCIAL UNIT

The evidence about settlement patterns, about the relationship of the seigneurie to roads, parishes, judicial and economic functions, added to that which has already been presented about the seigneurs, leaves little doubt that the generalized picture of the seigneurie as a social unit is incorrect at least for the preconquest period. Not only had few seigneurs any interest in leading; most habitants did not want to be led. A man who could travel many miles away from the St. Lawrence colony to intercept furs did not need protection on a farm near Quebec, especially when protection might have interfered with fur trading. The new freedom was attractive to the habitants, who quickly discovered that the authorities could do little to constrict it, and this discovery reshaped the social structure. The seigneur usually collected the slight annual dues, he built a gristmill, and in a few cases he conducted a seigneurial court, but unless he was a particularly attractive personality the habitants either had very little to do with him, or treated him as one of themselves. Lacking evidence to the contrary, and using the available evidence as carefully as possible, one is forced to conclude that the social structure of the colony would not have been markedly different if all rotures had been held directly from the king, and the Canadian seigneur eliminated. To the most important aspects of the habitant's living, and to much of the geography of his settlement, seigneur and seigneurie were simply irrelevant.

10: The Seigneurial System in Canada during the French Regime

WITH long, thin fields stretching away from the St. Lawrence and straggling rows of farmhouses along either bank of the river for two hundred miles and more, the landscape of rural Canada towards the end of the French regime presented a unique face. Visitors commented on its distinctive charm, and scholars since have assumed that its distinctiveness reflected the influence of the seigneurial system. Yet, as the previous chapters have demonstrated, the seigneurial system was largely irrelevant to the early geography of Canada. The pattern of rotures was an important part of the geography of the colony, and the imprint of these early concessions is still preserved in the landscape of rural Quebec, although these patterns, the possible by-products of many methods of land-granting, were not in themselves the seigneurial system or even a reflection of it. Neither settlement patterns nor those of social and economic activity reflected the influence of the seigneurs. Seigneuries were indefinite units on the land, and seigneurial boundaries neither enclosed nor altered any of the principal patterns of human activity in the colony.

The seigneurial system could have shaped much of the geography of early Canada only if it had provided a mold first for settlement and then for the social and economic development of the colony, but there is little indication that during the French regime the system was ever such a mold. Few seigneurs profited from their concessions in a colony where seigneuries were often divided among many coseigneurs, where seigneurial dues were low and, above all, where settlers were few and far

193

between. In the seventeenth century, when there was only a handful of censitaires in their seigneuries and the land was a potential expense rather than a source of revenue, the seigneurs often neglected their holdings for years. Their censitaires often paid no dues, and may have forgotten their seigneurs' names. The censitaires, who often came to Canada with vivid memories of a seigneur's social and economic role in France and who quickly decided that illegal participation in the fur trade was the easiest road to wealth in the colony, sought to avoid most contacts with their seigneur. Their uneasiness about the seigneurs waned in the eighteenth century, to be replaced largely by indifference, and they settled into a way of life which was little influenced by him one way or the other. To be sure, in the last decades of the French regime land was becoming scarce in some seigneuries near Quebec, and the population in a number of seigneuries near either Quebec or Montreal had risen to the point where seigneurial revenues were substantial. Seigneurs took a more active interest in their concessions; without cheap land nearby, censitaires were increasingly tied to their own rotures. But Canadian seigneurs, always closely supervised by royal officials, found it difficult if not impossible to extend their influence over their censitaires, and even in these later years the seigneurial system remained in the background of Canadian life.

Certainly some seigneurs may have thought of their titles as status symbols even when the seigneuries which they controlled were wilderness tracts. Some may have viewed their titles as entrées for themselves or their sons to appointments in the army or civil service. These are matters on which the geographical evidence sheds no light, but which cannot alter the conclusion that the seigneurial system was largely irrelevant to the general social and economic development of the colony.

In the years before the English conquest a French way of life had been recast in Canada. Canada and France were 3,000 miles apart, and the connection between them was a precarious voyage of several months' duration. Royal officials brought the king's authority to Canada and administered his laws as carefully as they could when the king's wishes were known often only after long delay, and often did not apply well to a Canadian situation. Frenchmen trickled across the Atlantic to settle in Canada, but the flow was so small that French ideas and customs were not replenished through immigration. The few who did come found a vastly different land. The colony was a ribbon of settlement in a wilderness of trees, rock, and water. Land was everywhere, and it was free. The fur trade was open to all able-bodied men and offered, in addition to the revenue from beaver pelts, complete independence from the traditional channels of authority. In these circumstances a French way of life had been transformed.

The principal change in Canada was towards more individual independence. Royal officials in Quebec and Montreal could regulate the commercial life of the towns and supervise the exports and imports which passed through Quebec, but exerted relatively little control over habitants who were spread out for more than two hundred miles along the banks of the St. Lawrence, and who could vanish into the interior to escape any unwelcome pressure. The seigneurs found control expensive, and equally difficult to administer. The Church may have become the strongest of the traditional sources of authority, although its influence on the habitants is extremely difficult to assess. Certainly the habitants never quarreled with its dogmas, but its controls and interdictions may have sat lightly on them. In later years an aged Philippe de Gaspé described the Canadian habitant as "l'homme le plus indépendant du monde," [1] and if this was an exaggeration, there is no doubt that his independence was such that the seigneurial system, one of the sources of control in France, quickly disintegrated in Canada.

When Frederick Jackson Turner's frontier thesis was first vigorously challenged, ripples of the debate reached back to New France, and Turner himself wrote a short defense of the relevance of his ideas to an understanding of the French colony.[2] Turner knew little enough about New France, and his critics probably knew even less. Although the evidence in this study suggests that Turner was closer to the truth than were his critics, no one would want to reopen the argument along the earlier lines. There can be little doubt that in 1760 Canada was not an enclave of French civilization. Ideas and institutions, the way of life, had changed, and if it is helpful to consider a colony which had not moved westward in a hundred years a frontier, then the frontier was a seat of change, albeit one without a cutting edge where the metamorphic force of the wilderness reshaped European ways with particular alacrity.

Turner's contention that the change was related to the availability of free land to the west, to isolation, and to the safety valve is both shrewd and misleading when applied to Canada. Settlement in early Canada filled in a line between Quebec and Montreal; it did not expand westward. The fact that free land within seigneuries along the lower St. Lawrence was more important than free land to the west meant that those aspects of a legal system which were designed to protect scarce land, and of the social hierarchy which were based on the control of scarce land were superfluous. It also led to the development of a much more extensive agricultural system than was characteristic in north-western France. In the sense that a French king and his ministers kept an interested if often poorly informed watch on Canada, and that his representatives in the colony maintained a closer vigilance, the colony was not isolated from France. And yet the very closeness of this contact inadvertently reinforced the collapse of a French institution; it must not be forgotten that the seigneurial system disintegrated in Canada in part because a French king reduced the prerogatives and the dues to which his Canadian seigneurs were entitled. When the conquest broke this French connection, seigneurial dues and seigneurial influence probably began to increase, and they might have done so long before if the seigneurs had been more isolated from French authority. There would not have been an explosion had safety valves in the direction of the Great Lakes or the American colonies not existed, but the alternative to farming and the ready escape from authority which they provided were fundamental ingredients in the Canadian situation.

And yet, Canada bore little resemblance to the unruly American settlements in the Appalachian valleys in the middle of the eighteenth century and, in the nineteenth century, in some areas farther west which had been settled before law and order were established. There were royal courts in Quebec, Trois-Rivières, and Montreal, as well as the intendant and Conseil Supérieur in Quebec, and the censitaire could appeal for justice to any one of them. When Canada was organized into parishes, a curé was seldom more than a few miles from any farm in his parish. Although a seigneur or coseigneur was usually no farther away, the censitaire needed little from him. However, he went to mass, and may have taken many problems to his curé. The records of all the colony's courts attest to the use the censitaire made of them. The machinery of control had come to Canada but its oppressive features were mitigated or atrophied from disuse because control was possible only to the degree that the censitaires would cooperate.

That the seigneurial system was not a way of life in Canada during the French regime is certain beyond reasonable doubt, but that much of it remained as a legal system is equally definite. Some French laws had been modified and new laws introduced, but on the whole Canadian law at the end of the French regime was little different from that at the beginning. Parts of this legal framework, as has been shown, came to have a substantial influence on the geography of Canada. Even the laws which treated the relationship between a seigneur and his vassals were often observed, although the original justification for them had long since vanished. In 1732 the seigneur of an arrière-fief in Lachenaie paid *foi et hommage* to his seigneur, who did not maintain a manor in the seigneurie, by knocking on the door of the miller's hut on three separate days, and crying to the surrounding wilderness: "Monsieur de Repentigny I bring and offer to you the *foi et hommage* that I am obliged to bring and offer to you by virtue of my fief located and situated in the said seigneurie of Lachenaie. . . ."[3] When this statement was drawn up by a notary and witnessed by the miller it constituted a legal title which was proof of ownership, and it had been made for this reason. The statement took the legal form of earlier French feudalism, and is but an extreme example of the decay of feudalism in all but legal form which had taken place in Canada.

Most of whatever flesh was added to these legal bones must have appeared after the conquest. Then the intendant was replaced by English officials who did not understand French civil law, and who relied on the seigneurs for interpretations of it. In this situation seigneurs may have begun to enlarge their influence by introducing new charges and by increasing the old. As the population grew, many seigneuries became profitable to their seigneurs for the first time. By the end of the eighteenth century, agricultural land had become scarce along the lower St. Lawrence, and expansion to the west was partially blocked by English settlement. The outlets to the fur trade could support only progressively smaller proportions of the total population. French Canada fell back upon the agricultural resources of the lower St. Lawrence, and as land became scarce a French social and economic system which was based in large part upon the organization and control of land was no longer completely incongruous. Moreover, some French Canadians may have seen in the seigneurial system a potential bastion against English cultural encroachment, and have encouraged its consolidation in the years after the conquest. Thus it is entirely possible that in the late eighteenth and early nineteenth centuries the seigneurial system became the social and economic framework of life in rural Canada which it had never been before, and that the preconquest geography of the seigneurial system was significantly altered. Several descriptions of seigneurial life which date from this later period pictured respectful habitants, kindly seigneurs involved in the development and maintenance of their seigneuries, and, after the middle of the nineteenth century, parish priests leading their flocks from the overpopulated St. Lawrence lowland to new homes along the margin of the Shield. If these pictures were correct, much had changed since the days of the French regime.

Reference Matter

Appendix : Key to Numbering
of Seigneuries

The numbers given to the seigneuries on the maps and used in referring to them in the text are listed here, grouped according to administrative division in the colony.

GOVERNMENT OF MONTREAL

1 Petite Nation
2 Argenteuil
3 Deux Montagnes
4 Mille Iles
5 Plaines
6 Terrebonne
7 Lachenaie (La Chesnaye)
8 L'Assomption, or Repentigny
9 St-Sulpice
10 Lavaltrie
11 Lanoraie
12 Ailleboust
13 Ramezay, or Jouette
14 Dautré
15 Berthier
16 Dorvilliers
17 Ile Dupas et Chicot
18 Pointe à l'Orignal
19 Rigaud
20 Nouvelle Longueuil
21 Vaudreuil
22 Soulanges
23 Ile Perrot
24 Ile Bizard
25 Ile Jésus
26 Ile de Montréal
27 Iles de la Paix

28 Iles Courcelles
29 Ile aux Hérons
30 Ile St-Paul
31 Ile Ste-Thérèse
32 Iles Bouchard
33 Ile St-Pierre
34 Beauharnois
35 Châteauguay
36 Sault St-Louis
37 La Salle
38 La Prairie de la Magdeleine
39 Longueuil
40 Rocbert
41 Daneau de Muy
42 Ramezay-la-Gesse
43 La Perrière
44 Beaujeu
45 Pancalon
46 La Moinaudière
47 La Gauchetière
48 Livaudière
49 Lacolle
50 Foucault
51 St-Armand
52 De Léry
53 Noyan
54 Sabrevois

55 Bleury
56 Tremblay
57 Boucherville
58 Montarville
59 Chambly
60 Monnoir
61 Varennes
62 Cap de la Trinité
63 Guillaudière
64 Belœil
65 Rouville
66 St-Blain
67 Verchères
68 Cournoyer
69 St-Charles-sur-Richelieu
70 Vitré
71 Cabanac
72 Contrecœur
73 St-Denis
74 St-Hyacinthe
75 St-Ours
76 Sorel
77 Bourgchemin
78 Bonsecours
79 St-Charles
80 Ramezay
81 Bourg Marie

GOVERNMENT OF TROIS-RIVIÈRES

1 Lac Maskinongé, or Lanaudière
2 Dusablé
3 Carufel
4 Maskinongé

5 St-Jean
6 Rivière du Loup
7 Grandpré
8 Dumontier
9 Grosbois-Ouest

10 Grosbois-Est, or Yamachiche
11 Robert
12 Gastineau
13 St-Maurice

14 Tonnancour, or Pointe du Lac
15 Not conceded
16 Boucher
17 Labadie
18 Vieuxpont
19 Jésuites
20 Seigneuries in or on outskirts of Trois-Rivières
21 Cap de la Madeleine
22 Champlain
23 Batiscan
24 Ste-Anne-Ouest
25 Ste-Marie
26 Ste-Anne-Est, or Dorvilliers
27 Yamaska
28 St-François
29 Lussodière
30 Pierreville
31 Deguire
32 Baie du Febvre, or St-Antoine
33 Courval
34 Nicolet
35 Roquetaillade
36 Godefroy, or Linctôt
37 Bécancour
38 Dutort
39 Cournoyer
40 Gentilly
41 Lévrard
42 Ile Moras
43 Ile Marie
44 Iles du St-Maurice

GOVERNMENT OF QUEBEC

1 Grondines
2 Les Pauvres
3 La Tesserie
4 La Chevrotière
5 Deschambault
6 Perthuis
7 Portneuf
8 Jacques Cartier
9 D'Auteuil
10 Bélair, or Pointe aux Ecureuils
11 Bourg Louis
12 Neuville
13 Fossembault
14 De Maure
15 Bonhomme, or Bélair
16 Gaudarville
17 St-Gabriel
18 Hubert
19 Sillery
20 St-Ignace
21 Seigneuries in or on outskirts of Quebec
22 Lespinay
23 Islets, or Comté d'Orsainville
24 Notre Dame des Anges
25 Beauport
26 Beaupré
27 Rivière du Gouffre
28 Les Eboulements
29 Malbaie
30 Deschaillons
31 Lotbinière
32 Ste-Croix
33 Bonsecours
34 Duquet
35 Belle Plaine, or Le Gardeur
36 Tilly
37 Gaspé
38 St-Gilles
39 Lauzon
40 St-Etienne
41 Jolliet
42 Ste-Marie
43 St-Joseph
44 St-François
45 Aubert Gayon
46 Aubin de l'Isle
47 Martinière, or Beauchamp
48 Vincennes
49 Livaudière
50 Beaumont
51 La Durantaye et St-Michel
52 St-Vallier
53 Bellechasse, or Berthier
54 Rivière du Sud
55 Lespinay
56 St-Joseph
57 Gagné, or Lafrenaye
58 Gamache
59 Ste-Claire
60 Vincelotte
61 Bonsecours
62 L'Islet
63 Lessard
64 Rhéaume
65 St-Roch des Aulnaies
66 La Pocatière
67 Rivière Ouelle
68 St-Denis
69 Kamouraska
70 Islet du Portage
71 Grandville Lachenaye
72 Verbois
73 Rivière du Loup
74 Le Parc
75 Villeray
76 Ile Verte
77 Trois Pistoles
78 Rioux
79 Ile d'Orléans
80 Ile Madame
81 Ile aux Ruaux
82 Ile aux Grues
83 Ile aux Oies
84 Ile aux Coudres
85 Ile aux Lièvres

Notes

Certain frequently cited sources appear in abbreviated form in the notes. In each case a more detailed description will be found in the Bibliography. The shortened forms are as follows:

AC, B refers to the official correspondence from France to Canada; AC, C 11 A refers to the correspondence from Canada to France. Copies of both sets of correspondence are in bound volumes in the National Archives of Canada.

AJQ means Archives Judiciaire de Québec.

APQ means Archives de la Province de Québec.

ASQ means Archives du Séminaire de Québec.

Edits et ordonnances refers to *Edits, ordonnances royaux, déclarations, et arrêts du conseil d'état du roi concernant le Canada* (2d ed., Quebec, 1854–56).

Pièces et documents refers to *Pièces et documents relatifs à la tenure seigneuriale* (Quebec, 1852–54).

RAPQ stands for *Archives de Québec, Rapport de l'Archivist.*

The *pièces détachées* cited so frequently are the unbound documents, in boxes arranged alphabetically by seigneurie in the APQ.

CHAPTER 1

1 Relevant parts of the letters patent as well as a discussion of their legal implications are in Edmond Lareau, *Histoire du droit canadien* (Montreal, 1888), I, 159–60.

2 The ratification of Feb. 28, 1626, can be found in *Pièces et documents*, II, 373.

3 Acte pour l'établissement de la Compagnie des Cent Associés pour le commerce du Canada, April 29, 1627, published in full in *Edits et ordonnances*, I, 5–11.

4 William B. Munro, *Documents Relating to the Seigniorial Tenure in Canada, 1598–1854* (Toronto, 1908), p. xxi.

5 See particularly Marcel Trudel, *Le Régime seigneurial* (Canadian Historical Association, brochure No. 6, Ottawa, 1956).

6 Léon Gérin, *Aux sources de notre histoire* (Montreal, 1946), particularly Chaps. 11, 13, 14, 15.

7 Lionel Groulx, *Histoire du Canada français depuis la découverte* (Montreal, 1950–51), I, 111.

8 William B. Munro, *The Seigneurs of Old Canada: A Chronicle of New World Feudalism* (Toronto, 1914), p. 105.

9 Gérard Filteau, *La Naissance d'une nation* (Montreal, 1937), I, 134.

10 Guy Frégault, *La Civilisation de la Nouvelle-France, 1713–1744* (Montreal, 1944), pp. 183–84.

11 Lionel Groulx, *La Naissance d'une race* (Montreal, 1919), pp. 278–80.

12 Mason Wade, *The French Canadians, 1760–1945* (Toronto, 1956), p. 66.

CHAPTER 2

1 See Raoul Blanchard, *L'Est du Canada français* (Paris and Montreal, 1935), I, 318, for a more detailed description.

2 *The America of 1750: Peter Kalm's Travels in North America . . .* , ed. A. B. Benson (New York, 1937), II, 459.

3 W. E. D. Halliday, *A Forest Classification for Canada* (Department of Mines and Resources, Forest Service Bulletin 89, Ottawa, 1937), is still the best brief description of Canadian forests.

4 *The Works of Samuel de Champlain*, ed. H. P. Biggar (Toronto, 1922–36), II, 176.

5 Denonville au Ministre, May 8, 1686, in AC, C 11 A, VIII, 22.

6 *Peter Kalm's Travels*, II, 515.

7 *Ibid.*, II, 531.

8 Charles A. Fontaine, "Les Sols du Québec," *L'Actualité économique*, XVII, Pt. 2, No. 5 (March, 1942), 401–42.

9 De Meulles au Ministre, Sept. 28, 1685, in AC, C 11 A, VII, 133–34.

10 Mémoire de M. Dubois d'Avaugour sur la colonie de Québec, 1663, in AC, C 11 A, I, 16–27.

11 Talon au Ministre, Nov. 13, 1666, in AC, C 11 A, II, 342; Aug. 25, 1667, in AC, C 11 A, II, 485.

12 Talon au Roy, Nov. 2, 1671, in AC, C 11 A, III, 181.

13 Projet du chevalier de Callières pour faire la guerre contre les anglais, 1689, in AC, C 11 A, X, 415–29.

14 Mémoire pour servir d'instruction à monsieur le comte de Frontenac sur l'entreprise de la Nouvelle York, June 7, 1689, in *RAPQ* (1927–28), pp. 12–16.

CHAPTER 3

1 Reference to the Coutume de Paris appears in seigneurial title deeds as early as 1637, and this coutume may well have been followed before that date. It is characteristic of the confusion of the early years that two other coutumes, the Norman and the Vexin, an offshoot of the Coutume de Paris, were followed in some concessions, and certain aspects of these coutumes, notably their provisions for the retrait, remained fixtures of the Canadian legal system to the time of the abolition of the seigneurial regime.

2 Acte pour l'établissement de la Compagnie des Cent Associés pour le commerce du Canada, April 29, 1627, *Edits et ordonnances*, I, 5–11.

3 *Ibid.,* I, 5.

4 Concession de Beauport à Robert Giffard, Jan. 15, 1634, in *Pièces et documents,* II, 386–87.

5 Thus both the Company and the seigneurs who held their land from the Company granted rotures in the proprietary period. Examples of such grants made by the Company are to be found in the Quebec Judicial Archives. See, for example, Concession par Louis Dailleboust gouverneur et Lieutenant général à Jean Sauvaget, Oct. 28, 1649, in AJQ, Guillaume Audouard, notary; Concession par Chas. Juault de Montmagny pour le Cie de la Nouvelle France à René Maheu, Oct. 19, 1639, in AJQ, Martial Piraubé, notary.

6 Marcel Trudel has prepared a series of maps showing seigneurial concessions during various periods. The back endpaper, showing seigneuries in 1760, is based almost entirely on one of Trudel's maps. The front endpaper and Figure 3–1 were drawn independently.

7 The last reference to Pinguet as a distinct seigneurie is in 1667. Shortly thereafter it was apparently absorbed by Portneuf. See P. G. Roy, *Inventaire des concessions en fief et seigneurie, fois et hommages, et aveux et dénombrements conservées aux archives de la province de Québec* (Beauceville, 1927), I, 166.

8 Concession à François de Chavigny Sr. Berchereau et Damoiselle Elénore de Grand Maison, sa Femme, Dec. 14, 1640, in *Pièces et documents,* I, 375.

9 I have not found the first ordinance establishing this *rhumb de vent,* but it must have been between 1634 and 1637. The Company's first concessions and the few that preceded it followed a slightly different *rhumb de vent.* See the seigneuries just north and east of Quebec on the front endpaper. All the concessions in 1637 followed a new line which was standard thereafter.

10 Sometimes these corner markers were quite elaborate. Michel Leneuf dug in a stone marker and added a cross and a ditch in which he placed some more stones and several lead plates to mark the boundaries of a seigneurie near Trois-Rivières. Cie de la Nouvelle France à Michel Leneuf . . . , June 17, 1641, in AJQ, Piraubé, notary.

11 Ordonnance du Gouverneur de Lauzon qui oblige tous les françois à se rendre à leur travail avec leurs armes à feu, Nov. 14, 1654, in *RAPQ* (1924–25), p. 390.

12 Ordonnance du Gouverneur de Lauzon qui fait défense à tous d'aller en traite sans avoir obtenu un congé, April 28, 1654, in *RAPQ* (1924–25), pp. 383–84.

13 Arrêt de Sa Majesté pour la révocation des concessions, March 21, 1663, in AC, C 11 A, II, 10–12; *Edits et ordonnances,* I, 33; William B. Munro, *Documents Relating to the Seigniorial Tenure in Canada* (Toronto, 1908), pp. 12–14.

14 Instructions données par Sa Majesté au Sieur Gaudais, au moment de s'embarquer pour aller examiner le Canada, May 7, 1663, in *Edits et ordonnances*, III, 23–27; Munro, *Documents*, pp. 14–17. Gaudais turned out to be more interested in the colony's politics than its land policy and was of no assistance in clarifying the king's ideas on this subject. The king was interested in but not informed about landholding in Canada, and his conclusions were not shrewd assessments of what was wrong.

15 Mémoire du Roi pour servir d'instruction au Sieur Talon s'en allant au Canada, March 27, 1665, in AC, B, I, 62–63.

16 Talon au Ministre, Oct. 27, 1667, in AC, C 11 A, II, 525–26; Munro, *Documents*, p. 27.

17 Ordonnance au sujet de l'arrêt du 4 juin 1672, Sept. 27, 1672, in P. G. Roy, *Inventaire des ordonnances des intendants de la Nouvelle-France conservées aux archives provinciales de Québec* (Beauceville, 1927), III, 271 ff.; Arrêt du Conseil d'Etat du Roi pour retrancher la moitié des concessions, June 4, 1672, in *Edits et ordonnances*, I, 70–71.

18 Ordinance of Sept. 27, 1672, in *Edits et ordonnances*, I, 70–71.

19 Whether Talon did not know about this large seigneurie or whether the grant was officially rescinded is not known; in any case Talon conceded seigneuries within La Citière as if it did not exist. The last record of La Citière in the documents is dated 1667.

20 Arrêt pour retrancher les Concessions d'une trop grande étendue et les concéder à de nouveaux habitants·. . . , June 4, 1675, in *Edits et ordonnances*, I, 81–82.

21 Duchesneau's ordinance is published in P. G. Roy, *Ordonnances, commissions, etc., des gouverneurs et intendants de la Nouvelle-France, 1639–1706* (Quebec, 1924), I, 210–11; and Colbert's response is in AC, C 11 A, IV, 304, and published in Munro, *Documents*, pp. 42–43.

22 Edit du Roy, May 9, 1679, in *Edits et ordonnances*, I, 233–34; Munro, *Documents*, pp. 43–45.

23 See, for example, Ordonnance de M. M. Le Febvre de la Barre et de Meulles, March 12, 1683, in APQ, Insinuations du Conseil Souverain, cahier 2; Ordonnance de M. M. Le Febvre de la Barre et de Meulles, May 26, 1683, in Roy, *Inventaire des ordonnances des intendants*, III, 72–73; Réunion au domaine de Sa Majesté par le Marquis de Denonville et Jean Bochart de Champigny, March 18, 1689, in *Pièces et documents*, I, 332.

24 This objection was raised in a letter from Vaudreuil and Bégon to the minister, Oct. 26, 1719, in AC, C 11 A, XL, 7; Munro, *Documents*, pp. 163–64.

25 Frontenac et Champigny au Ministre, Oct. 15, 1698, in AC, C 11 A, XVI, 20–21.

26 Frontenac et Champigny au Ministre, Nov. 5, 1694, in AC, C 11 A, XIII, 35.

27 Frontenac et Champigny au Ministre, Oct. 15, 1698, in AC, C 11 A, XVI, 20–21.

28 Frontenac et Champigny au Ministre, Nov. 10, 1695, in AC, C 11 A, XIII, 352.

29 Acte de concession du marquis de Denonville et de Jean Bochart Champigny . . . , April 24, 1688, in APQ, Pièce détachée, Rimousky.

30 Acte de Concession du marquis de Denonville et de Jean Bochart Champigny aux sieurs de la Chenaye et de Villeray, April 5, 1689, in APQ, Pièce détachée, Ile Verte.

31 On this point see W. J. Eccles, *Frontenac: The Courtier Governor* (Toronto, 1959), pp. 206–7.

32 *Ibid.,* pp. 278 and 292.

33 Raudot au Ministre, Nov. 14, 1709, in AC, C 11 A, XXX, 270.

34 Frontenac et Champigny au Ministre, Nov. 5, 1694, in AC, C 11 A, XIII, 35. Whatever the merits of their advice they paid little attention to it themselves, making more than thirty concessions during the next three years.

35 Catalogne, Mémoire sur Canada, Nov. 7, 1712, in AC, C 11 A, XXXIII, 278–368; Munro, *Documents,* pp. 94–151. Catalogne's was the most detailed description to reach France during the French regime and certainly conveys the general impression that there was very little development on too many seigneuries. The report contains little that cannot be obtained in more detail from other sources, but for the ministers in France, it was certainly a substantial addition to their information about the colony.

36 The Edicts of Marly are published in many different volumes, among them: *Edits et ordonnances,* I, 324–26; Munro, *Documents,* pp. 91–94.

37 Mémoire du Roy à Vaudreuil et Bégon, March 19, 1714, in AC, B, XXXVI, 342.

38 Instructions du Roy pour M. M. Vaudreuil et Bégon, May 23, 1719, in AC, C 11 A, XL, 243–45; Munro, *Documents,* pp. 160–62.

39 Mémoire du Roy à Vaudreuil et Bégon, June 26, 1717, in AC, B, IXL, 232(back)–233.

40 Vaudreuil et Bégon à Maurepas, Oct. 17, 1722, in AC, C 11 A, XLIV, 138; Vaudreuil et Bégon au Conseil de Marine, Oct. 26, 1720, in APQ, Correspondance de Vaudreuil (the Vaudreuil correspondence for the years 1703–16 has been published in the *RAPQ,* 1939–40, 1942–43, 1946–47, and 1947–48); Beauharnois et Hocquart au Ministre, Oct. 1, 1732, in AC, C 11 A, LVII, 8 ff., and in Munro, *Documents,* pp. 176–77.

41 Mémoire du Roy à Vaudreuil et Bégon, June 2, 1720, in AC, B, XLII, 432(back).

42 Jugement qui réunit au Domaine de Sa Majesté toutes les Seigneuries qui ne sont point mises en valeur, May 10, 1741, *Edits et ordonnances,* II, 555–61.

43 Guy Frégault, "Le Régime seigneurial et l'expansion de la colonisation dans le bassin du St-Laurent au dix-huitième siècle," *Canadian Historical Association Report* (1944), pp. 61–73; William B. Munro, *The Seigniorial System in Canada* (New York, 1907), p. 50.

44 Beauharnois et Hocquart au Ministre, Oct. 15, 1736, in AC, C 11 A, LXV, 76 ff.; Munro, *Documents,* pp. 178–80.

45 *Ibid.*

46 Concession d'Un arpent de terre au village En arrière-fief par Monsr. Boucher Seigr. de Boucherville Au Sieur de Montbrun Son fils, July 2, 1693, in APQ, Pièce détachée, Boucherville.

CHAPTER 4

1 For an example of the latter picture see Léon Gérin, *Aux sources de notre histoire* (Montreal, 1946). The other side of the coin is perhaps clearest in the work of Lionel Groulx.

2 D'Auteuil au Ministre, Oct. 17, 1705, in AC, C 11 A, XXII, 380–81.

3 Déclaration du Roi, concernant les Ordres Religieux et gens de mainmorte établis aux Colonies françaises, Nov. 25, 1743, *Edits et ordonnances*, I, 576–81.

4 Acte de cession et délaissement par le Père Dablon . . . en faveur de M. Berthelot, de l'Ile Jésus et iles adjacentes, Nov. 7, 1672, Romain Becquet, notary, in APQ, Pièce détachée, Ile Jésus.

5 Beauharnois et Hocquart au Ministre, Oct. 15, 1736, in AC, C 11 A, LXV, 76 ff.; Munro, *Documents,* pp. 178–80.

6 See, for example, Acte de vente de Charles Denys de Vitré à Pierre Boisseau, habitant demeurant en la seigneurie de Longueuil, du fief de Bellevue . . . moyennant la somme de deux cent quatre-vingt livres, Feb. 26, 1678, Romain Becquet, notary, in APQ, Pièce détachée, Vitré. Note the sale price.

7 Lettre de MM. de Beauharnois et Hocquart au Ministre appuyant une demande de Concession, Oct. 8, 1731, in APQ, Pièce détachée, Le Gardeur.

8 For an attempt to do this see Alfred Vanasse, "A Social History of the Seigniorial Regime in Canada, 1712–1739" (unpublished Ph.D. thesis, University of Montreal, 1958), II, Appendix E.

9 The most important Articles on inheritance are in Title I of the Coutume, particularly Articles 13–19. The easiest way to understand the spirit of the Coutume is to read some of it in, for example, M. Claude de Ferrière, *Nouveau Commentaire sur la Coutume de la Prévôté et Vicomté de Paris* (Paris, 1770).

10 See Title VIII of the Coutume, and especially Article 129, *ibid.,* I, 284–95.

11 See Article 298 of the Coutume, *ibid.,* II, 280–85.

12 Acte de foi et hommage de . . . tous propriétaires du Cap Saint-Michel, Aug. 18, 1736, in APQ, Fois et hommages, cahier 2, folio 182; Aveu et dénombrement . . . pour le fief et seigneurie du Cap St-Michel, Aug. 22, 1736, in APQ, Aveux et dénombrements, cahier 2, II, folio 490.

13 Mémoire instructif pour sérvir a MM. les arbitres nommés pour M. et Mme. DuBuisson . . . , March 10, 1725, in APQ, Pièce détachée, Ile Bizard.

14 Aveu et dénombrement de René Gaultier de Varennes . . . pour le fief de Varennes, July 13, 1723, in APQ, Aveux et dénombrements, cahier 2, I, folio 113(back).

15 Coutume de Paris, Title X, in Ferrière, *Nouveau Commentaire*, II, 1 ff.

16 Coutume de Paris, Article 337, *ibid.*, II, 405–9.

17 Partage fait par Mme. de Varenne à ses enfants, July 1, 1707, Greffe de Pierre Raimbault, notary, in APQ, Pièce détachée, Varennes.

18 See, for example, Acte de vente de Joseph Couillard . . . à Hughes-Jacques Péan, de deux parts en douze dans le fonds et propriété du moulin . . . , March 7, 1741, Greffe de Jacques Imbert, notary, in APQ, Pièce détachée, Beaumont.

19 Acte d'accorde de Monsr. Couillard avec les héritiers et cohéritiers pour la construction de nouveau moulin de la Rivière des Vases, July 4, 1738, in APQ, Pièce détachée, Rivière du Sud.

20 Jugement qui condamne le sieur Charest à faire construire un Moulin à Farine sur la Rivière Etchemin, Seigneurie de Lauzon, et qui oblige le sieur Charly d'y contribuer au prorata . . . , Feb. 12, 1746, *Edits et ordonnances*, II, 578–79.

21 Ordonnance qui décide que Joseph Amyot, seigneur de Vincelotte, jouira . . . de la place qu'il a toujours joui proche la balustrade de la dite église, Jan. 19, 1722, in APQ, Ordonnances des Intendants, VIII, 86–89.

22 Acte de vente des frères et sœurs Lemoyne à Jean-Baptiste Lemoyne de Martigny de tous leurs droits dans le fief de Notre-Dame ou Cap-de-la-Trinité, April 22, 1702, Greffe d'Adhémar, notary, in APQ, Pièce détachée, Notre Dame ou Cap de la Trinité.

23 Assemblé de Parens Et délibération pour la rente de la Seigneurie app't à la Succession de feu Sr. Joseph hertel Scize à Chambly, Feb. 23, 1730, in APQ, Pièce détachée, Chambly.

24 For the first of several sales, see Acte de vente de Thomas Fleury de la Jeannière à Joseph Fleury de la Gorgendière . . . de toutes les prétentions qu'il peut avoir en la succession de Jacques-Alexis Fleury Deschambault et Marguerite de Chavigny, Sept. 10, 1716, Greffe de Florent de la Citière, notary, in APQ, Pièce détachée, Deschambault.

25 P. G. Roy, *Inventaire des concessions en fief et seigneurie, fois et hommages et aveux et dénombrements conservées aux archives de la province de Québec* (Beauceville, 1927), IV, 185–86.

26 *Ibid.*, III, 224–30.

27 Acte de partage entre Michel Messier et Jacques Lemoyne du fief à eux accordé par M. de Courcelles le 14 May, 1668, Aug. 1, 1676, Greffe de Benigne Basset, notary, in APQ, Pièce détachée, Cap de la Trinité.

28 In 1686 the king issued a stern *arrêt* which required the seigneur to build a gristmill or forfeit the banal rights. Arrêt du Conseil d'Etat au sujet des Moulins Banaux, June 4, 1686, *Edits et ordonnances,* I, 255–56.

29 Acte de Foi et Hommage de Jean Leber de Senneville pour ses droits dans l'Ile St-Paul, Oct. 20, 1753, in APQ, Fois et hommages, cahier 2, folio 324.

30 Aveu et dénombrement de François Herault . . . fondé de pouvoir du sieur François Chorel Dorvilliers . . . , March 6, 1738, in APQ, Aveux et dénombrements, cahier 2, II, folio 634 (back).

31 Aveu et dénombrement de Jacques Brisset pour le fief de l'Ile Dupas et du Chicot, June 15, 1723, in APQ, Aveux et dénombrements, cahier 2, I, folio 102; Aveu et dénombrement de Louis Adrien Dandonneau Dusable pour le fief de l'Ile Dupas et du Chicot, July 22, 1724, in *ibid.,* cahier 2, I, folio 168.

32 In each case the relevant document closest to 1730 has been selected. The *aveux et dénombrements* are inclined to refer to a single seigneur when there may well have been several. On the other hand both *aveux et dénombrements* and statements of *foi et hommage* were commonly presented by a new seigneur shortly after his predecessor had died, that is, at a time when the fragmentation of seigneurial control could be expected to be at a maximum. In this period, however, most *aveux et dénombrements* were prepared in response to an intendant's ordinance which required all seigneurs to compile them, and usually do not reflect an unusual division of control. In any case, the two biases tend to cancel each other out.

33 Besides the seigneurie of Beauport, Robert Giffard was conceded St-Gabriel in 1647, St-Ignace in the same year, and Mille-Vaches, a seigneurie below Tadoussac, in 1653.

34 One of these was La Rivière au Griffon, conceded on July 30, 1936. The other was Dautré, conceded on December 1, 1637. Roy, *Inventaire des concessions en fief et seigneurie,* I, 141 and 160. The location of La Rivière Griffon, a seigneurie which disappeared shortly after 1667, is uncertain, and it is not shown on the endpaper maps.

35 For the record of these concessions, see Roy, *Inventaire des concessions en fief et seigneurie,* II, 30, 75; II, 14; II, 22, and III, 95; I, 125.

36 *Ibid.,* I, 53, 69, 54, 70, 64–66, 264; II, 127, 110, 34, 77, 140, 274; III, 133, 154, 170, 261, 283.

37 Abandon par la dame Ve De langloiserie à Ses Enfans Et partage Entr'eux relativement aux Seigneuries de l'Ile Ste-Thérèse et des Mille-Isles, July 8, 1734, in APQ, Pièce détachée, Ile Ste-Thérèse.

38 Acte de Foi et Hommage pour les fiefs de la Rivière du Loup et de Ma-doueska, March 19, 1756, in APQ, Fois et hommages, cahier 3, folio 47.

39 Acte de Foi et Hommage pour les fiefs de Repentigny et de La Chesnay, June 7, 1724, in APQ, Fois et hommages, cahier 2, folio 94–96.

40 Arrêt du Conseil Supérieur de Québec qui ordonne que Charles Amyot, maitre de barque en la ville de Québec, jouira pour son droit d'ainesse, outre le quart du fief qui lui à été adjugé par arrêt du Aug. 12, 1709, d'un demi-arpent de terre de préciput dans tel endroit qu'il voudra choisir dans le fief de Vignes, Aug. 26, 1710, in APQ, Jugements et délibérations du Conseil Souverain ou Supérieur, 1710, folio 115; *Jugements et délibérations du Conseil Souverain de la Nouvelle France*, VI, 107–8.

41 Acte de vente de François-Etienne Cugnet . . . aux Révérends Pères Jésuites . . . d'une portion du fief et seigneurie de Bélair . . . , Feb. 16, 1733, Greffe de Jacques Pinguet, notary, in APQ, Pièce détachée, Bélair.

42 Acte de vente du Sieur Boucher de Boucherville, au sieur Louis Gastineau du fief à lui concédé par M. Talon le 3ᵉ nov., 1672; July 28, 1712, Greffe de Lepallieu, notary, in APQ, Pièce détachée, Gastineau.

43 Vente par le chevalier d'Argenteuil à Joseph Gaultier du fief et seigneurie d'Ailleboust, Feb. 17, 1756, Greffe de Davre de Blanzy, notary, in APQ, Pièce détachée, Ailleboust.

44 Acte d'échange . . . du fief et seigneurie de la Chevrotière pour une habitation en l'Ile d'Orléans, April 7, 1674, Greffe de Romain Bocquet, notary, in APQ, Pièce détachée, La Chevrotière.

45 See, for example, Vente de Bertier au Sr. de Lestage, April 25, 1718, in APQ, Pièce détachée, Berthier-en-haut; Vente de Terrebonne à M. Le Page, Sept. 2, 1720, in APQ, Pièce détachée, Terrebonne.

CHAPTER 5

1 Six contrats de Concessions par Monsr. Dollier, trois à Gervaizes et trois à Teyssiers, Nov. 9, 1694, in APQ, Pièce détachée, Ile de Montréal, Château de Vaudreuil.

2 For some reason at least two of the Jesuits' concessions in La Prairie de la Magdeleine, one in 1720 and the other in 1732, were to be paid in turkeys rather than capons. Canadian turkeys must have been scrawny birds; the conversion rate on them was fifteen sols, which was less than the rate for capons.

3 Terres en censive au Détroit du Lac Erie données par Beauharnois et Hocquart, June 16, 1734, in *Pièces et documents*, I, Appendix XVII. Undoubtedly furs were sometimes paid along the St. Lawrence as well.

4 For example: Madame Simonet, seigneur of Grande Pré, who had been charging twenty sols and one capon or another twenty sols for every arpent of frontage, decided that the payment in capons or wheat was a nuisance, and added the twenty sols to the cash rente making it in future title deeds a fixed charge of forty sols for each arpent of frontage.

5 See, for example, Ordonnance qui permet aux Seigneurs de l'Isle-Jésus de se faire payer leurs Rentes en argent ou en chapons, suivant les Contrats de

concession, June 27, 1730, *Edits et ordonnances,* II, 512; or, Jugement qui condamne les Habitans de Port-Joly à payer au Sr. De Gaspé, leur Seigneur, les arrérages de Cens et Rentes et le Chapon en nature ou en argent, au choix du dit seigneur, Feb. 21, 1731, *Edits et ordonnances,* II, 521–22.

6 Lettre de M. de Pontchartrain à Jacques Raudot, June 13, 1708, in William B. Munro, *Documents Relating to the Seigniorial Tenure in Canada* (Toronto, 1908), pp. 80–81. In this connection see also Lettre de M. de Pontchartrain à M. Deshaguais à Fontainebleau, July 10, 1708, in *ibid.,* pp. 82–83.

7 Extrait de la concession faite par le Sieur de Vaudreuil . . . au Séminaire de Montréal, de la seigneurie du Lac de Deux-Montagnes, Oct. 17, 1717, *Titles and Documents Relating to the Seigniorial Tenure* (Quebec, 1852), pp. 210–11; and in the French edition, *Pièces et documents,* Appendix B, No. 103, p. 75.

8 M. M. de Beauharnois et Hocquart au Ministre, Oct. 6, 1734, *Correspondance entre le gouvernement français et les gouverneurs et intendants du Canada relative à la tenure seigneuriale* (Quebec, 1853), pp. 29–33.

9 See, for example, Concession par les jésuits à Michel Huppé, Henri Bancherons . . . en Notre-Dame-des-Anges, April 1, 1647, in AJQ, Guillaume Audouard, notary.

10 Raudot au Ministre, Nov. 10, 1707, in AC, C 11 A, XXVI, 7 ff.; Munro, *Documents,* pp. 70 ff.

11 For a discussion of Raudot's recommendations see Munro, *Documents,* p. xlviii.

12 Rapport des Commissionaires nommés pour s'enquérir des Lois et autres circonstances qui se rattachent à la Tenure Seigneuriale . . . , Oct. 4, 1843, *Pièces et documents,* I, 25–71; Munro, *Documents,* pp. 208–56.

13 When the king fixed the conversion rate from French to Canadian funds in 1717 so that the latter were only three-quarters of the value of the French and ordered Canadian money withdrawn, the censitaires were quick to fix upon this as reason for reducing their payments by a quarter. Almost invariably court cases resulted, and often the censitaires won.

14 See, for example, Jugement par lequel Nicolas Bissonnet est reçu opposant à l'exécution de l'ordonnance de M. Raudot, du 2 juillet, 1707, et que, par provision, il ne payera qu'un minot et demi de bled de rente, les droits seigneuriaux et la journée de commune, July 3, 1720, *Edits et ordonnances,* III, 177–78. Bissonnet's original contract had been for only 1.5 minots of wheat in rente, but in 1707 the seigneur had obtained in Bissonnet's absence an ordinance from Raudot permitting a charge of one sol per square arpent as well as the 1.5 minots, a rente which was fairly standard. Bissonnet appealed this change when he discovered it and, on presenting

his original contract, succeeded in having Raudot's ordinance reversed. The seigneur then appealed this decision but lost.

15 See, for example, Contrat de concession fait par Mlle. Le Gardeur à Joseph Marot, April 22, 1759, in APQ, Pièce détachée, Le Gardeur, rotures.

16 Rapport des Commissionaires, in Munro, *Documents*, p. 334.

17 Fragment concerning manipulated *cens et rentes* in an arrière-fief in Notre Dame des Anges, without date, signature, or title, in APQ, Pièce détachée, Notre Dame des Anges, arrière-fiefs.

18 Beauharnois et Hocquart au Ministre, Oct. 6, 1734, in *Correspondance entre le gouvernement français et les gouverneurs et intendants du Canada*, pp. 29–33.

19 Concession de Sieur Robert Choret seigneur de Notre-Dame-de-Bonsecour à Pierre Morisset, Jan. 2, 1708, in APQ, Pièce détachée, Bonsecours, rotures, A-B.

20 Jugement qui condamne les Habitans de la Chevrotière à donner à leur Seigneur leurs corvées franches . . . et qui défend à tous Seigneurs d'insérer à l'avenir cette clause de corvées, dans les Contrats de Concession qu'ils feront, à peine nullité, Jan. 22, 1716, *Edits et ordonnances*, II, 444–46. The intendant backed down somewhat on this rather severe judgment three months later. See Jugement qui ordonne que les Habitans de la Chevrotière payeront à leur Seigneur, au lieu de Corvées, chacun vingt sols par an, pour chaque Concession de trois arpens de front sur quarante de profondeur, March 5, 1716, *Edits et ordonnances*, II, 449–51.

21 Concession par le Marquis de Beauharnois à Pierre Hénault, June 2, 1733, in APQ, Pièce détachée, Villechauve ou Beauharnois, rotures, S-Z.

22 Vaudreuil et Beauharnois au Ministre, Nov. 15, 1703, in AC, C 11 A, XXI, 11.

23 The *droit de pêche* was not always one-eleventh of the catch as Munro suggests. Censitaires in Boucherville paid one-twentieth. See Ordonnance de M. Bochart Champigny au sujet de la commune de Boucherville, Aug. 18, 1688, in P. G. Roy, *Ordonnances, commissions, etc., des gouverneurs et intendants de la Nouvelle-France, 1639–1706* (Quebec, 1924), II, 178–81. Censitaires in La Pocatière paid one-tenth. See Jugement qui condamne les Habitans de La Pocatière à payer à leur Seigneur les Arrérages de cens et rentes et les lods et ventes dans un mois, et à lui tenir compte du Dixième du produit des pêches à marsouins, Nov. 10, 1736, *Edits et ordonnances*, II, 541–42.

24 Ordonnance qui maintient Joseph Crevier et ses cohéritiers, propriétaires du fief et seigneurie de Saint-François . . . dans le droit de pêcher dans certaines parties de la dite seigneurie sous le peine de cent livres d'amende contre les contrevenants et de confiscation des rets, engins, canots, et utensiles de pêche à eux appartenans, March 27, 1732, Ordonnances des Intendants, XX, 32–40; *Edits et ordonnances*, III, 269–73.

25 Jugement qui déboute les sieurs Marcot et Chastenay de la prétention qu'ils ont de s'arroger le droit de pêche . . . reservé par le sieur Robineau, seigneur de Portneuf . . . , July 25, 1723, *Edits et ordonnances,* III, 203–5.

26 Copie Collationnée du 20me mars, 1725, d'une Concession par les pères Jésuittes à Michel Baribaud, May 15, 1714, in APQ, Pièce détachée, Batiscan, rotures.

27 The reader will find some of these disputes published in the *Edits et ordonnances,* and there are many more in the Ordonnances des Intendants, and in the Jugements du Conseil Souverain.

28 See, for example, Ordonnance au sujet de la commune de la seigneurie de St-Ours, July 14, 1714, in APQ, Ordonnances des Intendants, VI, 112.

29 Arrêt du Conseil Supérieur qui règle les Moutures à la quatorzième portion, June 20, 1667, *Edits et ordonnances,* II, 39. Peter Kalm claimed that some seigneurs charged a quarter of all the grain they ground (A. B. Benson, ed., *The America of 1750: Peter Kalm's Travels in North America* [New York, 1937], II, 532), but this flagrant increase is hard to believe.

30 Ordonnance du Conseil Supérieur, déclarant Banaux les Moulins à vent et à eau, bâtis par les seigneurs, July 1, 1675, *Edits et ordonnances,* II, 62–63. In France windmills were not banal. See William B. Munro, *The Seigniorial System in Canada* (New York, 1907), pp. 110–13.

31 Arrêt du Conseil d'Etat au sujet des Moulins Banaux, June 4, 1686, *Edits et ordonnances,* I, 255–56.

32 Aveu et dénombrement . . . pour le fief et seigneurie de Terrebonne, May 20, 1736, in APQ, Aveux et dénombrements, cahier 2, II, folio 430–59.

33 ASQ, Grand Livre, 1701–23, folio 32.

34 Often the cost was very much more. In 1719 the Séminaire spent 2,629 livres on the mill at Petit Pré; in 1723 it spent 853 livres. In 1717 expenses for the mill at Le Sault à la Puce were 3,086 livres; in 1723 they were 573 livres. These changes reflect fluctuations in the value of money.

35 The relative flexibility of cereal prices in Canada was not unusual. See B. A. Slicher Van Bath, *The Agrarian History of Western Europe, A.D. 500–1850* (London, 1963), pp. 98–131, for a careful analysis of this phenomenon in western Europe.

36 In 1750, for example, the Séminaire de Québec rented the moulin de la Blondelle in St-Joachim for ten years at 235 minots a year.

37 The Coutume de Normandie as well as the Coutume de Paris had been employed in the colony during the proprietary years, and this retrait was one of its distinctive characteristics which remained in Canada after 1662.

38 Jacques Raudot au Ministre, Nov. 10, 1707, in AC, C 11 A, XXVI, 7 ff.; Munro, *Documents,* pp. 70 ff.; and Oct. 18, 1708, in AC, C 11 A, XXVIII, 175 ff.; Munro, *Documents,* pp. 85 ff.

39 Bégon au Ministre, Feb., 1716, in AC, C 11 A, XXVI, 90 ff.; Munro, *Documents,* pp. 153–57.

40 See François Joseph Cugnet, *Traité de la Loi des Fiefs* (Quebec, 1775), pp. 19–21 (comments on Articles 14 and 15 of the coutume) for an analysis by a Canadian of this retrait. See also, Jugement de Bégon, June 5, 1716, cited in Cugnet, *Traité*, p. 21.

41 See, for example, a concession rented for three years on the Ile d'Orléans in the 1660's when the seigneur agreed to pay his tenants twenty livres for each arpent they cleared. Bail à ferme par Claude Charron à Pierre Basset et Jean Jacquereau, March 7, 1660, in APQ, Pièce détachée, arrière-fief Charron, Ile d'Orléans. In 1653 Jean Lauzon sold a small arrière-fief in his seigneurie of Lauzon to the Jesuits for 1,000 livres, a price which would not have been paid unless there were some cleared land on the concession. Vente et concession par M. Jean de Lauzon en faveur des Jésuites de six arpents de front sur quarante de profondeur à titre de arrière-fief, Nov. 15, 1653, Greffe de Jean Durand, notary, in APQ, Pièce détachée, arrière-fief, Notre Dame de la Victoire, Lauzon. The Jesuits themselves sold arrière-fiefs in the same way in Notre Dame des Anges.

42 Examples of this type of transaction can be found in the roture boxes in the APQ. See, specifically, Vente de terre par Jacques Pasquel et sa femme aux Rds. pères Jésuites, 1710, in APQ, Pièce détachée, La Prairie de la Magdeleine, rotures; Vente par Jean Perrot aux R. P. Jésuites, Feb. 11, 1716, in APQ, Pièce détachée, La Prairie de la Magdeleine, rotures; Sentence du juge de N. D. des Anges pour la Réunion au Domaine des terres abandonnées, ou par disertion ou par mort ou qui avoient esté occupées par des vagabonds, March 12, 1693, in APQ, Pièce détachée, Notre Dame des Anges. Sometimes when a censitaire abandoned a concession he had a statement drawn up, no doubt on the seigneur's urging, returning his land to the seigneur. See, for example, Remise et abandon par Nicolas Rousselot de la prairie de son habitaon de la petite Rivière aux Rds. P. Jésuites, March 25, 1689, in APQ, Pièce détachée, Notre Dame des Anges, rotures.

43 Beauharnois et Hocquart au Ministre, Oct. 10, 1730, in AC, C 11 A, LII, 101 ff.; Munro, *Documents*, pp. 169–72.

44 See, for example, Vente par Jean Perrot aux R. P. Jésuites, Feb. 11, 1716, in APQ, Pièce détachée, Notre Dame des Anges. Constitution de Rente de 15 livres sur Paul Chalison, Oct. 24, 1710, in APQ, Pièce détachée, Notre Dame des Anges, rotures.

45 The obligation to plant a Maypole appears in roture contracts in Bonsecours and in Varennes. The habitants objected strenuously. See Concession du Sieur Robert Choret Seigneur de Notre-Dame de Bonsecours à Pierre Morisset, Jan. 2, 1708, in APQ, Pièce détachée, Bonsecours, rotures; Jugment qui, du consentement de la Dame et Seigneuresse de Varennes, décharge ses censitaires du Tremblay de l'obligation de porter leurs grains moudre à son moulin du Cap-de-Varennes, etc. . . . , June 29, 1707, *Edits et ordonnances*, III, 132–33.

46 Jugement qui déclare les offres faites par Pierre Lanouette à Mr. de la Pérade . . . sera bien et valablement déchargé . . . , Oct. 13, 1736, *Edits et ordonnances*, III, 316–18.

47 Jugement définitif rendu entre les Sieurs Gourdeaux . . . et le Sieur Noël . . . et qui condamne ce dernier à payer 21 années d'arrérages de Cens et rentes . . . , April 13, 1745, *Edits et ordonnances*, III, 348–60.

48 Ordonnance qui condamne Julien Rivard Lanouette, habitant de la seigneurie de Sainte-Anne à payer . . . les cens et rentes . . . , March 3, 1744, Ordonnances des Intendants, XXXII, 35–37.

49 Ordonnance de Gilles Hocquart, Intendant, qui oblige les habitants de la seigneurie de Demaure à représenter à la Dame veuve de la Chesnaye, leurs contrats, billets de concession, quittances d'arrérages de cens et rentes; à faute par eux de les représenter, la dite Dame autorisée à poursuivre le payement des dits arrérages jusqu'à concurrance de vingt-neuf années, March 18, 1734, *Edits et ordonnances,* III, 295.

50 Etat des Sommes dues aux R. P. Jésuites Seigneurs de Notre-Dame-des-Anges . . . pour arrérages de cens et rentes et droits de Los et ventes, 1754, in APQ, Pièce détachée, Notre Dame des Anges.

51 Marcel Trudel has also calculated the total cost of a roture to the censitaire. His figures differ somewhat from mine principally because he assumed an average price for wheat of four livres a minot, which seems a little high. *Le Régime seigneurial* (Canadian Historical Association, brochure No. 6, Ottawa, 1956), p. 14.

52 The large domain in Berthier was thirty by forty arpents, but as late as 1723 there was no settlement on it. Aveu et dénombrement de Pierre de Lestage . . . pour le fief et seigneurie de Berthier . . . , Aug. 9, 1723, in APQ, Aveux et dénombrements, cahier 2, I, folio 122.

Only the smaller seigneuries ever lacked a domain for long. One such was Guillaudière or Grandmaison in which there were two filled ranges in 1736 but no domain. Aveu et dénombrement de Maurice Blondeau pour le fief de la Guillaudière ou Blondeau, July 1, 1726, in APQ, Aveux et dénombrements, cahier 2, I, folio 291.

53 There were, for example, four domains on Terrebonne although there was only one seigneur. See Aveu et Dénombrement . . . pour le fief et seigneurie de Terrebonne, May 20, 1736, in APQ, Aveux et dénombrements, cahier 2, II, folios 430–59.

54 Aveu et dénombrement du Fief d'Argentenay, June 11, 1714, in APQ, Pièce détachée, Ile d'Orléans, Argentenay.

55 Aveu de dénombrement de Joseph Amyot de Vincelotte pour le fief et seigneurie de Vincelotte, June 27, 1724, in APQ, Aveux et dénombrements, cahier 2, I, folio 156.

56 See, for example, Acte de loyer de Charles Aubert de la Chesnaye fils, July 9, 1689, Greffe d'Adhémar, notary, in APQ, Pièce détachée, Lachesnaye ou L'Assomption.

57 Bail du domain des Jésuites à la Prairie de la Magdeleine à Charles Boyer, June 29, 1675, in APQ, Pièce détachée, La Prairie de la Magdeleine, rotures, I.

58 Acte de loyer . . . de la Chesnaye fils, cited in n. 56.

59 Aveu et dénombrement de Jean-Baptiste Coté pour le fief de l'Isle-Verte, Feb. 15, 1723, in APQ, Aveux et dénombrements, cahier 2, I, folio 1.

60 Aveu et dénombrement . . . pour le fief et seigneurie de Terrebonne, cited in n. 53.

61 Acte de vente de M. Lepage de Sainte-Claire à Louis de Chapt . . . , Jan. 15, 1745, Greffe de Blanzy et Adhémar, notaries, in APQ, Pièce détachée, Terrebonne.

62 The three domains are described in the *aveu et dénombrement* of 1732, in APQ, Aveux et dénombrements, cahier 2, II, 375 ff.

63 See the excellent study by Robert-Lionel Séguin, *L'Equipement de la ferme canadienne, aux XVII° et XVIII° siècles* (Montreal, 1959).

64 De Meulles au Ministre, Sept. 28, 1685, in AC, C 11 A, VII, 133–34.

65 Séguin, *L'Equipement de la ferme canadienne*, pp. 36–37.

66 J. N. Fauteux, *Essai sur l'industrie au Canada sous le régime français* (Quebec, 1927), II, Chap. XI.

67 These efforts were most persistent early in the 18th century, and a very good impression of the trials and tribulations of setting up an industry in Canada can be had by reading the Raudots' dispatches in the Correspondance Générale, AC, C 11 A, XXV to XXIX particularly. See also Fauteux, *Essai sur l'industrie*, II, Chaps. IV–VII.

CHAPTER 6

1 See Guy Frégault, "Le Régime seigneurial et l'expansion de la colonisation dans le bassin du St-Laurent au dix-huitième siècle," *Canadian Historical Association Report* (1944), p. 61, for one example among many.

2 Arrêt du Roi, June 4, 1672, *Edits et ordonnances*, I, 70–71; William B. Munro, *Documents Relating to the Seigniorial Tenure in Canada* (Toronto, 1908), pp. 32–34.

3 Arrêt du Roi, May 9, 1679, *Edits et ordonnances*, I, 70–71; Munro, *Documents*, pp. 43–45.

4 William B. Munro, *The Seigniorial System in Canada* (New York, 1907), p. 61.

5 Arrêt du Roi qui déchoit les habitants de la propriété des Terres qui leur auront été concédées, s'ils ne les mettent en valeur, en y tenant feu et lieu, dans un an et jour de la publication du dit Arrêt, July 6, 1711, *Edits et ordonnances*, I, 324–26; Munro, *Documents*, pp. 91–94.

6 This conclusion was reflected in many of the king's early *arrêts*. See particularly the *arrêt* of 1672, the reissue of 1675, the *arrêt* of 1679, and the many instructions to grant smaller seigneuries which have been cited in Chap. 3 above.

7 See, for example, Contrat de vente fait par Jean le May à Michel Marie fils, April 23, 1711, in APQ, Pièce détachée, rotures, A-B, Bonsecours. In this case a roture of three by forty arpents was sold for twelve livres. A sale of forty square arpents for twelve days work was the Vent d'habitation de Jacques Denlau à Gilles Luton, Nov. 27, 1678, in APQ, Pièce détachée, rotures, La Prairie de la Magdeleine, II. In later years prices were somewhat higher.

8 See particularly Raudot's report to the minister in 1707, in AC, C 11 A, XXVI, 7–34; Munro, *Documents,* pp. 70–80.

9 Vaudreuil et Bégon au Ministre, Oct. 26, 1719, in AC, C 11 A, XL, 7; Munro, *Documents,* pp. 163–64.

10 Jugement rendu par le Gouverneur et l'Intendant . . . par lequel ils concèdent à la Dame Veuve Petit, une terre dans la seigneurie de Saint-Ignace, Oct. 13, 1721, *Edits et ordonnances,* III, 184–87.

11 Beauharnois et Hocquart au Ministre, Oct. 10, 1730, in AC, C 11 A, LII, 101 ff.; Munro, *Documents,* pp. 169–72.

12 *Ibid.*

13 Arrêt faisant défense aux seigneurs de vendre les terres qui ne sont pas défrichées . . . , March 15, 1732, *Edits et ordonnances,* I, 531.

14 Registre des titres de concession en la ville de Québec et autres concessions en censive, circa 1702, in APQ, Pièce détachée, Rivière du Sud.

15 Mémoire du Roy aux Srs. Marquis de Vaudreuil et Robert sur les affaires de la Colonie, May 30, 1724, in AC, B, XLVII, 149.

16 Hocquart et Beauharnois au Ministre, Oct. 11, 1737, in AC, C 11 A, LXVII, 11 ff.; Munro, *Documents,* pp. 181–85; Guy Frégault, *La Civilisation de la Nouvelle-France* (Montreal, 1944), pp. 204–6.

17 Emile Salone, *La Colonisation de la Nouvelle-France* (Paris, 1905), pp. 56–57; Benjamiñ Sulte, *Histoire des canadiens français* (Montreal, 1882–84), II, 57.

18 Salone, *La Colonisation,* pp. 57–58.

19 Mémoire du Roi pour servir d'instruction au Sieur Talon s'en allant au Canada, March 27, 1665, in AC, B, I, 48–75. In this memoir the king likened the Canadians to "presque ses propres enfans," which was another way of stating the ideal seigneur-vassal relationship.

20 The size and wealth of the Canadian bourgeoisie during the French regime has been considerably debated. Several historians, particularly Guy Frégault, have maintained that there was a small but prosperous bourgeoisie, on a reduced scale not unlike the bourgeoisie in New England. This view is well summarized in Frégault, *La Société canadienne sous le régime français* (Canadian Historical Association, brochure No. 3, 1954). On the other hand, Jean Hamelin, in *Economie et société en Nouvelle-France* (Laval University Press, 1960), has amassed evidence pointing to the fact that this group was much smaller and less prosperous than had been

thought. Hamelin claims that most of those who profited from Canada lived in France. This latter view seems closer to the truth.

21 My own estimate, and only a calculated guess. Some people were transported to Canada for considerably less, but the average total bill for recruiting settlers in France, transporting them to and provisioning them in the New World cannot have been less than 100 livres.

22 Paul-Emile Rénaud, *Les Origines économiques du Canada* (Mamers, 1928), p. 285.

23 Concession à Jean Maignay, Sept. 13, 1672, in APQ, Pièce détachée, La Prairie de la Magdeleine, rotures. This was the first concession at the lower rate.

24 Rentes were returned to the higher level in 1693. See any of the rotures for this date in the APQ, Pièce détachée, La Prairie de la Magdeleine.

25 Concession à Pierre Hérault, June 2, 1733, in APQ, Pièce détachée, Beauharnois, rotures.

26 Jugement qui réunit au domaine du sieur Neveu . . . trois terres abandonnées, July 3, 1720, *Edits et ordonnances*, III, 178–81.

27 Lettre de Mgr. Dosquet au Ministre, Oct. 14, 1730, in APQ, Pièce détachée, Dosquet.

28 As there were several mills on some seigneuries, not more than a third of all the seigneuries conceded for agricultural development had mills in 1734. The number of mills is given in most of the censuses, and many of these are printed in *The Census of the Dominion of Canada* (1871), IV.

29 Boucher placed at least thirty-eight families on his seigneurie in 1673, an accomplishment which represented an enormous effort on his part. Concessions par Mr. Boucher Seigneur de Boucherville Pr Servir à Trente Huit Personnes Denommées au pied dud. Contract, April 4, 1673, in APQ, Pièce détachée, Boucherville.

30 Jugement qui réunit au Domaine de Sa Majesté les seigneuries de François Daine . . . , May 10, 1741, *Edits et ordonnances*, II, 555–61.

31 The market was formally established in Quebec in 1676. See Réglemens généraux du Conseil Supérieur, 1676, *Arrêts et Réglements*, II, 65 ff. A similar market was established in Montreal in 1706 (*Edits et ordonnances*, II, 258–62), and another, on a much smaller scale, in Trois-Rivières in 1722 (*Edits et ordonnances*, III, 443).

32 Mémoire concernant l'Estat présent du Canada par Denonville, Nov. 12, 1685, in AC, C 11 A, VII, 204.

CHAPTER 7

1 At least one such roture was granted by Frontenac. Occasionally individual seigneurs granted rotures with a river frontage of twenty to thirty arpents.

2 It would be extremely difficult to demonstrate this conclusion statistically, and I have not tried. There is no record of complaints because a seigneur

was giving less land than another, and in reading many hundreds of roture contracts, I have rarely noticed sustained differences in the size of rotures conceded by different seigneurs.

3 Projets des Réglemens qui semblent être utiles en Canada, proposés . . . par Talon, Jan. 24, 1667, *Edits et ordonnances,* II, 29–34.

4 For example, when Pierre Boucher began his drive for settlers for his new seigneurie, he granted them plots of 2 × 25 arpents which, like the Talon grants, were substantially smaller than the earlier or later averages. Acte de concession de Pierre Boucher . . . aux personnes ci après nommées . . . , April 4, 1673, Greffe de Gilles Durand, notary, in APQ, Pièce détachée, Boucherville.

5 During the 1660's the king frequently inveighed against seigneurs who granted rotures which he considered to be too large. The first of these complaints is in Extrait du Registre du conseil d'état, March, 1663, in William B. Munro, *Documents Relating to the Seigniorial Tenure in Canada* (Toronto, 1908), pp. 12–14; *Edits et ordonnances,* I, 33; and AC, C 11 A, II, 10–12.

6 Concession par Robert Giffard à Noel Langlois, June 29, 1637, Lespinasse, notary, in AJQ, Pièce détachée.

7 Uncatalogued map in the Archives du Séminaire de Québec.

8 As early as 1682 there were complaints about this practice. See Ordonnance qui décrète que les habitants ne pourront tenir et faire valoir que deux concessions, April 24, 1682, in P. G. Roy, *Ordonnances, commissions, etc., des gouverneurs et intendants de la Nouvelle-France, 1639–1706* (Quebec, 1924), I, 308–10.

9 *Ibid.*

10 Some of these can be found in the Ordonnances des Intendants. See, for example, an ordinance requiring the habitants of St-Ours to *tenir feu et lieu,* July 7, 1710, Ordonnances des Intendants, IV, 102–4.

11 Arrêt du Roi qui déchoit les habitants de la propriété des Terres qui leur auront été concédées, s'ils ne les mettent en valeur, en y tenant feu et lieu, dans un an et jour de la publication du dit Arrêt, July 6, 1711, *Edits et ordonnances,* I, 326; Munro, *Documents,* pp. 91–94.

12 It is often pointed out that at the beginning of his intendancy Hocquart withdrew several hundred rotures, but it is not realized that in this Hocquart was not particularly exceptional. The reader will find most of the ordinances on this subject in the Ordonnances des Intendants.

13 References to such censitaires appear from time to time in the documents. See, for example, Concession Par Mrs. du Séminaire à Pierre Bandry Père et fils, Nov. 20, 1731, in APQ, Pièce détachée, Lauzon, rotures. Bandry was a censitaire in the seigneurie of Tilly, and abandoned this concession in Lauzon sometime between 1731 and 1739.

14 Réunion de la terre de la chêne au Cap de la Madeléine, June 22, 1723, in APQ, Pièce détachée, Cap de la Madeleine.

15 Jugement qui condamne les nommés Jean Boutin, Pierre Guignard, et Guillemet Lemieux à travailler dans un an au défrichement de leurs terres, et qui donne défaut contre Antoine Guillemen et la veuve Guignard . . . , March 1, 1723, *Edits et ordonnances,* III, 196–97. Note the order to clear rather than to *tenir feu et lieu.*

16 Ordonnance sur La Commune de la Prairie de la Magdeleine, June 29, 1720, in APQ, Pièce détachée, La Prairie de la Magdeleine, rotures, I.

17 The *douaire* was much less common than the *communauté des biens,* but it did appear from time to time. See, for example, Ordonnance qui donne acte à Robert Dufour de la renonciation qu'il fait à la succession d'Ignace Gagnon, March 22, 1707, Ordonnances des Intendants, I, 94.

18 See, for example, Ordonnance qui approuve la donation faite par Antoine Toupin et Louise Cloutier, sa femme, à Antoine Toupin, leur fils, Feb. 8, 1710, Ordonnances des Intendants, IV, 12–13.

19 See, for example, Ordonnance qui permet à Laurent Levasseur . . . , July 6, 1708, Ordonnances des Intendants, II.

20 Aveu et dénombrement, Beaupré, 1733, in APQ, Aveux et dénombrements, cahier 2, II, 375 ff.

21 Ordonnance du Roi portant entr'autres choses défenses aux habitans de bâtir sur les terres, à moins qu'elles ne soient d'un arpent et demi de front sur trente à quarante de profondeur, April 28, 1745, *Edits et ordonnances,* I, 585–86.

22 See, for example, Ordonnance qui commet le sieur de Rouville pour faire démolir les maisons bâties, au préjudice de l'Ordonnance du Roi de 1745, sur des terrains moindre d'un arpent et demi de front et de trente de profondeur, June 25, 1749, *Edits et ordonnances,* II, 400. These buildings were demolished in Beaupré.

23 Aveu et dénombrement, La Prairie de la Magdeleine, March 4, 1733, in APQ, Pièce détachée, La Prairie de la Magdeleine.

24 Aveu et dénombrement, Ile de Montréal, Sept. 10, 1731, in APQ, Aveux et dénombrements, cahier 2, I; *RAPQ* (1941–42), pp. 2–163.

25 These and the following figures have been calculated from Léon Roy's inventory of the parish, "Les Terres de l'Ile d'Orléans; les terres de la Sainte-Famille," in *RAPQ* (1949–51), pp. 147–260.

26 Census of the Government of Quebec, 1762, in *RAPQ* (1925–26), pp. 1–143.

27 *Ibid.,* pp. 3–5.

28 *Ibid.,* pp. 108–13.

CHAPTER 8

1 Marcel Trudel, *L'Esclavage au Canada français* (Laval University Press, 1960). Robert-Lionel Séguin, "Les conditions techniques de l'habitant canadien-français aux XVII° et XVIII° siècles" (Thesis for *le diplome d'étude supérieure en histoire,* Laval University, 1958); *L'Equipement de*

la ferme canadienne aux XVIIe et XVIIIe siècles (Montreal, 1959); *Les Granges du Québec* (Ottawa, 1963). Luc Lacourcière, director of the Archives de Folklore series published intermittently by the Laval University Press since 1946.

2 When an habitant could not pay the *lods et ventes,* his seigneur might lend him the money on the security of the land, an arrangement which transferred title of the roture to the seigneur until the habitant had repaid the loan plus interest, and which must have discouraged many prospective buyers. In 1716 Jean Perrot bought a roture in La Prairie de la Magdeleine for 4,800 livres and sold it to the Jesuits for 400 livres in order to pay the *lods et ventes.* Perrot worked the land, and would regain legal possession of it when he had paid off the 400 livres. Vente par Jean Perrot aux R. P. Jésuittes, Feb. 11, 1716, in APQ, Pièce détachée, La Prairie de la Magdeleine, rotures, I.

3 There is no way of knowing how frequently the retrait was used, but because the retrait was essentially a threat, it did not have to be used frequently to fulfill a useful function. From time to time the threat materialized. See, for example, Jugement qui valide le Retrait Seigneurial exercé par la Dame Veuve de Varenne . . . , June 15, 1714, *Edits et ordonnances,* II, 438–40.

4 In the 17th century deeds of sale commonly stipulated that the price would be paid either in *argent monneye* or in kind (usually beaver or wheat); in the 18th century these arrangements became less frequent. The interested reader will find the deeds of sale in the roture boxes of the APQ, and a quick perusal of a few of them will give an idea of the variety of agreements worked out to pay for land.

5 The *Inventaires de Biens,* those inventories of a man's estate drawn up after his death, are most revealing in this regard. More often than not a censitaire owed money to a number of creditors and might, in turn, have been the creditor in several other transactions. Because he was accustomed to paying for purchases over a number of years, the debts he contracted to buy land might not have seemed particularly onerous.

6 Aveu et dénombrement, Notre-Dame-des-Anges, 1678, in APQ, Pièce détachée, Notre Dame des Anges.

7 Ordonnance de M. Talon qui oblige les concessionnaires de terre à abattre le bois et à mettre deux arpents en Culture chaque année, May 22, 1667, in P. G. Roy, *Ordonnances, commissions, etc., des gouverneurs et intendants de la Nouvelle-France, 1639–1706* (Quebec, 1924), I, 66–68.

8 Concession de l'Ile aux Ruaux par les Révérends pères Jésuites à Charles Campagna, March 6, 1708, in APQ, Pièce détachée, Ile aux Ruaux.

9 *Ibid.*

10 Marcel Rioux, *Description de la culture de l'Ile Verte* (Musée National du Canada, Bulletin 133, No. 35 de la série anthropologique, Ottawa, 1954), pp. 40–42.

11 See, for example, Ordonnance pour Pierre Retou . . . , July 11, 1710, Ordonnances des Intendants, IV, 107.

12 See, for example, Ordonnance qui permet à Joseph Huot . . . tuteur des enfants mineurs . . . de faire crier à bail à ferme la terre . . . pour six années consécutives au plus offrant et dernier enchérisseur, Dec. 7, 1737, Ordonnances des Intendants, XXVI, 52–53.

13 R. G. Thwaites, ed., *The Jesuit Relations and Allied Documents* (Cleveland, 1897), IX, 154–55. In one year twenty men could clear thirty arpents suitable for plowing.

14 See, for example, De Meulles au Ministre, Sept. 28, 1685, in AC, C 11 A, VII, 133–34.

15 Séguin, *L'Equipement de la ferme canadienne*, p. 40.

16 *The America of 1750: Peter Kalm's Travels in North America*, ed. A. B. Benson (New York, 1937), II, 458.

17 B. A. Slicher Van Bath, *The Agrarian History of Western Europe, A.D. 500–1850* (London, 1963), pp. 18–23.

18 Vaudreuil et Raudot au Ministre, Nov. 14, 1709, in AC, C 11 A, XXX, 3; Séguin, *L'Equipement de la ferme canadienne*, pp. 40–42; Boucault, "Etat présent du Canada," 1754, in *RAPQ* (1920–21), p. 20.

19 Slicher Van Bath, *The Agrarian History of Western Europe*, p. 177.

20 See, for example, M. de La Pause, Rapport sur la Population et sur la Culture des Terres, 1759, in *RAPQ* (1933–34), pp. 211–12.

21 Slicher Van Bath, *The Agrarian History of Western Europe*, p. 18.

22 *Peter Kalm's Travels*, II, 438.

23 *Ibid.*, II, 510.

24 Boucault, in *RAPQ* (1920–21), p. 20.

25 *Peter Kalm's Travels*, II, 508–9; The engineer Gideon de Catalogne reported peach trees in Canada in 1712, but there cannot have been many. Catalogne, Mémoire sur Canada, Nov. 7, 1712, in AC, C 11 A, XXXIII, 299. Catalogne's report is printed in full in William B. Munro, *Documents Relating to the Seigniorial Tenure in Canada* (Toronto, 1908), pp. 94–151.

26 Catalogne wrote of cherry trees, but there are few other references to them in Canada. The best description of the vineyards is again in *Peter Kalm's Travels*, II, 514.

27 *Ibid.*, II, 458.

28 When Pierre Boucher wrote his description of Canada in 1664 there were still no horses in the colony. Pierre Boucher, *Histoire véritable et naturelle des mœurs et productions du pays de la Nouvelle-France*, ed. C. Coffin (Montreal, 1882), p. 137; or the English translation, *Canada in the Seventeenth Century*, ed. E. L. Montizambert (Montreal, 1873), p. 70.

29 Champigny au Ministre, May 26, 1699, in AC, C 11 A, XVII, 87.

30 These regulations were imposed by a series of ordinances:
     Ordonnance contre ceux qui courent à cheval dans les grands chemins, Nov. 10, 1706, Ordonnances des Intendants, I, 239–40.

Ordonnance pour les carioles et chevaux dans les grands chemins, Jan. 21, 1708, Ordonnances des Intendants, II, 54–55.

Ordonnance qui défend aux habitants du gouvernement de Montréal d'avoir chez-eux plus de deux chevaux et un poulain, June 13, 1709, Ordonnances des Intendants, III, 74–76.

Ordonnance qui défend aux habitants de prendre les chevaux des autres, Oct. 29, 1710, Ordonnances des Intendants, IV, 4–5.

31 Vaudreuil et Raudot au Ministre, Nov. 2, 1710, in AC, C 11 A, XXXI, 22.

32 Mémoire de Vaudreuil à Pontchartrain, 1710, in AC, C 11 A, XXXI, 88; Vaudreuil et Bégon au Ministre, Nov. 12, 1712, in AC, C 11 A, XXXIII, 32.

33 Denonville urged the minister to agree to an ordinance requiring every habitant to keep two or three sheep. Denonville au Ministre, Nov. 13, 1685, in AC, C 11 A, VII, 59.

34 Raudot au Ministre, Nov. 19, 1705, in AC, C 11 A, XXII, 288.

35 Séguin, *Les Granges du Québec*, pp. 1–30.

36 *Ibid.*, p. 113.

37 *Ibid.*, p. 12.

38 Séguin, *L'Equipement de la ferme canadienne*, pp. 9–34; and Séguin, "Nos premiers instruments aratoires sont-ils de bois ou de fer?" *Revue d'Histoire de l'Amérique Française*, XVII, No. 4 (March, 1964), 531–36.

39 The census taken by the English from 1762 to 1765 lists additional help, and these listings suggest the percentage indicated, *RAPQ* (1925–26), pp. 1–143.

40 Trudel, *L'Esclavage au Canada français*, p. 156.

41 Ordonnance de l'Intendant, March 17, 1707, Ordonnances des Intendants, I, 311–12.

42 *Peter Kalm's Travels*, II, 411.

43 *Ibid.*, II, 479.

44 J. N. Fauteux, *Essai sur l'industrie au Canada sous le régime français* (Quebec, 1927), II, Chap. 4.

45 Les habitants de l'île de Montréal au sujet de la réserve que les seigneurs ont fait dans les concessions pour le bois de chauffage, July 2, 1706, Ordonnances des Intendants, I, 183–84.

46 Catalogne, Mémoire, 1712, in AC, C 11 A, XXXIII, 277–368; Munro, *Documents*, pp. 138 and 140.

47 *Rélations des Jésuites*, XL, 214, cited in Fauteux, *Essai sur l'industrie*, II, 500–501.

48 Boucher, *Histoire*, pp. 19 and 44–47; Boucault, in *RAPQ* (1920–21), pp. 14–15.

49 *Peter Kalm's Travels*, II, 423–24, 494.

50 Boucault, in *RAPQ* (1920–21), pp. 14–15.

51 Jean Lunn, "The Illegal Fur Trade out of New France," *Canadian Historical Association Report* (1939), pp. 61–76.

52 See, for example, the following descriptions of the ills wrought by the coureurs de bois: Duchesneau au Ministre, Nov. 10, 1679, in AC, C 11 A, V, 52–53; Denonville au Ministre, Nov. 13, 1685, in AC, C 11 A, VII, 42–46; Mémoire Instructif sur le Canada joint à la lettre de M. de Champigny, Intendant, May 10, 1691, in AC, C 11 A, XI, 468.

53 Ordonnance qui défend la chasse hors l'étendue des terres défrichées, May 12, 1678, in AC, C 11 A, IV, 276–87.

54 Mémoire de Frontenac au Ministre, in AC, C 11 A, IV, 170–73.

55 Duchesneau au Ministre, Nov. 10, 1679, in AC, C 11 A, V, 52–53.

56 Mémoire Instructif . . . joint à la lettre de M. de Champigny, May 10, 1691, in AC, C 11 A, XI, 468.

57 It may be impossible to determine the number of habitants who were attracted to a life, or even to a season, in the forest, but the question of the influence of the fur trade on the development of agricultural Canada, which H. A. Innis (*The Fur Trade in Canada*) introduced, and W. J. Eccles (*Frontenac: The Courtier Governor*) has expanded on, still needs a great deal of work. Certainly, the fur trade required a lot of manpower, almost all of which had to come from Canada.

58 Catalogne, Mémoire, 1712, in AC, C 11 A, XXXIII, 299.

59 Raudot au Ministre, Nov. 2, 1706, in AC, C 11 A, XXIV, 90.

60 *Peter Kalm's Travels,* II, 511.

61 *Ibid.,* II, 510.

62 Ordonnance qui défend à tous les habitants d'aller sur les terres des autres enlever les fruits, Aug. 4, 1707, Ordonnances des Intendants, I, 433–34.

63 Boucher, *Histoire,* pp. 71–72; Fauteux, *Essai sur l'industrie,* II, 379–80.

64 Talon established a tannery in the 1660's; and, unlike his other industries, it did not collapse when he departed. By the 1680's there were tanneries in Montreal and Quebec. Denonville au Ministre, Nov. 13, 1685, in AC, C 11 A, VII, 59. Fauteux, *Essai sur l'industrie,* II, 405–43.

65 See, for example, Champigny au Ministre, Nov. 16, 1686, in AC, C 11 A, VIII, 338.

66 Raudot au Ministre, Nov. 2, 1706, in AC, C 11 A, XXIV, 87.

67 Mme. de Repentigny au Ministre, Oct. 13, 1705, in AC, C 11 A, XXII, 348–52.

68 Denonville au Ministre, May 8, 1686, in AC, C 11 A, VIII, 22.

69 The tools which were used for carding, spinning, and weaving are described by Séguin, *L'Equipement de la ferme canadienne,* pp. 93–99; the best discussion of the weaving industry during the French regime is in Fauteux, *Essai sur l'industrie,* II, 444–82.

70 On architecture in the colony see particularly: Nora Dawson, *La Vie traditionnelle à Saint-Pierre* (Quebec, 1960), pp. 23–29; Gérard Morisset, *L'Architecture en Nouvelle-France* (Quebec, 1949).

71 *Peter Kalm's Travels,* II, 460.

72 *Ibid.* These stoves had been made at the iron works near Trois-Rivières.

73 C. S. Grant, *Democracy in the Connecticut Frontier Town of Kent* (New York, 1961), p. 29.

74 Mémoire concernant le Canada par Denonville, Jan., 1690, in AC, C 11 A, XI, 319.

75 R. M. Saunders, "The Emergence of the Coureurs de Bois as a Social Type," *Canadian Historical Association Report* (1939), pp. 22–33.

CHAPTER 9

1 William B. Munro, *Documents Relating to the Seigniorial Tenure in Canada,* p. xvii; Guy Frégault, "Le Régime seigneurial et l'expansion de la colonisation dans le bassin du St-Laurent au dix-huitième siècle," *Canadian Historical Association Report* (1944), pp. 62–63; Thomas Gérin, *Feudal Canada: The Story of the Seigniories of New France* (Montreal, 1926), p. 117. Filteau tends to stress the influence of the seigneur, Groulx that of the curé. Gérard Filteau, *La Naissance d'une nation* (Montreal, 1937), II, Chaps. 2 and 3; Lionel Groulx, *Histoire du Canada français* (Montreal, 1950–51), I, 103–11; II, 158–66.

2 Raisons de la Compagnie de Canada pour empêcher sa dépossession ou pour de meilleures conditions, circa 1663, in AC, C 11 A, II, 64–67.

3 Arrêt qui ordonne que les habitants du Canada feront défricher les terres de leur concessions sinon révoque les concessions à eux faites, March 21, 1663, in AC, C 11 A, II, 10–12.

4 Instructions données par Sa Majesté au Sieur Gaudais . . . , May 7, 1663, *Edits et ordonnances,* III, 23–27; Munro, *Documents,* pp. 14–17.

5 Arrêt du Conseil Supérieur de Québec, qui ordonne, avant faire droit, que l'arrêt concernant la réunion des terres non défrichées, sera communiqué au syndic des habitans, Aug. 6, 1664, *Edits et ordonnances,* II, 18–19.

6 Mémoire du Roi pour servir d'instruction au Sieur Talon s'en allant au Canada, March 27, 1665, in AC, B, I, 62.

7 Talon au Ministre, Oct. 4, 1665, in AC, C 11 A, II, 214–15; and Talon au Ministre, Nov. 13, 1666, in AC, C 11 A, II, 324–25. The *aveu et dénombrement* for Notre Dame des Anges in 1678 indicates that all the rotures in Charlesbourg and Petit Auvergne were conceded in 1665 and 1666. It makes no mention of Bourg Royal, and there is some doubt if it was established as early as the others.

8 The village project is discussed in most of Talon's dispatches, but most fully in Projets des Réglemens qui semblent être utiles en Canada proposés à Mrs. de Tracy et de Courcelles par M. Talon, Jan. 24, 1667, *Edits et ordonnances,* II, 29–34; AC, C 11 A, II, 553 ff.

9 Frontenac au Ministre, Nov. 2, 1672, in AC, C 11 A, III, 337; and also, Frontenac au Ministre, Nov. 12, 1674, in AC, C 11 A, IV, 168–69.

10 Résumé des lettres de M. M. de Denonville et Champigny, Aug. 20, Aug. 31, Nov. 6, 1688, in AC, C 11 A, X, 302–3.

11 Mémoire instructif sur le Canada par Champigny, May 10, 1691, in AC, C 11 A, XI, 469.

12 Remarques sur ce qui parroit important au Service du Roy pour la conservation de la nouvelle france, circa 1689, in AC, C 11 A, X, 556–57.

13 Réponse du Ministre au marge des lettres de Denonville et Champigny, Aug. 20, Aug. 31, Nov. 6, 1688, in AC, C 11 A, X, 302–3.

14 Ordonnance du Roi, portant . . . défenses aux habitans de bâtir sur les terres, à moins qu'elles ne soient d'un arpent et demi de front sur trente à quarante de profondeur, April 28, 1745, *Edits et ordonnances*, I, 585–86.

15 Marcel Trudel, *Le Régime seigneurial* (Canadian Historical Association, brochure No. 6, Ottawa, 1956), p. 9.

16 These were requested by the seigneurs of Beaupré, Ile Jésus, La Durantaye, L'Assomption, Lotbinière, Neuville, Soulanges, and Contrecœur, between 1753 and 1758 inclusive. All are printed in *Edits et ordonnances*, II, 410–12, 412–13, 414, 415, 419, 420, and III, 401–2.

17 See any of the applications cited in n. 16.

18 Jugement qui enjoint aux . . . seigneurs de Chambly . . . de convenir d'experts pour constater les dommages faits . . . par les bois qui se répandent sur leurs terres, June 7, 1714, *Edits et ordonnances*, III, 164–66.

19 Frontenac au Ministre, Nov. 2, 1672, in AC, C 11 A, III, 337.

20 Aveu et dénombrement de Jean-Baptiste Gaultier de Varennes . . . pour le fief et Seigneurie de Boucherville, Aug. 28, 1724, in APQ, Aveux et dénombrements, rég. fr., cahier 2, I, fols. 186–97.

21 St-Joachim and Château Richer. In 1753 the Séminaire proposed to enlarge the latter.

22 The village of Fargy is referred to in the *aveu et dénombrement* for the seigneurie of Beauport of 1659 (APQ, Pièce détachée, Beauport). There were eleven rotures in it, each of them one by ten arpents. The village was mentioned again in 1713, but like many another "village" was probably no more than a straggling line of houses. Arrêt du Conseil Supérieur de Québec portant réglement qui fait défense au Sieur Duchesnay de concéder aucun emplacement dans le Bourg de Fargy à Beauport, à plus haut titre de redevance qu'à celui d'un sol de cens et un poulet de rente seigneuriale par chaque arpent, May 29, 1713, *Edits et ordonnances*, II, 161–62.

23 Remarques sur ce qui parroit important au Service du Roy, circa 1689, in AC, C 11 A, X, 557.

24 This point was suggested by Fernand Ouellet during a conversation with him. It is also alluded to by Louis-Edmond Hamelin, "Le Rang à Saint-Didace de Maskinongé," *Notes de Géographie*, No. 3 (Laval, 1953), p. 7.

25 De Meulles au Ministre, Nov. 4, 1683, in AC, C 11 A, VI, 290–91. In this connection see, also, Denonville au Ministre, Nov. 13, 1685, in AC, C 11 A, VII, 50–51.

26 Frontenac au Ministre, Nov. 12, 1674, in AC, C 11 A, IV, 168–69.

27 The clearest exposition of the reasons for establishing a village is in

Ordonnance qui établit un Village sur la Pointe de l'Est de l'Isle Jésus, d'environ vingt arpens en superficie, Aug. 25, 1753, *Edits et ordonnances,* II, 412–13.

28 Frontenac et Champigny au Ministre, March 5, 1694, in AC, C 11 A, XIII, 26–27.

29 Denonville au Ministre, Nov. 13, 1685, in AC, C 11 A, VII, 50. Probably these cabins were less common than Denonville thought, and certainly their principal *raison d'être* was the fur trade.

30 The reader will find some of the intendants' judgments relating to these disputes in the *Edits et ordonnances,* and many more in the Ordonnances des Intendants.

31 Procès Verbaux sur la commodité et incommodité dressés dans chacune des paroisses de la Nouvelle-France par Mathien-Benoit Collet, Procureur Général du Roi au Conseil Supérieur de Québec, Jan., 1721, in *RAPQ* (1921–22), pp. 262–362.

32 The population level is not mentioned in the documents, but it is clear from an analysis of census data that an attempt was made to keep the population of a parish within these limits.

33 See William B. Munro, *The Seigniorial System in Canada* (New York, 1907), pp. 145–58, for a good analysis of the Canadian seigneur's judicial prerogatives.

34 A comparison of the census figures for 1739 suggests this difference in living standard.

CHAPTER 10

1 Philippe A. de Gaspé, *Mémoires* (Quebec, 1885), p. 530.

2 F. J. Turner, "The Rise and Fall of New France," *Minnesota History,* XVIII (Dec., 1937), 383–98.

3 "Monsieur de Repentigny je vous fais Et Portte La foy et homage que je suis tenue de vous faire Et Porter à cose de mon fief scise et Citué en lad[ite] Seigneurie de Lachainay . . . ," Act de foy Et hommage à Monsieur de Repentigny par le Sr Pierre Martelle, June 14, 1732, in APQ, Pièce détachée, Lachenaie.

Glossary

Arrière-fief A seigneurie conceded within a larger seigneurie, and held from the seigneur of the larger seigneurie rather than from the king.

Aveu et dénombrement A list of the landholdings within a seigneurie, including the buildings, cleared land, and livestock on them, and the dues with which the landholdings were charged. This list was required of the seigneur after any change in seigneurial control, or on the special request of the intendant.

Banality A charge which a seigneur levied for a service which he provided.

Cens A token cash payment always levied on rotures, and on no other type of landholding.

Censitaire One who paid a cens for a roture.

Communauté des biens A marriage contract automatically entered into unless another contract was specified, in which all fixed property other than that acquired through direct inheritance belonged jointly to both parties.

Côte A short line of settlement along a river or a road.

Coureurs de bois Small-scale fur traders of French stock.

Coutume A codification of French customary law.

Douaire A marriage contract by which the wife received a sum of money or the rights to half of her husband's inheritance.

Droit de retrait The right to take over land which had been sold by paying the purchase price within a specified time to the buyer.

Foi et hommage A statement of vassalage owed by a seigneur to a seigneur of higher order from whom he held his land.

Légitime An individual's right to half his rightful inheritance.

Lods et ventes A tax of one-twelfth of the sale price which was levied by the seigneur on a sale of a roture out of the line of direct succession.

Minot A measure of volume equal to 1.05 bushels.

Papier terrier A list of documents pertaining to the ownership of a given piece of land.

Pièce sur pièce A type of construction in which squared logs are laid horizontally and the corners are flush.

Quint A tax of one-fifth of the sale price of a seigneurie.

Rang A row of rectangular rotures with the short side fronting on the same river or road.

Rente A charge which a seigneur frequently levied for a roture held from him.

229

Retrait lignager   The right of one whose inheritance was affected by a sale, to take over the alienated property on payment of the purchase price within a specified time to the buyer.

Retrait roturier   The right of a seigneur to take over a roture after its sale by paying the sale price within a specified time to the purchaser.

Rhumb de vent   A fixed survey line.

Roture   A concession of land which could not be subconceded, and which was held by a censitaire from a seigneur.

Tenir feu et lieu   To keep home and hearth, that is, to live on the land.

Toise   A linear measure equal to 6.4 feet.

Bibliography

There is now an enormous body of primary and secondary material on Canada during the French regime, in which the neophyte researcher can wander unproductively for months. Too many such months of my own time have convinced me that there is a need to list, not all the materials available, but rather the principal studies and sources and the means by which they can be utilized effectively. Most of the documentary evidence is available in archives in Quebec City, Montreal, and Ottawa, and nothing that can be said here will supplant an archivist's advice. Nevertheless, much can be accomplished away from these archives, and first contact with them can be a dismaying experience unless the student comes properly prepared and forewarned. The following bibliographic essay is a brief discussion of the more important literature on the seigneurial system, of the archival material, and of the published documents.

SECONDARY MATERIALS

The best working bibliography of secondary materials on the French regime is a perceptive article by André Vachon, "Etat des recherches sur le régime français, 1632–1760," in *Situation de la recherche sur le Canada français: Premier colloque de la revue* Recherches Sociographiques *du Département de Sociologie et Anthropologie de l'Université Laval*, eds. Dumont and Martin (Laval University Press, 1962), a volume which is a must for the personal library of every serious student of French Canada. This bibliography does not include, however, the geographical literature which is relevant to the study of the French regime, of which the following should be read at the onset of any geographical analysis: Raoul Blanchard, *L'Est du Canada français, Le Centre du Canada français, L'Ouest du Canada français* (3 vols., Paris and Montreal, 1935–53), for the best general description of the physical geography of the St. Lawrence Valley; W. E. D. Halliday, *A Forest Classification for Canada* (Department of Mines and Resources, Forest Service Bulletin 89, Ottawa, 1937), for a brief description of the forests of the lower St. Lawrence Valley; Jacques Rousseau, *La Trame forestière de l'histoire canadienne* (Montreal, 1962), and "La Forêt mixte du Québec dans la perspective historique," *Cahiers de Géographie de Québec*, No. 13 (March, 1963), for more detailed discussions of the forests as they existed during the French regime; and C. A. Fontaine, "Les Sols du Québec," in *L'Actualité économique*, Vol. XVII, Pt. 2, No. 5 (March, 1942), 401–42, for a regional analysis of the province's soils.

Introductory analyses of the settlement geography of early Canada are in: Gérard Barette, "Contribution de l'arpenteur-géometre à la géographie du Québec," *Canadian Geographer,* II (1952), 67–71; Pierre Deffontaines, "Le Rang, type de peuplement rural du Canada français," *Cahiers de Géographie,* V (1953); Max Derruau, "A l'origine du 'rang' canadien," *Cahiers de Géographie de Québec,* I (1956), 39–47; and Louis-Edmond Hamelin, "Le Rang à Saint-Didace de Maskinongé," *Notes de Géographie,* No. 3 (Laval, 1953), 8 pp., map.

The principal study of the seigneurial system is still William Bennett Munro's, *The Seigniorial System in Canada: A Study in French Colonial Policy* (New York, 1907), although it is exactly what its title claims to be, a study of policy and not of achievement. Munro must be read cautiously, for many of his legal arguments are misleading and others are wrong. A more succinct analysis by the same author is in the introduction to *Documents Relating to the Seigniorial Tenure in Canada, 1598–1854* (Toronto, 1908). The lack of information in either of the two above volumes about the social, economic, and geographical implications of the seigneurial system is not filled by Munro's more popular study, *Crusaders of New France: A Chronicle of the Fleur-de-lis in the Wilderness* (New Haven, 1918).

Of three more recent volumes devoted to the seigneurial system, Dorothy A. Heneker's *The Seigneurial Regime in Canada* (Quebec, 1927); Victor Morin's *Seigneurs et censitaires, castes disparues* (Montreal, 1941); and Thomas Gérin's *Feudal Canada: The Story of the Seigniories of New France* (Montreal, 1926), none contributes a great deal of additional information. Much better is Marcel Trudel's pamphlet, *Le Régime seigneurial* (Canadian Historical Association Special Publications, brochure No. 6, Ottawa, 1956), although it is too short to push many important questions to their conclusion.

Two articles describing the seigneurial system in romantic terms are Benjamin Sulte, "La Tenure seigneuriale," *Revue Canadienne* (July–August, 1882); and Rodolphe Lemieux, "Le Régime seigneurial au Canada," *Mémoires et comptes rendues de la Société Royale du Canada* (Ottawa, 1913). Honorius Provost, the archivist at the Séminaire de Québec, has defined some of the terms used during the French regime to denote certain types of landholding in a short article, "En parlant de colonisation seigneuriale," *Revue de l'Université de Laval,* III, No. 8 (April, 1949), 672–78. Guy Frégault has examined the relationship between the seigneurial regime and colonization in "Le Régime seigneurial et l'expansion de la colonisation dans le bassin du Saint-Laurent au dix-huitième siècle," *Canadian Historical Association Report* (1944), pp. 61–73.

An attempt by Alfred Vanasse to analyze the social and economic corollaries of the seigneurial system in Canada in "A Social History of the Seigniorial Regime in Canada, 1712–1739" (unpublished Ph.D. thesis, University of Montreal, 1958) is a failure. On the other hand, a study along similar lines by Léon Gérin, *Aux sources de notre histoire: Les conditions économiques et sociales de la colonisation en Nouvelle-France* (Montreal, 1946), contains many new thoughts and a provocative analysis of the role of the Canadian seigneur.

Many more general studies contain useful material on the seigneurial system. Francis Parkman's chapter on "Canadian Feudalism" in *The Old Regime in Canada* (Boston, 1901), brought the system to the attention of many English-speaking scholars, although earlier histories in French such as E. Rameau, *La France aux colonies* (Paris, 1859), or Benjamin Sulte, *Histoire des canadiens français* (8 vols., Montreal, 1882–84), had dealt with it in considerable detail.

Among the more recent histories of early Canada, the following are particularly important for their treatments of the seigneurial system: Gérard Filteau, *La Naissance d'une nation* (Montreal, 1937); Guy Frégault, *La Civilisation de la Nouvelle-France, 1713–1744* (Montreal, 1944); and Lionel Groulx, *Histoire du Canada français depuis la découverte* (Montreal, 1950–51). Two studies of the colonization of the colony, Emile Salone, *La Colonisation de la Nouvelle-France* (Paris, 1905), and Ivanhoe Caron, *La Colonisation du Canada sous la domination française* (Quebec, 1916), have much to say about a system which was intended to provide a framework for colonization.

There are many studies which do not deal directly with the seigneurial system but which, because of the light they shed on the economic and social development of early Canada, are important background reading. In this class are two detailed analyses of the economic development of the colony, one by Joseph-Noel Fauteux, *Essai sur l'industrie au Canada sous le régime français* (2 vols., Quebec, 1927); the other by Paul-Emile Rénaud, *Les Origines économiques du Canada: L'œuvre de la France* (Mamers, 1928). One side of a debate over the size and wealth of the Canadian bourgeoisie, a debate of much relevance to an understanding of the position of the Canadian seigneur, is in Guy Frégault, *La Société canadienne sous le régime français* (Canadian Historical Association Special Publications, brochure No. 3, 1954); and the other in Jean Hamelin, *Economie et société en Nouvelle-France* (Laval University Press, 1960).

The fur trade, which profoundly influenced much of the colony's development, is analyzed by H. A. Innis in *The Fur Trade in Canada: An Introduction to Canadian Economic History* (New Haven and London, 1930); and by H. P. Biggar in *The Early Trading Companies of New France* (Toronto, 1901). A fascinating picture of the political background of the trade is painted by W. J. Eccles, in *Frontenac: The Courtier Governor* (Toronto, 1959). An article by R. M. Saunders, "The Emergence of the Coureurs de Bois as a Social Type," *Canadian Historical Association Report* (1939), pp. 22–33; and another by Jean Lunn, "The Illegal Fur Trade out of New France," *ibid.*, pp. 61–76, deal with two of the aspects of the trade which created much of its appeal for the Canadian habitants.

Some of the detail of farm life which is indispensable to the clear understanding of agriculture in the colony has been described by Robert-Lionel Séguin in three works: *L'Equipement de la ferme canadienne aux XVIIe et XVIIIe siècles* (Montreal, 1959); *Les Granges du Québec* (Ottawa, 1963); and "Les Conditions techniques de l'habitant canadien-français aux XVIIe et XVIIIe siècles" (unpublished thesis for *le diplome d'études supérieures* in history, Laval University, 1958). A study by Nora Dawson, *La Vie traditionnelle à Saint-Pierre* (Quebec, 1960), is also useful in this regard, although it is primarily concerned with the 19th and 20th centuries. Finally, the *Revue de l'Histoire de l'Amérique Français* should be perused for articles on the economic development of early Canada, particularly those by Roland Sanfaçon, E. Z. Massicotte, and R. L. Séguin.

Before examining any of the documents pertaining to the seigneurial system the researcher would be well advised to acquaint himself with some of the cardinal tenets of French customary law. This subject is introduced in three histories of Canadian law: B. A. Testard de Montigny, *Histoire du droit canadien* (Montreal, 1869); Edmond Lareau, *Histoire du droit canadien* (2 vols., Montreal, 1888–89); and Rodolphe Lemieux, *Les Origines du droit franco-canadien* (Montreal, 1901). However, I found it most helpful to go directly to commentaries on the *Coutume de Paris*. Most serviceable of these are Charles Dumoulin, *Coutumes de la Prévôté et Vicomté de Paris* (Paris, 1681); and M. Claude de Ferrière, *Nouveau Commentaire sur la Coutume de la Prévôté et Vicomté de Paris* (Paris, 1770). Shorter commentaries drawn up after the conquest by a Canadian jurist are F. J. Cugnet's *Traité de la Loi des Fiefs* (Quebec, 1775) and *Traité de la Police* (Quebec, 1775). The close comparison of Cugnet with either Dumoulin or Ferrière will reveal some of the distinctive characteristics of Canadian law.

PRIMARY MATERIALS

The voluminous documentary evidence on the French regime which is relevant to a study of the seigneurial system can be divided into several types: censuses; maps; documents pertaining to the concession, alienation, and maintenance of seigneuries; documents pertaining to the concession, alienation, and maintenance of rotures; official correspondence; court records; and travellers' accounts. There is a lifetime's reading in these documents, almost all of which are available in archives in eastern Canada, but useful information can be gathered relatively quickly if the many indexes and inventories which are available are used to full advantage.

One of the corollaries of the introduction of a French governmental bureaucracy to Canada was the regular compilation of censuses throughout all but the last two decades of the French regime. Each of these censuses divides the population into men, women, boys, and girls, and lists livestock, quantities of various crops, and arpents of cultivated land in each enumeration area. Three are nominal censuses (those of 1666, 1667, and 1681), and give the name and age of each inhabitant. The censuses are frustrating to use because enumeration areas were often vaguely delimited and were rarely the same for two censuses in succession, and because careful analysis of them reveals many inaccuracies. Nevertheless, they contain much information which is not available elsewhere, and are probably the best starting point for most geographical studies of the French regime. The originals or copies of all the important censuses are available in Series G¹ in the National Archives of Canada.

A great many maps dating from the French regime are preserved in the National Archives and in the Archives in Quebec City. Many of these are small-scale maps of eastern North America which are of little use for the geographical analysis of the St. Lawrence colony, but others which show individual seigneuries and the rotures within them are invaluable. Neither of these collections is well indexed, and several days should be allowed for making an inventory of the maps in either archives. The National Archives will make photostats of any of its maps for a nominal charge.

The documents relating to the concession, alienation, and maintenance of individual seigneuries comprise title deeds, acts of partition of seigneuries, deeds of sale, statements of *foi et hommage, aveux et dénombrements,* and *papiers terriers.* The key to this material is the *Inventaire des concessions en fief et seigneurie, fois et hommages, et aveux et dénombrements conservées aux archives de la province de Québec* (Beauceville, Quebec, 1927–29), prepared by P. G. Roy. The six volumes of the inventory are an indication of the quantity of material involved. Most of the title deeds, deeds of sale, and acts of partition are in boxes arranged alphabetically by seigneurie in the Archives de la Province de Québec, although a few which pertain to the holdings of the Séminaire de Québec are in its archives, and others are in the Archives Judiciaires in Quebec and Montreal. Most of the statements of *foi et hommage* are in several large volumes in the Archives de la Province de Québec, and the *aveux et dénombrements* and *papiers terriers* are in other bound volumes in the same archives. Copies of some of these documents are in the National Archives, and a few, which are not in the Archives de la Province, are the property of the Séminaire de Québec. The acts of concession are useful primarily to indicate the land which a seigneur held and the conditions by which he held it, the acts of partition shed much light on the fragmentation of seigneurial control, and the deeds of sale are the best indication of the value of seigneuries and of the reasons for and conditions of their sale. Of the three bound series, the *aveux et dénombrements* are the most useful. Included in each of these inventories of seigneurial property is a description of the seigneur's domain and of the buildings and cleared land on each of the rotures in his seigneurie. The statements of *foi et hommage* often contain evidence of the fragmentation of seigneurial control; and the *papiers terriers,* lists prepared by the seigneur of his censitaires and the dues they owed, are sources of information about seigneurial revenue.

The thousands of documents relating to the concession, alienation, and maintenance of rotures are a crucial source of evidence about the seigneurial system. Many of these documents are loose in boxes in the Archives de la Province de Québec, but perhaps more are in the Archives Judiciaires in Quebec and Montreal, and a few are in the Archives du Séminaire de Québec. They comprise principally acts of concession, donation, or partition, deeds of sale, and occasionally, inventories of a censitaire's property, and are the principal source of information about the sizes of rotures, the conditions by which they were held, and the frequency with which they were divided or sold. There is no index or inventory of this collection, although most of the documents are listed in the *Inventaire des greffes des notaires du régime français* (Quebec, 1942), a mammoth compilation which was begun by P. G. Roy and continued by his successors at the Archives de la Province de Québec. This inventory is an attempt to list chronologically by individual notary all the existing notarized documents which were drawn up during the French regime. Those pertaining to the concession, mutation, or maintenance of rotures are interspersed among marriage contracts, wills, and so on. I found that the best approach to the documents relating to rotures was to work through the many boxes of them which are arranged alphabetically by seigneurie in the Archives de la Province de Québec, and to use the *Inventaire des greffes des notaires* to locate specific documents in the Archives Judiciaire de Québec.

The official correspondence to and from Canada includes the *lettres envoyées* (Series AC, B: correspondence sent from France to Canada) and the *correspondance générale* (Series AC, C 11 A: that travelling in the other direction). The original manuscripts of this correspondence are in the Archives du Ministre des Colonies in Paris, but all of them have been copied by hand and, more recently, microfilmed, and both copies and microfilm are available in the National Archives of Canada. Series AC, B comprises forty-six feet of shelf space, but only the first volumes, containing the king's instructions to Talon, are indispensable reading for any study of the seigneurial system. For the most part, the king's policy is clearly revealed in AC, C 11 A; and this series, which occupies thirty-one feet of shelf space, cannot be avoided. In it are important analyses of many problems relating to the seigneurial tenure, and invaluable descriptions of social and economic conditions in the colony. An index for C 11 A is available at the National Archives, and with it a quick but productive run-through of the series is possible in several months.

Perhaps the most important of the court records are the Ordonnances des Intendants, which comprise, for the most part, the intendants' judgments on the cases brought to them. Appeal to the intendant was free, and after 1705 when the Intendant Jacques Raudot took the judging of many civil disputes into his own hands, the intendant became the most popular jurist in the colony. A great variety of disputes were brought to him, and the cases of each of the disputants as well as the intendant's ruling can be found in these ordinances. The manuscripts are in the Archives de la Province de Québec, and there are longhand copies in the National Archives. Use of the Ordonnances des Intendants is facilitated by another inventory prepared by the indefatigable P. G. Roy, *Inventaire des ordonnances des intendants de la Nouvelle-France conservées aux archives provinciales de Québec* (4 vols., Beauceville, Quebec, 1927). Ordinances issued before 1706 are available in P. G. Roy, *Ordonnances, commissions, etc., des gouverneurs et intendants de la Nouvelle-France, 1639–1706* (Quebec, 1924).

Complementing the Ordonnances des Intendants are the Registres de la Prévôté de Québec, 1666–1759. Civil as well as criminal cases were judged by the Conseil de la Prévôté, and copies of its judgments fill fourteen feet of shelf space at the National Archives. These judgments could be appealed to the Conseil Souverain, and the records of its judgments and deliberations are almost as voluminous. Those for the years from 1663 to 1716 are available in *Jugements et délibérations du Conseil Souverain de la Nouvelle-France* (6 vols., Quebec, 1885–1940); and P. G. Roy has prepared an inventory of the remainder, *Inventaire des jugements et délibérations du conseil supérieur de la Nouvelle-France de 1717 à 1760* (7 vols., Beauceville, Quebec, 1885–1940). And yet the size of these two collections—the Registres de la Prévôté and the Jugements du Conseil Souverain—have made them virtually unused sources. The *correspondance générale* can be skimmed, but these intricate legal arguments cannot. A month's work with the Ordonnances des Intendants yielded many dividends, I found, but much more time would be required with each of these larger collections.

Finally, and most welcome for their brevity, are the records of the seigneurial courts. The most complete collection of documents from these courts is for the Jesuits' seigneurie of Notre Dame des Anges, a collection which comprises only a few inches of shelf space. The manuscripts are in the Archives de la Province de Québec, and there are copies in the National Archives.

A number of visitors to Canada wrote accounts of what they saw, and some of these descriptions contain valuable information about the colony's social and economic development. Easily the most important of these is Peter Kalm's *Travels into North America* (London, 1772, and subsequent editions). Baron de Lahontan's *Nouveaux Voyages* (The Hague, 1705, and subsequent editions) is a delightful if exaggerated account. More reliable are Pierre Boucher, *Histoire Véritable et Naturelle des Mœurs et productions du pays de la Nouvelle-France Vulgairement dite Canada* (Paris, 1664, and subsequent editions); N. G. Boucault, "Etat présent du Canada, dressé sur nombre de mémoires et connaissances acquis sur les lieux," 1754, *Archives de Québec, Rapport de l'Archivist* (1920–21), pp. 11–51; Louis Franquet, *Voyages et mémoires sur le Canada* (Quebec, 1889); and J. C. Bonnefonds, *Voyage au Canada dans le nord de l'amérique septentrionale, fait depuis l'an 1751 à 1761* (Quebec, 1887).

Published Documents

Only a very small fraction, perhaps a hundredth, of the documents relevant to a study of the seigneurial system in Canada have been published, and consequently these published materials serve principally to give an impression of the documentary evidence which is available. The student would be well advised to peruse the published collections carefully before visiting the archives in Ottawa, Quebec, and Montreal, but should remember that most of these publications are fragmentary compilations which do not include representative samples of the documentation.

Summaries of most of the censuses taken during the French regime are published in the *Census of the Dominion of Canada, 1871*, Vol. IV. The three nominal censuses are published in full, that of 1666 in the *Archives de Québec, Rapport de l'Archivist* (1935–36); that of 1667 in B. Sulte, *Histoire des canadiens français* (Montreal, 1882–84), IV, 64–79; and that of 1681 in the same history, V, 53–90. The careful census taken by the English shortly after the conquest has been published in the *Archives de Québec, Rapport de l'Archivist* (1925–26), pp. 1–144; (1936–37), pp. 1–121; (1946–47), pp. 3–55. Some of the totals in the published censuses differ slightly from those in the original documents, but generally the modern editors have added more accurately than the census-takers, and published censuses can be used for mapping and for statistical compilations with few qualms.

The only sizable collection of maps of Canada drafted during the French regime which has been published to date is in Marcel Trudel's *Atlas historique du Canada français* (Laval University Press, 1961). The large-scale seigneurial maps are still available only in the archives.

Most of the seigneurial title deeds have been published in full in *Pièces et documents relatifs à la tenure seigneuriale* (2 vols., Quebec, 1852–54), in English and French editions, but acts of partition and deeds of sale are still available only in the archives. A few of the *aveux et dénombrements* and statements of *foi et hommage* are printed in the *Archives de Québec, Rapport de l'Archivist* (vols. for 1941–42, 1943–44, 1945–46, 1948–49, 1949–51). Of the thousands of documents relating to the concession, alienation, and maintenance of rotures, only a handful are published, almost all in parish histories.

Some of the correspondence in AC, B, and C 11 A which is relevant to a study of the seigneurial system is now in print. The first publication of this material was ordered by the Legislative Assembly of Canada, and appeared in 1853 under the title *Correspondence between the French Government and the Governors and Intendants of Canada Relative to the Seigniorial Tenure* (Quebec), in English and French editions. Several important dispatches which were overlooked in this compilation were published by the Champlain Society in a volume of *Documents Relating to the Seigniorial Tenure in Canada, 1598–1854*, edited by William Bennet Munro (cited earlier). Other fragments of C 11 A have appeared in a *Collection de manuscrits contenant lettres, mémoires, et autres documents historiques relatifs à la Nouvelle-France, recueillis aux archives de la Province de Québec, ou copiés à l'étranger* (4 vols., Quebec, 1883–85); and in Pierre Margry's *Relations et mémoires inédits, pour servir à l'histoire de la France dans les pays d'outre-mer, tirés des archives du Ministère de la Marine et des Colonies* (Paris, 1867). The Talon correspondence is available in the *Archives de Québec, Rapport de l'Archivist* (1930–31), and much of that of Vaudreuil appeared in the same publication between 1938 and 1948.

Some documents from AC, B were published in two volumes of *Edits, ordonnances royaux, déclarations, et arrêts du conseil d'etat du roi concernant le Canada* (Quebec, 1803–6). This compilation was enlarged and republished from 1854 to 1856 in three volumes under the same title. The first volume contains royal edicts, ordinances, and *arrêts* pertaining to Canada, and the second and third contain judgments and ordinances of royal officials and courts in the colony. The three volumes are carefully indexed, and are an admirable introduction to the documents, but it cannot be too strongly emphasized that they contain only a fraction of the archival material. Not nearly as reliable is a hasty compilation in English and French editions of *Edicts, Ordinances, Declarations, and Decrees Relative to the Seigniorial Tenure* (Quebec, 1852). All the *Jugements et délibérations du Conseil Souverain de la Nouvelle-France* from 1663 to 1716 have been printed in a six-volume compilation which has been masterfully edited. Future publications of documents from the French regime should be of this type, solid blocks of material rather than selections which can only reflect the interest and point of view of the selectors.

Perhaps it does not need to be mentioned that evidence about the French regime can still be seen on the land, and that hours spent in the delightful countryside of Quebec can be more than a tonic to be taken after exposure to too many documents.

Index

All seigneuries are listed, with administrative division and identifying number given in parentheses.

Agriculture: limits of, 11, 113–14; and forests, 14; markets for products of, 114, 161–62, 182; extensive nature of, 150–51; crops, 151–55; livestock, 155–58; farm buildings, 158–59; implements, 159; labor, 159; income from, 160–62. *See also* Farms

Ailleboust (*12 Montreal*): sale of, 57

Appalachian Roughlands: agricultural potential of, 10

Argenteuil (*2 Montreal*): concession of, 34

Arpent: definition of, x

Arrière-fiefs: number of, 39; size of, 39; types of, 39–40

Artisans: habitants as, 162; in Boucherville, 177; distribution of, 182

Assomption (*8 Montreal*): acquired by La Chesnaye, 56; settlement in, 94, 105, 184–85

Assomption River: settlement along, 100, 123

Aubert Gayon (*45 Quebec*)

Aubin de l'Isle (*46 Quebec*)

Auctions: of seigneuries, 50–51; of rotures, 132

Augmentations: frequency of, 31; requests for, 32–33; to Ste-Marie, 108

Avaugour, Governor: proposal for fort on Hudson, 18

Aveu et dénombrements, 41 n

Baie du Febvre (*32 Trois-Rivières*)

Baie St-Paul: settlement of, 10; domain at, 83

Banalities: bake oven, 72; gristmill, 72, 77–79

Barley: cultivation of, 154

Barns: types of, 158–59

Batiscan (*23 Trois-Rivières*): size of, 24; concession of, 42; charges for wood in, 71

Batiscan River: settlement along, 100, 101

Beauchamp (*47 Quebec*)

Beauharnois (*34 Montreal*)

Beauharnois, Governor: concession to, 35; seigneurial policy, 37, 44; on cens et rentes, 65, 69, 111; corvées levied by, 70; on sale of rotures, 76

Beaujeu (*44 Montreal*)

Beaumont (*50 Quebec*): mill in, 50; settlement in, 95

Beauport (*25 Quebec*): shape of, 23; mill revenue in, 73; settlement of, 108; concession in, 119; size of rotures in, 138; spacing of houses in, 172; village sites in, 179. *See also* Giffard, Robert

Beaupré (*26 Quebec*): size and shape of, 24; arrière-fiefs in, 39; early control of, 43, 45, 56; mills in, 72; domains in, 83–85, 87; settlement of, 89, 94, 100, 101, 108, 146–47, 172; subdivision of rotures in, 133, 135; village sites in, 179; hamlet in, 182; côte in, 186; living standards in, 191

Bécancour (*37 Trois-Rivières*)

Bégon, Intendant: on retrait roturier, 75; on seigneurial grants, 107

Bélair (*10 Quebec*)

Bélair (*15 Quebec*): sold to Jesuits, 43, 57

Bellechasse (*53 Quebec*), 150

Belle Plaine (*35 Quebec*)

Belœil (*64 Montreal*)

Berthier (*15 Montreal*): charges for common in, 71

Bleury (*55 Montreal*)

Bonhomme (*15 Quebec*)

Bonsecours (*33, 61 Quebec, 78 Montreal*)

Boston merchants: trading advantage of, 18

Boucher (*16 Trois-Rivières*)

Boucher, Pierre: seigneur of Grosbois, 48; as colonizer, 113

Boucherville (*57 Montreal*): arrière-fief in, 39–40; subdivision of, 48–49; charges for common in, 71; settlement of, 94, 95, 101, 104; village in, 176–79

Bourdon, Jean: seigneurial concessions to, 55

Bourgchemin (*77 Montreal*)

Bourg Louis (*11 Quebec*)

Bourg Marie (*81 Montreal*)

Bourg Royal: plans for, 172

Boyer River: settlement along, 100

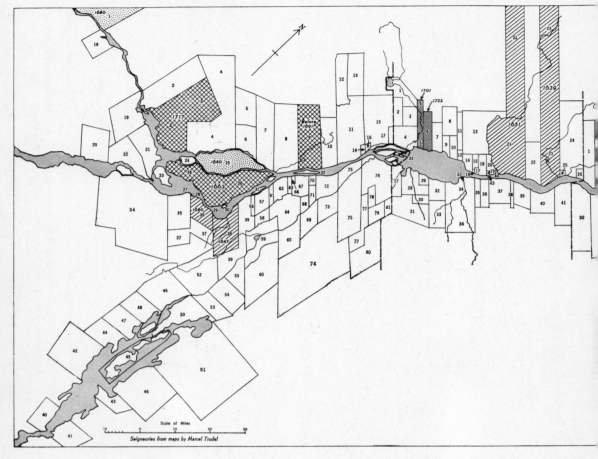

Seigneuries from maps by Marcel Trudel

GOVERNMENT OF MONTREAL

1	Petite Nation	27	Iles de la Paix	55	Bleury
2	Argenteuil	28	Iles Courcelles	56	Tremblay
3	Deux Montagnes	29	Ile aux Hérons	57	Boucherville
4	Mille Iles	30	Ile St-Paul	58	Montarville
5	Plaines	31	Ile Ste-Thérèse	59	Chambly
6	Terrebonne	32	Iles Bouchard	60	Monnoir
7	Lachenaie (La	33	Ile St-Pierre	61	Varennes
	Chesnaye)	34	Beauharnois	62	Cap de la Trinité
8	L'Assomption, or	35	Châteauguay	63	Guillaudière
	Repentigny	36	Sault St-Louis	64	Belœil
9	St-Sulpice	37	La Salle	65	Rouville
10	Lavaltrie	38	La Prairie de la	66	St-Blain
11	Lanoraie		Magdeleine	67	Verchères
12	Ailleboust	39	Longueuil	68	Cournoyer
13	Ramezay, or	40	Rocbert	69	St-Charles-sur-
	Jouette	41	Daneau de Muy		Richelieu
14	Dautré	42	Ramezay-la-Gesse	70	Vitré
15	Berthier	43	La Perrière	71	Cabanac
16	Dorvilliers	44	Beaujeu	72	Contrecœur
17	Ile Dupas et Chicot	45	Pancalon	73	St-Denis
18	Pointe à l'Orignal	46	La Moinaudière	74	St-Hyacinthe
19	Rigaud	47	La Gauchetière	75	St-Ours
20	Nouvelle Longueuil	48	Livaudière	76	Sorel
21	Vaudreuil	49	Lacolle	77	Bourgchemin
22	Soulanges	50	Foucault	78	Bonsecours
23	Ile Perrot	51	St-Armand	79	St-Charles
24	Ile Bizard	52	De Léry	80	Ramezay
25	Ile Jésus	53	Noyan	81	Bourg Marie
26	Ile de Montréal	54	Sabrevois		

GOVERNMENT OF TROIS-RIVIÈRES

1	Lac Maskinongé,	22	Champlain	
	or Lanaudière	23	Batiscan	
2	Dusablé	24	Ste-Anne-Ouest	
3	Carufel	25	Ste-Marie	
4	Maskinongé	26	Ste-Anne-Est, or	
5	St-Jean		Dorvilliers	
6	Rivière du Loup	27	Yamaska	
7	Grandpré	28	St-François	
8	Dumontier	29	Lussodière	
9	Grosbois-Ouest	30	Pierreville	
10	Grosbois-Est, or	31	Deguire	
	Yamachiche	32	Baie du Febvre,	
11	Robert		or St-Antoine	
12	Gastineau	33	Courval	
13	St-Maurice	34	Nicolet	
14	Tonnancour, or	35	Roquetaillade	
	Pointe du Lac	36	Godefroy, or	
15	Not conceded		Linctôt	
16	Boucher	37	Bécancour	
17	Labadie	38	Dutort	
18	Vieuxpont	39	Cournoyer	
19	Jésuites	40	Gentilly	
20	Seigneuries in or	41	Lévrard	
	on outskirts of	42	Ile Moras	
	Trois-Rivières	43	Ile Marie	
21	Cap de la Mad-	44	Iles du St-Maurice	
	eleine			